Christian Punk

Bloomsbury Studies in Religion and Popular Music

Series editor: Christopher Partridge

Religion's relationship to popular music has ranged from opposition to "the Devil's music" to an embracing of modern styles and subcultures in order to communicate its ideas and defend its values. Similarly, from jazz to reggae, gospel to heavy metal, and bhangra to qawwali, there are few genres of contemporary popular music that have not dealt with ideas and themes related to religion, spirituality and the paranormal. Whether we think of Satanism or Sufism, the liberal use of drugs or disciplined abstinence, the history of the quest for transcendence within popular music and its subcultures raises important issues for anyone interested in contemporary religion, culture and society. *Bloomsbury Studies in Religion and Popular Music* is a multi-disciplinary series that aims to contribute to a comprehensive understanding of these issues and the relationships between religion and popular music.

Christian Metal, Marcus Moberg
Mortality and Music, Christopher Partridge
Mysticism, Ritual and Religion in Drone Metal, Owen Coggins
Religion in Hip Hop, edited by Monica R. Miller, Anthony B. Pinn and Bernard "Bun B" Freeman
Religion and Popular Music, edited by Andreas Häger
Sacred and Secular Musics, Virinda Kalra
U2 and the Religious Impulse, edited by Scott Calhoun

Christian Punk

Identity and Performance

Edited by
Ibrahim Abraham

BLOOMSBURY ACADEMIC

LONDON • NEW YORK • OXFORD • NEW DELHI • SYDNEY

BLOOMSBURY ACADEMIC
Bloomsbury Publishing Plc
50 Bedford Square, London, WC1B 3DP, UK
1385 Broadway, New York, NY 10018, USA
29 Earlsfort Terrace, Dublin 2, Ireland

BLOOMSBURY, BLOOMSBURY ACADEMIC and the Diana logo
are trademarks of Bloomsbury Publishing Plc

First published in Great Britain 2020
Paperback edition first published 2021

Copyright © Ibrahim Abraham and Contributors, 2020

Ibrahim Abraham has asserted his right under the Copyright,
Designs and Patents Act, 1988, to be identified as Editor of this work.

For legal purposes the Acknowledgements on p. ix constitute
an extension of this copyright page.

Cover image © Kjetil Kolbjørnsrud/Alamy Stock Photo

A catalogue record for this book is available from the British Library.

Library of Congress Control Number: 2019949114.

ISBN: HB: 978-1-3500-9479-6
PB: 978-1-3502-7237-8
ePDF: 978-1-3500-9480-2
eBook: 978-1-3500-9481-9

Series: Bloomsbury Studies in Religion and Popular Music

Typeset by Integra Software Services Pvt. Ltd.

To find out more about our authors and books visit
www.bloomsbury.com and sign up for our newsletters.

Contents

Figures

Contributors

Ibrahim Abraham is the Hans Mol Research Fellow in Religion and the Social Sciences at the Australian National University, Canberra. He is the author of *Evangelical Youth Culture: Alternative Music and Extreme Sports Subcultures* (2017).

Joshua Kalin Busman is Assistant Professor of Music at the University of North Carolina at Pembroke, with appointments in the Music Department and the Esther G. Maynor Honors College. His research focuses on contemporary evangelicalism, particularly worship, affect, and mass media.

Michael J. Iafrate is a theologian, musician, activist, doctoral candidate at the University of St. Michael's College, University of Toronto, and Co-coordinator of the Catholic Committee of Appalachia. His most recent album is *Christian Burial* (2017).

Eileen Luhr is Professor of History at California State University, Long Beach. She is the author of *Witnessing Suburbia: Conservatives and Christian Youth Culture* (2009).

Amy D. McDowell is Assistant Professor of Sociology at the University of Mississippi. Her research focuses on American evangelicalism, gender, sexuality, and race.

Andrew Mall is Assistant Professor of Music at Northeastern University, Boston, where he teaches courses in ethnomusicology, popular music studies, and music industry. His current book project is titled *Music on the Margins: Niche Markets, Christian Rock, and Popular Music*.

Maren Haynes Marchesini holds a PhD in ethnomusicology from the University of Washington. She serves as part-time faculty at Carroll College in Helena, Montana, where she directs worship and music at St. Paul's United Methodist Church.

Nathan Myrick is Assistant Professor in the Townsend School of Music at Mercer University in Macon, Georgia. His work focuses on music and human flourishing in the context of Christian communities.

Francis Stewart is the Implicit Religion Research Fellow at Bishop Grosseteste University, Lincoln, UK. She is the author of *Punk Rock Is My Religion: Straight Edge Punk and "Religious" Identity* (2017).

Eric Strother holds a Master's degree in music theory and a PhD in musicology from the University of Kentucky. He is currently serving as a part-time faculty member at Anderson University, Indiana.

Acknowledgments

This book would not have been possible without the enthusiasm of the series editor, Christopher Partridge at Lancaster University, and the support of Lucy Carroll, Camilla Erskine, and Lalle Pursglove at Bloomsbury. The editor is also grateful for the support of the discipline of social and cultural anthropology at the University of Helsinki, the Humanities Research Centre at the Australian National University, and the Christian Congregational Music network through which many of the contributors became acquainted.

This book draws upon two publications. Chapter 1, "Rebel with a Cross: The Development of an American Christian Youth Culture," by Eileen Luhr, contains material previously published by the University of California Press in *Witnessing Suburbia: Conservatives and Christian Youth Culture*. Chapter 9, "Christian Punk in (Post)secular Perspectives," by Ibrahim Abraham, contains material previously published by Bloomsbury Academic in *Evangelical Youth Culture: Alternative Music and Extreme Sports Subcultures*.

Introduction: Studying Christian Punk

Ibrahim Abraham

Introduction

Performing in Florida in 1977, rebelling against her strict Jehovah's Witness upbringing, punk poet Patti Smith called out to God, "Gimme your best shot, I can take it!" She then tumbled into the orchestra pit and broke her neck (Strongman 2007: 185). Thirty years later in an episode of the drama series *Friday Night Lights*, a teenage hardcore punk/heavy metal crossover band, Crucifictorious, thrashed their way through a metalcore dirge in front of a handful of baffled patrons in a Texas bar. "I can count on your scars to set me free!" (*Friday Night Lights*, 2007).

These are just two examples of the relationship between punk rock and Christianity, two cultural forms that are so apparently antithetical that Mark Sinker's (1999: 120) essay on punk etiquette invites us to "imagine the ensuing centuries of Judaeo-Christian moral debate had Moses returned from the mountain carrying not two stone tablets inscribed with five commandments each, but the first Siouxsie and the Banshees LP." Much like Siouxsie Sioux's stream-of-consciousness meditation on salvation, mashing together the Lord's Prayer and "Twist and Shout" (*Join Hands*, 1979), there is humor in juxtaposing the sacred and profane, but also a message about the deeper significance of rock 'n' roll. Punk has developed and debated the boundaries of its own moral orthodoxy and performative orthopraxy, and one genre rule has been skepticism or hostility toward religion, specifically the dominant religion of the Establishment, Christianity.

Like the bewildered audience at the Crucifictorious show, the idea of punk rock celebrating and spreading faith in Jesus Christ may seem like an oxymoron. In the seemingly secularizing, late capitalist Western societies this book is concerned with, religion is more often associated with the threat of censoring culture than inspiring the kinds of innovative and subversive self-expression associated with punk for the last four decades. After all this time, the most famous punk lyric remains "I am an Antichrist / I am an anarchist," the opening lines from the Sex Pistol's "Anarchy in the UK" (*Never Mind the Bollocks, Here's the Sex Pistols*, 1977). Christian punk is not a contradiction in terms, however, but an international subculture that exits within and between countless local secular punk scenes and the prosperous contemporary Christian music (CCM) industry. Focusing on the performance of Christian punk music and identity, primarily within the United States, the ten chapters in this book demonstrate the compatibility of punk's expressive, do-it-yourself (DIY) ethic with the youthful energy of evangelicalism, even or especially in the face of the decline of organized religion.

Christian punk is not unique to the United States, and far from only an Anglophone phenomena. Christian punk and metal have spread rapidly in Latin America, for example, with the rise of Pentecostalism in the region. However, this book is largely focused on Christian punk in the United States, where it first emerged out of the American CCM scene and Californian evangelical youth culture in the wake of the countercultural Jesus Movement of the 1960s and 1970s, explored in Chapter 1, and where it reached the peak of its success in the first decade of the twenty-first century. Christian punk has both exceeded and remained bound to these origins; its musical diversity encompasses lighthearted pop-punk, aggressive hardcore, and apocalyptic metalcore, but it is almost uniformly evangelical in outlook, albeit enlivened by Pentecostalism and the occasional Calvinist controversy, noted in Chapter 6. There is no escaping the moral malaise around American evangelicalism—David Gushee (2019: 14) wonders whether the word means anything other than "aggrieved white conservative" these days—but as is the case with music, reducing religion to politics is reductive to the point of totalitarian. Historian David Bebbington's (1989: 1–17) four pillars of evangelicalism remain definitive, emphasizing activism, Bible-centrism, conversion, and—as in Crucifictorious's screamed lyrics—a focus on Christ's crucifixion atoning for the sins of humanity.

Articulating these shared evangelical beliefs through a shared range of aesthetic practices, the Christian punk subculture responds to shared experiences of the complexities of life in late capitalism, notably the rise of individualism and the decline of communities of support, including churches, discussed in Chapter 4. Primarily attracting young men, punk scenes are also spaces for new and old gender identities to be performed or contested, and Christian punk is hardly immune from debates on the changing nature of gender norms, as explored in detail in Chapters 2, 5, 6, and 7. Since most Christian punk bands would conceive of their music as some form of "mission," designed in part or whole to share their beliefs by word and by action, either directly from the stage or through friendships formed in local scenes or on the road, Christian punk is also directly confronting the secularization of Western societies in trying to communicate an evangelical message to increasingly irreligious audiences, analyzed in Chapters 3, 8, and 9.

After sketching the histories and foundational features of Christian punk's parent genres, secular punk and CCM, and highlighting some of the more interesting existing studies of these topics, but making no claim to thoroughness, this Introduction will offer a brief overview of Christian punk, noting several turning points, and preview the following ten chapters.

Studying Punk

"Punk" is a term contested by fans, musicians, and scholars alike; in a subculture obsessed with authenticity punk's boundaries can be policed with an intensity that belies its diversity. The word itself can evoke a specific place and time—particularly London in the late 1970s—but also signify "a never-ending chord, a feedback whine that stretches out across the years" (Strongman 2007: 11). Globalizing and syncretizing beyond its origins in the rock clubs of New York and London, punk has become a vast and contradictory metagenre that encompasses a wide variety of musical subgenres—from acoustic folk-punk to electronic nintendocore—and many nonmusical subgenres: fashion, film, literature, visual art, politics, and pornography all have their punk expressions (Thompson 2004; Diehl 2007). In addition to Christianity, Buddhism, Hinduism, Islam, and Judaism have all been expressed in punk forms (Abraham and Stewart 2017). Garnett's (1999: 22) claim that punk is the most inclusive category in popular culture, incorporating "mutually exclusive tendencies [and] styles," seems accurate, therefore, because what unites punk culture is not a common style or sound but common approaches to creative practice and self-expression, with some shared tropes and touchstones.

The most useful approach to defining punk I have encountered is Stacy Thompson's (2004) focus on punk's core "desires." Focusing on desire emphasizes cultural processes, such that there is no specific style that must be precisely reproduced for the end result to be punk, so long as these desires are in evidence and punk identity is invoked. Three desires can be distilled from Thompson's study. Firstly, resistance to commercialization; this is punk's DIY ethic aimed at maintaining creative autonomy, born out of frustration with the music industry, of which many punk bands were initially enthusiastic participants. The second punk desire is the critique of the norms of rock music and a commitment to creating new styles of subcultural identity and subjectivity. Like popular culture in general, punk is a site of social contestation that mediates, rather than articulates, particular political positions. Punk was not initially inherently political, but progressively developed a normative radical position through responses to social and political issues in the 1980s (Moore and Roberts 2009), then taking an inward turn in the 1990s and 2000s to focus on individual alienation (Azerrad 2007). Punk expressions, from straight edge abstinence to emo Romanticism, perform these critical subjectivities. The final punk desire is its continuous development of communities of males in which the desire for DIY cultural production and the exploration of critical and subversive subjectivities take place. This male domination of punk is a continuation of basic rock norms, and even though punk's DIY ethos nominally invites women into the subculture, women have rarely been accepted as equals (Leblanc 1999; O'Brien 1999).

In spite of these certain continuities, such as ongoing gender inequality, a key claim of many histories of punk is that it signifies a radical departure from past approaches to popular music and culture. Punk's most baroque chronicler, Greil Marcus (1989: 3), gives punk the messianic role of creating a "breach in pop culture" and splitting popular music history in two. Clive Erricker's (2001: 77) theological reflection on punk argues that the capital-P Punk "turns the world upside down by ironically and deliberately challenging the imposed order of things by asserting that it is just that—imposed." Doing so, the first wave of punk looked backward and forward simultaneously to criticize what popular music and youth culture had become in the mid-1970s. "Young people everywhere look like young people everywhere," Phil Strongman (2007: 17) recalls of that period, noting the standardization of countercultural music and fashion into inauthentic expressions of individualistic conformity. By the mid-1970s, the baby boomers were beginning to turn thirty, and amid the economic stagnation of the period, punk turned against them for betraying the countercultural possibilities of life "outside of the hegemonic reality" (Grossberg 1990: 117), translated by the Sex Pistols into the warning "never trust a hippie." On the one hand, punk was looking backward to 1960s garage rock, with its rejection of musical complexity and a desire to get back to rock 'n' roll basics. On the other hand, punk was taking inspiration from the subversive style of David Bowie and the New York Dolls, preventing it from being a purely backward-facing cultural movement.

Accurately described as an example of "Anglo-American syncretism," punk's pendulum initially swung between London and New York (Lentini 2003). This first wave of punk reached the height of notoriety in 1977, thanks to the antics of the Sex Pistols, but a loosely labeled collection of bands and individual artists continued along increasingly diverse paths, through forms of innovation and back-to-basics re-creation. Francis Stewart (2017: 6) views this as a series of self-critiquing "new waves" that respond to particular social situations, building on what has come before, as well as what has been neglected or forgotten. Key examples are the straight edge movement that reimagined punk ethics, and later the Riot Grrrl movement that partly remedied punk's exclusion of female voices. Two notable tendencies emerged in the 1980s that largely framed future innovations: a "plebeian" strain of punk emphasized amateur DIY music and lyrical aggression, particularly in the hardcore subgenre, which mutated in the suburbs and small towns of the United States, while "post"-punk forms emphasized musicianship and introspective lyrics that one could at least understand, if not always comprehend (Borthwick and Moy 2004).

This tension between raw, DIY self-expression and artistic experimentation and sophistication has been foundational to punk. In 1976 the British punk publication *Sideburns* printed crude drawings of three guitar chords and instructed readers to "now form a band" (Savage 2002: 279). New York's pop-punk pioneers the Ramones also illustrated this DIY ethic, making a virtue of their lack of technical ability by emphasizing speed, volume, and distortion. The idea was that if your guitarist can't play lead guitar, "fuck lead"; if your vocalist can't sing in tune, "fuck tunes"; and so on (Gendreon 2002: 255). Henry Rollins (1997: 11), an influential American hardcore vocalist, jokes that debates about musical quality in punk can always be short-circuited with the cry of "This isn't Van Halen!" Analyzing this precise relationship between punk and heavy metal, two counter-genres that balance excesses in the other, Steve Waksman (2009: 257–9) notes that punk has had some serious difficulties with fostering innovation, talent, and hard work, without considering the end result to be elitist and therefore selling out punk values. But at the same time as some punks were stripping away the pretensions of rock virtuosity, others were drawing influences from radical political and cultural theory. Stewart Home (1995: 22) may well be justified in critiquing writers such as the "lumpen-intellectual" Greil Marcus for trying to legitimize punk for bourgeois tastes by folding it into the artistic avant-garde, but that a serious intellectual (and serious lumpen-proletarian) like Home can find a place in punk is testimony to its ability to occupy the cultural high and low ground simultaneously.

As the preceding paragraphs suggest, the literature available to scholars on punk is quite expansive. Literature on punk can be roughly divided into two categories: essays on the deeper cultural meaning of punk, and studies of punk in particular times and places (Leblanc 1999: 33–4). The latter category is dominated by historical studies of punk's origins in London or New York, with Jon Savage (2002) and Clinton Heylin (2005) the most thorough, and also more recent studies of punk's ever-multiplying secondary scenes and subcultures. In the former category, more concerned with the deeper meaning of punk than with the banalities of everyday punk life, Thompson (2004: 2) recognizes a strong idealist current, notable in the influential work of Dick Hebdige (1979) and of course Greil Marcus (1989). We can also roughly divide literature on punk into academic and general (or fan) studies. In addition to monographs and edited collections such as this one, the academic literature on punk includes journal articles from across the humanities and social sciences, a minority of which are published in the scholarly journal *Punk & Post-Punk*, established in 2011, and vast amounts of gray literature: student essays, dissertations, and conference papers, often uploaded to databases such as Academia or ResearchGate. General and fan studies include conventional biographies of individual musicians, bands, and scenes, but also countless interviews and reviews published over the decades online and especially in zines, fan-made DIY magazines eschewing concerns with objectivity or grammar.

This division of literature sits uncomfortably with some punk scholars, who seek to erase the divide between fandom and academia, just as punk often tries to erase the divide between artist and audience, consumer and producer (Beer 2014: 40). Punk scholars have found their collective voice in the years since the founding of the *Punk & Post-Punk* journal, and the idea of the "punkademic" as a distinct kind of scholar-activist-pedagogue has begun to take shape. A state-of-the-field paper by *Punk & Post-Punk* editor Russ Bestley (2015) demonstrates a considered resistance to the theorization necessary in scholarly approaches, drawing closer to the norms of biographical rock journalism to emphasize punks' individuality. Similarly, quintessentially punk approaches to university teaching appear to be prioritizing one's own experiences and opinions, while deprioritizing prior scholarship in general, and concerns with theory and methodology in particular (Lamb 2017; Parkinson 2017). This may be largely the stuff of staffroom daydreams, but it is one possible way of translating *Sideburns* zine's invitation to learn three guitar chords and start a band into higher education.

In addition to their pedagogical experimentation, punkademics have critically interrogated the representation of punk in conventional academic studies, just like the conventional studies in this conventional book. Tom Astley's (2017: 43) endeavor to "write punk, rather than just write about punk" offers the most considered example of translating punk practices into scholarship. In lieu of a conventional journal article, reedited and redrafted into a final form, Astley publishes a facsimile of a conference paper script, full of scribbles and subtractions, self-doubt and self-criticism. The idea is that to write in a punk method is "to critically address—and make more visible—the processes of writing, editing and presenting the paper, perhaps by deemphasizing the content of the paper" (Astley 2017: 42). Returning to Stacy Thompson's (2004) punk desires, we can see that this process follows the values of DIY cultural production, as well as offering critical reflection on the norms of academia and commercial publishing. In focusing on his own anxieties and frustrations—"that familiar feeling that it might not come together at all, that everything I write is shit" (Astley 2017: 45)—there is something inescapably communal about this practice, too. "A punk is not afraid of their own limitations and vulnerabilities," Dave Beer (2014: 28) writes consolingly, reminiscent of the Ramones's "fuck tunes" attitude (Gendreon 2002: 255). Thompson's (2004) punk desires are also implicitly highlighted in Astley's (2017) lack of concern with content; his point is not that punks must utilize a particular theory or study a particular subject, but that the process of scholarship is demystified and, as with the music industry, the norms of academic life are shown to be imposed norms (Erricker 2001: 77).

Looked at from a certain perspective, this is an unremarkable example of the general "crisis of representation" ongoing in the social sciences for the last half century. This crisis of representation has a political edge to it when it concerns representations of the cultures of others, especially cultures of the marginalized, even including the evangelicals this book concerns itself with, theorized by Susan Harding (1991) as "repugnant cultural others" indigestible to decent-minded scholars. It is also a matter of representational politics if fan-scholars representing their own culture fear that, by adhering to scholarly convention, they are misrepresenting or undermining that culture. Applying influential essays by the anthropologists James Clifford (1983) and Paul Rabinow (1986) on tensions around the "totalizing" tendency of ethnographic representation, we can note that whenever scholars move from research to writing, in this case, from experiencing punk culture to communicating punk culture to others in a different medium, something goes missing. Their aversion to theory means they may not name it as such, but it is clear that what many punkademics are pushing toward in seeking a way to represent the "messy, disparate, deliberately antagonistic, uncontrollable and downright bloody awkward" nature of punk (Bestley 2015: 118) is a version of Clifford's (1983) idea of "dialogic" or, more ambitiously, "polyphonic" ethnographic writing wherein, just like the Ramones, the author is not concerned with keeping all the disparate voices in tune. Dave Beer's (2014: 37–8) proposal for a "punk sociology" also addresses this topic, approached through the work of Howard Becker, arguing that the punk sociologist should "accept and embrace" the varieties of social knowledge that researchers have available to them and "curate" the ideas circulating in society, especially in the media, rather than offer a totalizing social analysis.

Much of this is in accordance with the general turn in subcultural (and post-subcultural) studies in the 1990s, away from the grand ambitions of Marxist scholarship seeking to understand seemingly ephemeral youth subcultures within the broader horizon of the changing nature of capitalism and toward an appreciation of individual meaning-making within a consumer capitalist culture now considered unassailable (Abraham 2017: 22–9). On the other hand, however, punk studies' particular crisis of representation is remarkable for what it suggests about the vitality, or the thickness, of punk culture, which is not in keeping with ideas of (post-)subcultural identities as fluid and individual. What is it about punk that makes some scholars insist that it cannot only be "the subject of punk writing," but that punk must also be "the process too, the vehicle, the sound and intention" (Astley 2017: 42)? Aside from hip hop, perhaps, I cannot conceive of any other genre of music whose scholars would make such a claim. The answer must be that punk is both a positive culture, in the sense of—protestations to the contrary—certain accepted orthodoxies and something approaching a canon or shared tradition, and a negative, deconstructive cultural force that critiques and reimagines the traditions it comes into contact with, including academia and Christianity.

Studying Contemporary Christian Music

As strange as it may seem, punk and CCM have a profound commonality: their shared suspicion toward the mainstream culture industry, specifically, a shared suspicion that one cannot authentically express oneself within such a commercial culture. Each metagenre holds that there is something corrupting about the commercial mainstream and something pure about one's own creative vision that must be protected. The commercial mainstream must be resisted, therefore, or at least very carefully negotiated, with a great deal of suspicion (that word again!) directed to those appearing too eager for commercial success. It is not only punks who are in constant danger of selling out.

A purely ideological metagenre, one with no strictly musical boundaries, CCM is in essence the label given to popular music created largely by and for white American evangelicals—and those evangelicals around the world who look, with varying degrees of critical distance, to America for inspiration—as they have negotiated their relationship to the culture industry in the context of comparative affluence. Many evangelical artists reject or contest the CCM or "Christian band" label, a matter analyzed in Chapter 3, fearing being pigeonholed, but insofar as artists embed themselves within CCM infrastructure—its labels, festivals, venues, retailers, broadcasters, and publications—the term is hardly unreasonable for scholars or fans to employ or even impose. As an evangelical analogue of secular popular music, to avoid suspicion of being mere superficial distraction or commercial exploitation of believers, CCM artists must perform at least one of two religious services: either evangelize non-Christians or provide Christians with faith-strengthening alternatives to secular music (Romanowski 2000: 112–3). It is hard enough to find a receptive audience in the secular (or "general") market, even when one is not tethered to the Christian music industry and its evangelical expectations, so CCM artists who do achieve "crossover success" with non-evangelical audiences are rare indeed, and Christian punk bands have been unusually successful in this regard.

Just one example of American evangelicals embracing a form of culture they were "simultaneously demonizing" (Young 2017: 105), CCM emerged in the late 1960s, hand-in-hand with the evangelical faction of the hippie counterculture called the Jesus Movement. There has been significant recent interest in documenting the Jesus Movement, analyzed at length in Chapter 1 by Eileen Luhr, whose *Witnessing Suburbia* (Luhr 2009) is one of a number of titles, including books by David W. Stowe (2011) and Shawn David Young (2017), exploring the relations and tensions between fundamentalist revivalist religiosity and countercultural expression, and why so many Jesus Movement alumni ended up living lives of such apparent suburban conformity. *Hippies of the Religious Right*, by Preston Shires (2006), sums up this tension in its very title. Arguably the key figure in early CCM was Larry Norman, whose music embodied values common to the Jesus Movement; he was socially conscious but socially conservative. Norman expressed attitudes that would become associated with both the evangelical left and right (Gushee 2008), as discussed in Chapter 2, raising awareness of poverty while preaching apocalyptic warnings to repent from moral laxity (Powell 2002: 632–41; Young 2015). Norman's first album was recorded with his folk-rock band People!—peopled largely by Scientologists—which he titled *We Need a Whole Lot More of Jesus and a Lot Less Rock and Roll*. According to Norman, the title was changed at the last minute by Capitol Records to the less confrontational *I Love You* (1968), prompting Norman to quit the band and begin his own unapologetically Christian projects (Powell 2002: 633).

Norman may well have been exaggerating Capitol's censorship (Stowe 2011: 25), but the idea of major label interference provided a reverberating and energizing origin story for CCM, establishing its belief that professing evangelicals can only succeed as sellouts in the commercial mainstream. This mirrors punk's experiences with the music industry a decade later, documented on tracks such as the Clash's "Complete Control" (1977): "They said we'd be artistically free / When we signed that bit of paper / They meant let's make a lots of money / And worry about it later." Both metagenres had the same solution: DIY. Just as the punks did, evangelicals created their own musical infrastructure: labels, retailers, venues, and so on. As a consequence of its separation from the broader music scene, CCM came to reflect the culture of evangelical churches far more than it reflected the culture of broader popular music scenes, such that in the 1980s "the assumption became rooted that all evangelicals, even the rockers, are Republicans" (Stowe 2011: 247). Recognizing the commercial possibilities of both punk and CCM, thriving in their largely separate independent scenes in that decade, a commercially successful faction of both CCM and punk was coaxed back by the major labels in the early 1990s, prompting claims that artists who embraced the commercial possibilities this new relationship entailed were selling out their fans and their faith (Howard and Streck 1999: 75–110; Diehl 2007). Since the CCM industry had claimed itself to be the voice of evangelical authenticity and the secular mainstream to be hostile to true Christianity, this was hardly unexpected, and yet the rise to prominence of CCM coincided with the rise to prominence of televangelism and evangelical politics (Stowe 2011: 247–8).

The now well-established commercial side to CCM has attracted some of the metagenre's fiercest internal criticism—the standard tensions between artists, audiences, and corporations that any popular music studies textbook or university course is predicated upon, but with added religious righteousness—as well as insightful scholarly analysis. Drawing on Marxist cultural studies, so foundational in the study of punk and proximate youth subcultures at the University of Birmingham's Centre for Contemporary Cultural Studies (Hall and Jefferson 1976; Hebdige 1979), Eric Gormly (2003) argues that CCM could have been a tool to contest America's cultural hierarchies and values. He recognizes that since evangelicals are culturally marginalized, CCM and other forms of Christian popular culture are engaged in hegemonic contestation, not least through the obsession with Christian artists allegedly selling out for fame and fortune. But the "virtually indistinguishable" nature of CCM and secular music negates this possibility, Gormly argues, as CCM has been incorporated into the "hegemonic culture" of American capitalism (2003). Indeed, while the popular CCM artists Barry Alfonso (2002) interviews are critical of most aspects of the industry—including demands on women to be physically attractive but not sexually desirable and demands on everyone to be commercially successful without desiring worldly acclaim—they identify the industry's focus on money as the root of its evils. When I interviewed a former CCM industry insider in Nashville in 2010, his complaint was that the Christian music industry has its values precisely backward; its real focus is industry, music, and lastly Christianity.

As with literature on punk, literature on and around CCM can be divided into scholarly and general (or fan) studies, including the Christian music zines discussed in Chapter 1, plus a third category of religious literature, largely of the "Christian living" variety discussed in Chapter 7. This latter category has, of course, included some notorious ideas illustrating the discomfort many evangelicals have had with popular music. The most infamous example of this genre is probably Jacob Aranza's (1983) *Backward Masking Unmasked*, which accuses pretty much every successful pop musician of the time of sneaking subliminally Satanic messages into their songs, revealed by playing their music backward. More recently, however, popular Christian literature on popular music and culture has preferred critical engagement, with a good example being William Romanowski's (2001) *Eyes Wide Open: Looking for God in Popular Culture*. These texts, often titled *The Gospel according to ...*, in which one can insert the name of most popular media franchises, seek to demonstrate that compatible Christian values or themes can be found within secular music, film, and television; that Christianity is perennial; that secular media can be consumed through a Christian lens; and that secular media can form the basis for evangelization.

The content of these books, as sketched above, offers the best illustration of precisely why it is that American evangelical Protestants have created their own parallel popular culture. The desire to evangelize through popular culture, the basic unease with secular popular culture, and the desire to differentiate from secular education and media is simply not found to anything like the same degree among "mainline" and progressive Protestants. As Ian, a former Christian ska-punk musician from Seattle, told me, "People on the left in this country who believe in what I call the hippie Jesus thing, they don't talk about that; they don't feel they need to talk with you about that. All you see across the country is these conservative Christians who are really loud." Furthermore, Roman Catholics have historically been more concerned with integrating into the cultural and economic mainstream in the United States, rather than seeking pious exclusion. In his excellent comparative study *The Juvenilization of Christianity*, Thomas E. Bergler (2012) notes the futility of clergy's attempts to inculcate an evangelical-like suspicion of secular popular culture and the permissive society in post–Second World War minority Catholic youth who idolized Frank Sinatra. This explicit evangelical otherness has attracted the curiosity of journalists, as in Daniel Radosh's (2008) humorous study of the "parallel universe" of Christian pop culture and Andrew Beaujon's (2006) *Body Piercing Saved My Life*, which profile a number of Christian punk figures on the cusp of the genre's commercial high point.

Turning to scholarly literature in the broad field, we see that theologians can be just as focused on religious themes and secular content as more popular Christian writers; Tom Beaudoin's (2013) collection *Secular Music and Sacred Theology* is exemplary, including a chapter by Michael J. Iafrate (2013) on "staying punk" in the church. Many secular scholars are equally concerned with finding religious content or analogues in secular popular music. For Francis Stewart (2017), straight edge punk, the focus of Chapter 4, can function as a form of imminent religion—religion stripped of its sacredness—or as a surrogate, wholly material meaning system. Rupert Till (2010) stretches the analogy between religion and music fandom as far as possible in *Pop Cult*, with more than a little help from the fans themselves, such as the Prince obsessive wondering if he is the only one with a spiritual connection to his little purple idol: "When you cry, do you feel he is crying at the same time?" (2010: 65–6). Marcus Moberg (2012) offers a sober assessment of scholarship on popular music in and as religion, and his study of Christian heavy metal (Moberg 2015) offers some clear parallels to this current study, although with the exception of the hardcore punk/heavy metal crossover genre metalcore, Christian metal does not seem to have attracted the non-evangelical audiences as much as contemporary Christian punk has. Indeed, reviewing the related entries in the *Bloomsbury Handbook of Religion and Popular Music* (Partridge and Moberg 2017), Christian punk stands out in this regard for its ability to attract secular audiences.

Studying Christian Punk

A brief history of Christian punk must begin before the genre gained any kind of secular success. The first Christian punk bands emerged out of the post-Jesus Movement milieu of Californian evangelicalism in the early 1980s, with the support of the Calvary Chapel church in suburban Orange County. An early example of an evangelical megachurch, with a congregation of 25,000 in the late 1970s, Calvary Chapel's "youthful membership and relaxed style" contrasted with the apocalyptic prophecies of its lead pastor Chuck Smith, evidence of evangelical discomfort with growing affluence (Lahr 2007: 174–5). Notable in this milieu was Undercover, "perhaps the first Christian punk band" (Howard and Streck 1999: 51), whose eponymous pop-punk debut album was released under Calvary Chapel's Ministry Resource Center label (*Undercover*, 1982). The band was the focus of debate in CCM circles not only over whether punk was a genre Christians could appropriate or not but also over whether the band was authentically punk or not (Powell 2002: 974–5). This was shrugged off by the band, which admitted that if young people wanted to be cowboys, "then we'd be wearing cowboy hats" (Powell 2002). Nevertheless, Jay R. Howard, an important scholar of Christian rock, argues that Undercover signified something more than a preference for leather jackets over cowboy hats. Their punk recording of the nineteenth-century hymn "Holy, Holy, Holy" (*Boys and Girls Renounce the World*, 1984) demonstrated identification with the church and its traditions, but also critique of institutional stagnation (Howard 1992: 128), while the band's exclusive evangelical focus differentiated them from secular punk: "You can feed the world, you can disarm the world and still go to hell," said one band member (Howard and Streck 1999: 211).

Christian punk existed on the margins of even CCM throughout the 1980s, and the few bands that achieved some subcultural prominence, such as One Bad Pig and the Crucified, remained unknown beyond Anglophone evangelical churches. The 1990s signaled a radical shift in Christian punk, through the emergence in the United States of the Spirit-filled hardcore movement of teenage Pentecostals, growing up with one foot in their local church and, unlike earlier bands, the other foot in their local secular hardcore scene. As Tomas, a vocalist involved with the Spirit-filled movement, said:

> Mostly we were playing local shows [but] I did some small tours with the band. We did what I would classify as secular shows and they were in basements and warehouses—fear-for-your-life kind of places—and half were Christian venues. Our original intent was not to play Christian venues, but the Christian venues afforded us the opportunity to tour. Not to make money, but to pay our bills.

These bands also frequented Christian music festivals, most importantly the Cornerstone festival, organized between 1984 and 2012 by a remnant of the Jesus Movement, the Jesus People USA, discussed in Chapter 3 and at length in Chapter 8.

An equally significant development was the creation of Tooth & Nail Records by Brandon Ebel in 1993, around the time of secular punk's commercial second coming. One of the label's earliest releases was the compilation *Helpless amongst Friends* (1994), which captured the sound of Spirit-filled hardcore. Modeled on independent secular labels such as Rough Trade, Tooth & Nail focused specifically on Christian punk and alternative rock, providing a focal point for musicians and fans (Thompson 2000: 175–6). Initially aimed at evangelical audiences, the label soon became a home for artists such as pop-punk band MxPx who were criticized for not being exclusively evangelical enough for the CCM industry (Beaujon 2006: 56). Their album *Slowly Going the Way of the Buffalo* (1998) was certified gold, indicating 500,000 sales, and it is a good example of a less aggressively evangelistic approach; licensed to the secular A&M label the lighthearted album offers positive spiritual encouragement, and unlike Undercover, the band were not damning anyone to hell in their interviews. Tooth & Nail established a hardcore and metal-focused subsidiary in 1997, Solid State, and the Christian subsidiary of transnational major label EMI—the first company to sign, then drop, the Sex Pistols—purchased a 50 percent stake in Tooth & Nail in 2000, providing greater access to secular retailers and better production technology.

In the new millennium, Christian punk solidified itself within the subcultural secular mainstream, as the model of Spirit-filled hardcore bands simultaneously embracing Christian and secular scenes proved effective and permanent. As noted above, American evangelicalism was also changing its approach to secular popular culture, and Christian bands were consequently no longer playing to naïve and captive Christian audiences, but audiences used to professional production standards and more sophisticated content. Many evangelical churches were themselves exploring the spectacular potentialities of the culture industry in their Sunday services, providing free and effecting training in popular music performance. It may be a world away from punk, but the success of evangelical worship musicians on the various *Idol* talent shows is instructive. Young people raised in megachurches, in particular, "have had instruments shoved into their hands since they've been able to walk," said Will, an Australian metalcore guitarist who also plays in a megachurch worship band. "So by the time you're fifteen or sixteen and you're ready to play in a band and gig around, you know your instrument, you know how to play in front of people, you have a real head start," he added.

From the early 2000s onward, Christian punk bands achieved significant commercial and critical success, notably in the crossover metalcore genre; August Burns Red, The Devil Wears Prada, and Underoath each released albums that charted in the top ten of the (secular) Billboard 200 albums chart and found themselves feted in secular magazines such as *Alternative Press* in the United States and *Kerrang* in the UK. One consequence of this success was questions around authenticity and selling out, inevitable given the shared obsession of Christian punk's parent genres. Suspicion crept in that bands were driven by money, not ministry, and that religious identity was merely a matter of public image. Success requires almost constant touring, placing these groups of popular young men beyond the purview of their families and churches, analyzed in Chapter 5 in relation to Underoath's negotiation of Christian and secular rock norms. At this point, "you could no longer tell whether a band was Christian or not by what label they were on, by who booked them, by who they toured with, or by where they played," said Jeff, a Nashville-based pastor and former grunge musician, in noting the previously unthinkable diffusion and popularity of Christian punk bands within the secular subculture, but also voicing the common suspicion of fans and musicians alike about evangelical authenticity.

Identifying Christian punk bands is therefore not just a complex spatial matter—are they signed to Christian labels; do they perform at Christian venues and festivals; are they sold through Christian retailers; are they tagged on iTunes as subgenre #1098 Christian Rock?—but a temporal matter. Beliefs and identities are changeable, especially in the context of a largely youth-based subculture. As discussed in Chapter 4, individual spiritual "seeking" is the dominant model of religion in the societies we are concerned with in this book (Wuthnow 1998; Roof 1999), so just as some young people embrace Christianity, many young people alter or abandon their Christian beliefs and identity. As analyzed from a theological perspective in Chapter 10, some musicians come to question just how "Christian" the Christian scene actually is. One notable example is Underoath, whose difficult relationship with Christianity is analyzed in Chapter 5. Another is Ojo Taylor, songwriter for Undercover, who received nasty comments from "disgruntled fans" who learned of his changing beliefs (Taylor 2012). MxPx's similar move away from Christianity is satirized by just such a disgruntled fan:

> MxPx has a brand-new album out, but this time around they're offering something exclusively for their early evangelical fans: a "Special Christian Edition" of the record that adds several vague references to God and scrubs the

mild language found on the secular version ... "We wanted to show respect to the Christian fans that got us started," bassist and frontman Mike Herrera said. "This is our little way to say 'thank you' for following us through all these years: a special edition of the record just for you. We toss out every reference to 'baby' and replace it with 'Jesus'". (*Babylon Bee* 2018)

Although satirizing Christian music, the fan's sense of abandonment is evident here. If music's significance lies not in recordings but in the relationships music creates (Small 1998), then Christian music will sometimes signify broken relationships and abandoned faith.

We begin Chapter 1 by analyzing the particular relationships that laid the groundwork for Christian punk through the Jesus Movement of popular music and youth-focused evangelicalism. As Eileen Luhr makes clear, when documenting the rise of Christian zine culture in the chapter, there was an evident affinity between early punk aesthetics and the revivalist religious tradition of American evangelicalism. This affinity was performed in early Christian punk music, the focus of Chapter 2, in the form of prophetic protest. Eric Strother identifies concerns from the evangelical right and left in the music of this era, aimed at challenging increasingly affluent evangelical audiences. There is also something of the prophetic in more recent Christian hardcore, insofar as Strother identifies the "aggressiveness" of God in prophetic performance; in Chapter 3 Amy McDowell demonstrates how the punk ethic of outspokenness can be mobilized to counter the stigma of evangelicalism in these hardcore scenes in which Christians are a minority voice. Christians are also a minority within punk's straight edge sub-subculture, the focus of Chapter 4 by Ibrahim Abraham and Francis Stewart, but as in hardcore they have largely been successful in fusing religious beliefs and secular subcultural identity. When placed alongside spiritual and therapeutic individualism, the chapter reveals both continuities and contradictions between contemporary Christianity, straight edge punk, and hegemonic liberal individualism.

Chapter 5 begins the book's focus on gender, with Joshua Kalin Busman analyzing the successful metalcore band Underoath, recognizing how the band, the subgenre, and venues such as Nashville's Rocketown "open up a kind of radical futurity" for young men creating and negotiating their identity. Similar themes are dealt with in Chapter 6, in which Maren Haynes Marchesini engages with the controversial Mars Hill megachurch in Seattle, which built close relations with punk and alternative musicians, but collapsed under the weight of the aggressive masculinity of its lead pastor, Mark Driscoll. Nathan

Myrick confronts questions of masculinity and Christian punk more broadly in Chapter 7, critically analyzing his own experiences growing up in an evangelical culture hostile to the perceived feminization of church and society, as well as contrasting attitudes toward gender in Christian punk and metal music. Similarly emphasizing the diversity within Christian punk, Andrew Mall closely engages with the Celtic folk-punk band Flatfoot 56 in Chapter 8. Veterans of the Christian festival scene, the band are equally at home in Chicago's bars and nightclubs, differently performing an identity that is "simultaneously punk and Christian," he argues. This ease with which Christian punk bands move between sacred and secular spaces is one focus in Chapter 9, in which Ibrahim Abraham analyzes Christian punk from the perspective of three different sociological approaches to secularization. The topic of secularization appears again in Chapter 10, but as a process of "deconversion," in Michael J. Iafrate's bracing analysis of Christianity and punk from the perspective of liberation theology. Challenging scholars, musicians, and fans alike to look beyond the limited conservative evangelical genre of Christian punk if they want to locate Christian truths in punk music, Iafrate finds greater theological wisdom and liberating potential in the anticapitalist punk performances of Pussy Riot and Crass.

1

Rebel with a Cross: The Development of an American Christian Youth Culture

Eileen Luhr

Introduction

In 1969, the burgeoning Jesus Movement revival added a new icon to the pantheon of counterculture rebels of the Sixties: Jesus Christ. Two of the evangelical youth movement's underground papers, *Right On!* and the *Hollywood Free Paper*, printed a Western-style "Wanted" broadside that described Jesus as the "notorious leader of an underground liberation movement," charged with "practicing medicine, wine-making, and food distribution without a license." This outlaw had other identities: "Messiah, Son of God, King of Kings, Lord of Lords, Prince of Peace." Worse, he was notorious for "associating with known criminals, radicals, subversives, prostitutes, and street people." The poster concluded with a generalized warning to its targeted readers, the young people of the counterculture: "His insidiously inflammatory message is particularly dangerous to young people who haven't been taught to ignore him yet." The accompanying sketch of Jesus depicted him looking to his left with long hair and a beard—in line with the "hippie type" appearance described in the text (*Hollywood Free Paper* 1969; Judson Press 1971: 10–11).

The figure of Jesus as a symbol of youthful rebellion who challenged the Establishment—both within the Church and society at large—came to serve as an inspiration for members of the Jesus Movement and subsequent generations of young believers, including Christian punks. This countercultural Jesus—a subversive in a society that celebrated rebels—demonstrates the inroads young evangelicals made into "Christianizing" American culture within a youthful vernacular. In doing so, they successfully fused popular religious traditions to cultural forms that valued authenticity. These efforts at cultural activism proved that young adults could be agents rather than victims in the moral and cultural debates waged in the late twentieth century. This chapter contextualizes the origins of an American Christian youth culture that celebrated a dissenting, outsider ethos, beginning with the Jesus Movement and continuing through the development of a Christian punk culture in the late twentieth century.

Awakening a Christian Youth Culture

Earlier American revivals also enlisted young people in their missions. Enthusiastic religions offered young people an intense religious experience, personal salvation, and a strict moral code, which were often combined with an anti-institutional rhetoric. During the Great Awakening of the mid-eighteenth century, revivals found broad support among ethnically and economically diverse populations—and among young people (Isaac 1982; Bonomi 1986: 126, 153). Similarly, during the Second Great Awakening, Southern evangelical clergy recognized the power of peer pressure and dearth of outlets for youthful imagination, and consequently targeted young people in their proselytizing (Heyrman 1997: 80–1). As industrialization drew more Americans into the cities in the late nineteenth century, organizations such as the YMCA and the Salvation Army established a clear moral order for young people (Boyer 1978; Taiz 2001). Moreover, early Pentecostal periodicals in the early twentieth century recounted tales of children between the ages of 10 and 12 who were moved by the Holy Spirit—and permitted by adults—to offer exhortations and speak in tongues at services and, in a few cases, on the revival circuit (Wacker 2001: 105).

Concern for the state of young souls continued throughout the twentieth century, as religious conservatives voiced a general apprehension about the undermining of morality within homes, schools, and churches alike. Following the infamous Scopes Trial of 1925, centered on whether evolution could be taught to school-aged children in Tennessee, fundamentalists were so apprehensive about the impact of modern culture on American youth that they established a network of nondenominational organizations dedicated to fostering religiosity among young people. In the wake of the Second World War, rallies held by groups such as Youth for Christ drew hundreds of thousands of young people to concerts all over the nation during a period of heightened anxiety over juvenile delinquency (Carpenter 1997: 165–6; Ammerman 1998: 84; Turner 2008). The youth-driven Jesus Movement and its successors in the subsequent Christian punk scene therefore signaled a continuation of evangelical interest in the state of young people's souls.

Although Protestantism has tended to be linked to concepts such as "work," "thrift," and "sobriety," American revivalists long ago began to incorporate commercial entertainment styles that featured intense emotion and theatricality (Moore 1986, 2003). Through magazines, books, and music, young Protestants learned "values, norms, behaviors, and attitudes" that were important to their faith (McDannell 1995: 2). After the Second World War, these practices fostered a thriving network of independent Christian bookstores that catered to a growing evangelical population that believed Christianity was a "lifestyle" as well as a belief system. This trend was driven in part by the Jesus Movement, which from the late 1960s to the 1970s boosted the sales and improved the overall quality and range of Christian products, particularly music, available on the market (Stowe 2011: 168–78). The number of independent Christian bookstores grew from 725 to 1,850 between 1965 and 1975, with merchandise becoming less theological and more nondenominationally "Christian" (McDannell 1995: 246, 259).

The enthusiasm for cultural goods coincided with a critical shift in American religious practices and institutions during the postwar era. The lines of cultural conflict in the late twentieth century were drawn around the issue of "moral authority" (Hunter 1991: 42). In particular, the 1960s opened up new terms of public discourse that validated social criticism based on experience—including spirituality and morality—rather than on objectivity and rationality (Connolly 1999). Rather than marginalizing religion, this experiential shift resulted in a new configuration of public religiosity in which "power and authority are less centered" (Harding 2000: 79–80). In this new order, "born-again Christians" maintained their separate theological identities, but focused their Bible-based supernaturalist rhetoric on moral, social, and political issues such as the Equal Rights Amendment, school busing, pornography, abortion, homosexuality, public school curricula, and popular culture. These changes in the religious and political culture created opportunities for young evangelicals to critique "mainstream" beliefs in culturally relevant—yet often defiant—forms.

American Christian youth culture in the late twentieth century reveals three changes that helped young evangelicals disseminate their message. First, Christian youth culture emphasized the messages of personal salvation and morality, while de-emphasizing denominational differences, allowing young evangelicals to unite behind a simplified version of Christianity. Beyond discussions about specific religious beliefs, the culture emphasized that social change could only occur through individual regeneration and therefore attached a high value to personal piety. Second, as in the case of the "Wanted: Jesus Christ" poster, Christian youth culture offered young people certainty and empowerment, often with a "rebellious" edge—but one that attempted to inculcate young people into "traditional" beliefs. Christian youth culture often articulated evangelical identity as "radical" or outside the mainstream. Third, by expressing beliefs within the vernacular of contemporary culture, evangelical youth culture created opportunities for young people to "witness" to their peers. These cultural products were not simply appropriation or co-optation of secular styles: rather, they demonstrate the genuine passion many young people felt for both their music and beliefs. They also provided young people with the opportunity to become active "speakers" in cultural conversations about values and beliefs. In this third step, devout youths became agents who, by reintroducing religiosity into public spaces, could be agents of positive change in the world.

The Jesus Movement: The Counter to the Counterculture

The emergence of the Jesus Movement, a youth revival that began in California in the late 1960s, signaled that political progressives did not hold a monopoly over youth or rebellion. In other periods of American history, enthusiastic religion's focus on individual salvation and the "self-validating nature" of spiritual experience also provided a challenge to established hierarchies (Wigger 1994: 173). Moreover, evangelicals' long-standing sense of dispossession from the dominant culture in society allowed them to portray themselves as disenfranchised populists whose beliefs countered those in the American mainstream (Moore 1986). In other words, the evangelical nonconformist was a rebel with a cross.

   This oppositional outlook blended with the alienation that arose in the Sixties, when white middle-class youths of the New Left drew upon their feelings of cultural disaffection to articulate a vision of democracy that vowed to restore "authenticity" through radical social change. As recent historians have shown, however, youth movements of the Sixties might be better understood primarily as an existentialist search for self-meaning and a rejection of the rational and scientific technocracy that had come to characterize modern life in the postwar era (Rossinow 1998: 8; Shires 2006: 10–12). As the decade wore on, many disillusioned youths turned from leftist political engagement toward efforts that allowed them to shift the focus of transformation from social structures to the self, including both "Eastern" and "Western" religions (Kent 2001). When the Sixties are recast this way, the Jesus Movement's embrace of authenticity and marginality becomes a critical piece of the culture of the decade. As Preston

Shires (2006: 20) argues, the Jesus Movement represented a "spiritual rebellion" in which young converts defied "the accommodation liberalism had made with scientism" by demanding "the right to tap into the supernatural and to allow the supernatural to tap into the world." In this revised formulation, the concepts of transformation that characterized the decade—"rebellion," "revolution," "liberation," "freedom," and "self-definition"—appealed to a range of young people, including evangelicals, who sought to articulate their beliefs in ways that differentiated themselves from their elders (Luhr 2013: 64).

The religious crisis of the Sixties ultimately rested in liberal Christianity's failure to minister to the generation that came of age during the decade. Young converts sought out alternative spaces where they could develop their beliefs. According to Paul Baker (1979: 23), a Christian deejay and journalist, dissatisfied youths "were trying desperately to find answers which technology could not provide, and solutions which American Christianity had failed to convey to them." Baker presented the Jesus Movement, an "underground church," as a solution amid the confusion that hoped to "communicate Christ to millions of stranded and confused young people caught in the middle of a Generation Gap," as well as "instilling joy and excitement about true Christian living" to youths who had grown up as Christians but who had "grown tired of church life" (1979: 25).

The Jesus Movement included wide range of groups, including the Berkeley-based Christian World Liberation Front, which was involved in both campus and street evangelism, and Jesus People USA, an intentional living community in Chicago, discussed in Chapter 8. The most famous church associated with the Jesus Movement may have been Orange County, California's Calvary Chapel, whose pastor, Chuck Smith, invited young converts into his church, and in doing so helped transform the worship practices of evangelical Christianity. The movement also witnessed the arrival of leaders such as Duane Pederson, the publisher of the *Hollywood Free Paper*, and Arthur Blessitt, the founder of a Sunset Strip-based coffeehouse named "His Place," both of whom offered a "Christ-centered freedom" based on a faith-filled "rebellious activism" (Shires 2006: 93). Young converts engaged in street witnessing and gathered to celebrate their experiential faith at coffee shops, storefront churches, and on the beach. They spurred sales of Hal Lindsey's (1970) *The Late Great Planet Earth*, which prophesied the end of the world based on readings of current events and had 9 million copies in print by 1978, and *The Living Bible* (1971), a paraphrased translation, which sold over 3 million copies in its first year of publication alone (McDannell 1995: 248).

Music became by far the most important product created by members of the Jesus Movement, as they sought ways to express their religious beliefs. Free from the organizational hierarchy of established churches, young converts established their own record labels, convened their own music festivals, and started their own music magazines. In his history of Christian pop music, David W. Stowe (2011: 32) posits that the continuity between the culture and politics of the Jesus Movement and the overall social and political attitudes of the baby boomers and the countercultural left represented a "structure of feeling" for the Sixties generation; like secular members of the counterculture, converts emphasized individual experience, the significance of expression in music and arts, a sense of generational identity, a crusading sense of mission that often countered government control, and alienation from the accepted contours of modern life. Young converts believed, as rock critic Steve Rabey (1998) explained, "God could redeem and use their music just the same as He had done with them." Christian activist Randy Matthews claimed, "For the masses today, the greatest medium for expressing the gospel is rock 'n' roll … It's not even a musical form anymore; it's a culture, and it's a lifestyle. The pulpit of this generation and the next is the guitar" (Rabey 1998). When musician Larry Norman recorded the song "Why Should the Devil Have All the Good Music?" (*Only Visiting This Planet*, 1972), he captured the spirit of a youth movement that sought to infuse their faith into all aspects of popular culture.

Others, noting that rock music had originated in the gospel tradition, argued that their actions were not a redemption but a reclamation. Within this understanding of rock, the stories of legends such as Elvis Presley, Little Richard, and Jerry Lee Lewis, all of whom were raised in churches in the southern United States, were cautionary tales about the tensions between the world and the spirit. At the same time, critics were encouraged by the references to God and Jesus as well as the "fascination with eternity" in the music of the moment: for example, even if George Harrison's "My Sweet Lord" did not refer to Jesus (*All Things Must Pass*, 1970), his song reflected a "journey of self-discovery" (Seay 1986: 6–8). The Jesus Movement also praised musicals such as *Jesus Christ Superstar* (1970) and *Godspell* (1971), which positioned Jesus as "a gentle rebel who reluctantly challenges the powers that be, lionized by his young acolytes but deeply ambivalent about the role he was expected to occupy" (Stowe 2011: 7). *Rock in Jesus*, a magazine created by members of the Jesus Movement to provide information about Christian rock releases, reflected believers' simultaneous interests in secular and Christian music. The first issue featured a full-page advertisement for Joan Baez's folk album *Blessed Are …* (1970), which included songs written by Mick Jagger, and John Lennon and Paul McCartney. Yet the magazine also profiled key figures from the Jesus Movement such as Larry Norman and Love Song and printed lyrics to Christian rock songs and advertisements for Christian rock radio shows.

In addition to musical styles, the Jesus Movement spawned a series of "Jesus papers," a variation on the theme of Sixties-era underground papers (Peck 1985). This print culture, which included the *Hollywood Free Paper* and *Right On!*, demonstrates how young converts engaged in the era's rhetoric of generational social rebellion. At times, the papers expressed anger at ways that evangelists had been slighted, marginalized, harassed, or repressed by government officials. For example, after city officials in Glendale, California, closed down a prayer meeting in a private home for violating county zoning ordinances, the paper angrily published an op-ed that stated, "You can throw a beer-bust, a pot-party, or a swingin' sex orgy—but you can't have a prayer meeting in your home! ... Is America the America of our founding fathers meant for it to be or have we allowed it to slip from us?" (*Hollywood Free Paper* 1970a: 1). In adapting this dispossessed rhetoric, the (unnamed) author drew upon long-standing Judeo-Christian traditions of apocalyptic prophecy, dissent, and deliverance articulated by a "righteous remnant" (Cohn 1957: 20–3).

The underground papers also railed against mainstream churches and secular authorities that interfered with their quest for what they believed was an authentic spirituality that would revitalize Christianity. Many texts suggested parallels between the Jesus Movement's troubles with the institutional church and Jesus's confrontations with the Pharisees and Sadducees (Lawhead 1981: 93). Arthur Blessitt (1972: 9) proudly labeled the Christians of the New Testament as "revolutionaries," Jesus as a "rebel against the established order," and he speculated that Paul "probably caused more riots and arrests than any other person in his day." Some authors used contemporary slang to describe their antichurch stance. In an article entitled "Can You Dig It?" Rich Schmidt (1971: 30–3) criticized churches for presenting Jesus as "some kind of a prejudiced, middle-class materialist" or a "milk-toast [*sic*] character that wants to spoil your bag with a bunch of rules and regulations." Schmidt told readers, "Jesus Christ is truly the Cool One because He took the rap for you and me on the cross, so that we could have life—the real down-inside kind of life that hits at the very core of your being" (1971).

In addition to reprinting the rebel Jesus in the "Wanted: Jesus Christ" poster, the *Hollywood Free Paper* ran full-page illustrations positing "Jesus is the Liberator" (*Hollywood Free Paper* 1971a). Drawing from the iconography of the Black Panthers, the paper ended articles by exclaiming, "JESUS PEOPLE UNITE!

ALL POWER THROUGH JESUS!" and by publishing illustrations with the same phrase, as well as one labeled "3rd World Liberation: All Power to the People Thru Jesus" (*Hollywood Free Paper* 1970b, 1971b). These iconographic and rhetorical devices demonstrate a redirection of certain kinds of political activism toward intense religious experience, often through the figure of Jesus, who provided the movement with a subversive edge even as it rejected elements of the transgressive behavior endorsed by the wider counterculture.

The "Jesus concerts" that originated in the movement provide a glimpse of how converts believed that religious revival could transform the nation; they also served as an important legacy for later evangelicals who came together at the Cornerstone festivals that began in the mid-1980s, discussed in Chapter 8. In 1972, Campus Crusade for Christ organized Explo '72, a multiday event in Dallas for young Christians that culminated with an assembly at the Cotton Bowl headlined by Billy Graham and followed by a Christian concert. In the wake of the concert, one author reflected on the utopian possibilities of the concert. He admitted that a survey taken by a Dallas newspaper had identified the majority of concertgoers as "middle-class, conservative Christians," but argued that "regardless of whether the delegates were low-class, middle-class, upper-class or no-class; regardless of whether they were conservative or liberal, short or tall, tan or white, brown or black, young or old, one fact remains: they got along" (Edmondson 1972). He implicitly contrasted the orderliness exhibited at Explo to the Rolling Stones' tragic Altamont concert in 1969 and concluded that the young people and adults at Explo had been practicing "Christ-like living" (Edmondson 1972).

As the members of the Jesus Movement aged and the first generation of contemporary Christian music faded, the Sixties remained a model for Christian critics and young fans. By the 1990s, Christian music had become a multimillion dollar business, with a chart in *Billboard* magazine and non-Christian ownership of Christian record labels (McDannell 1995: 265–6). Yet the sense that social change could only occur through individual conversion and personal action remained, as did the belief that young evangelicals' cultural activism served as an important counter to mainstream values.

"Christian Punk?": Christian Zine Culture, 1984–2000

The network of Christian rock bands, labels, music festivals, and venues established by young believers during the Jesus Movement flourished in the 1970s. The products became professionalized in quality and corporatized in distribution, with labels such as Myrrh, Solid Rock, and Sparrow dedicated to releasing Christian recordings. By the late 1980s, fueled by pop artists such as Amy Grant and Michael W. Smith, the genre's solid sales were beginning to attract secular investors. Yet even with wider recognition, the importance of countering mainstream values remained. The Christian video market for children also expanded, as series such as Focus on the Family's *McGee and Me* and Big Ideas Productions' *VeggieTales* sold briskly after their debuts in the early 1990s. In her analysis of Christian media, Heather Hendershot (2004: 28, 30, 37) suggests that evangelicals drew upon heavily commodified forms of resistance identities intended to make kids feel "less alienated from American consumer culture." Conservative Christians' acceptance of commercial culture added to a growing desire for solid middle-class respectability that was expressed in consumerist terms: these products appealed to Christian parents because they were legible to adult interpretation through their engagement with the broader mass culture.

Over the years, a number of church and parachurch organizations established youth-targeted publications aimed at integrating Christian teenagers into church, home, and society. These magazines included *Brio*, a girls' magazine established by Focus on the Family, and *Campus Life*, a teen magazine founded in 1944 and owned by the periodical *Christianity Today*. With a circulation of nearly 120,000 in 1994, *Campus Life* resembled a Christian version of teen-themed magazines like *Seventeen*. Like its secular counterparts, the glossy magazine covered a range of issues ostensibly of interest to teens, including dating, music, school, and family relationships. The magazine placed a special emphasis on the issue of self-control and chastity among teenagers, with an overall tone that was inescapably prescriptive.

As with the Jesus Movement, not every Christian teenager lived by the exact tenets set forth by religious elders. Indeed, many young Christians expressed feelings of alienation from "establishment" conservatives and the normative religious values they professed to defend, finding little solace in adult-endorsed Christian publications for teens. There were, however, magazines where young Christians developed their identities with a less direct adult filter. Just as the underground publications of the 1960s inspired young converts to start their own papers, young evangelicals during the 1980s established an array of zines that echoed the style of punk publications of the same era.

Zines are photocopied magazines created by fans from their homes. Overall, amateur participation in the creative process is intended to democratize cultural production as part of a broader punk critique of passive consumerism (Duncombe 1997: 117–30). Like early punk musicians who rejected the notion of "professionalism" in sound, zine producers embraced a do-it-yourself aesthetic that spurned slick layouts, journalistic distance, and glossy paper for cut-and-paste layouts, confrontational editorials and reviews, rough drawings, and photocopied pages. The language and layout of the original zines like *Sniffin Glue* or *Ripped and Torn* suggested the urgency of "memos from the front line" (Hebdige 1979: 111–12). Young Christians writing in a later moment found the genre well suited to amateur (but not necessarily angry) evangelists who viewed themselves as soldiers on the moral front lines. The personal—often emotional—style of the medium, as well as its participatory nature, provided young Christians with a way to express their faith. With titles such as *Gospel Metal, Heaven's Metal,* and *White Throne,* the zines were usually written by and for young believers who were interested in the Christian music scene; these zines, in turn, helped build a grassroots network of fans. Some zines, including *Heaven's Metal,* began as photocopies but became more professionalized; others remained steadfastly simple—if they continued to be published at all. Between 1980, when Chris Yambar started *The Activist,* and the late 1990s, when internet access and personal websites became widespread, American evangelicals established nearly 200 zine titles.

Christian zines showed their secular influence in layout style, tone, subject matter, and musical preference, but they reflected a strongly moralistic outlook. On the one hand, many of these zines, like the media that Hendershot (2004) discusses, allowed kids to engage in mild rebellion that, for example, poked fun at self-satisfied churchgoers and fundamentalist "squares" while otherwise attempting to integrate young people into church, home, and society. On the other hand, the youth culture's anti-institutional language also drew upon a long-standing evangelical rhetorical tradition of dissent that had also been a feature of the Jesus Movement. Other zines were determined to position themselves as heirs to both the "come-outer" religious tradition of American evangelical dissenters dating to the Second Great Awakening of the early nineteenth century and secular expressions of alienation like punk. Despite contrasting rhetorical positions, the Christian zines shared the goal of creating a distinct Christian youth identity that advocated strict doctrinal and moral codes.

While some zines attempted to attract non-Christians, most published under the assumption that their small readership was composed entirely of Christians, with content offering models for religious inspiration, often in the form of music reviews, band interviews, and alerts about upcoming concerts. One zine, *Take a Stand,* provided Bible study guides and also offered a correspondence directory, which provided a list of names, ages, and musical influences for people who wanted to hear "from other Christian rockers" (*Take a Stand* 1987). Many zines followed the example of *Contemporary Christian Music (CCM)*—the glossiest and most professional Christian music magazine—by offering profiles on metal groups like Stryper and Barren Cross and on "lifestyle Christianity." If readers failed to draw inspiration from the stories of Christian musicians, they could focus on the personal testimonies about personal salvation published in zines like *Rizzen Roxx* and *The Narrow Path*. Converts described how Christianity— usually in the figure of Jesus—guided them through difficult periods of their lives when they considered suicide or developed a drug addiction.

The zines also covered Cornerstone, an annual event that came to define contemporary Christian music. Jesus People USA, a residential religious community in Chicago, began Cornerstone at the Lake County fairgrounds in Illinois in 1984. During its most popular period in the 1990s and 2000s, the festival provided a venue for alternative Christian artists who sought to "bridge the differences" between younger, more radical believers and their older peers (Mall 2015a: 102). Advertisements for the event appeared in nearly every Christian music publication, and enthusiastic first-person accounts of fans willing to endure interminable road trips, miserable camping accommodations, and adverse weather conditions for the opportunity to partake in three days of concerts by the genre's biggest acts became required reading.

Zine editors, like revivalist preachers, outlined a shortened path to salvation and regeneration, leaving little need for doctrinal or theological disquisition. Most tended to equate Christianity with evangelicalism. For example, in an issue of *Rizzen Roxx*, the editor explained the basic requirements for a church to follow Jesus: salvation through Jesus, belief in the Bible's literal truth, and an emphasis on fellowship and community; these basic tenets made worship practices flexible, allowing music to assume a primary role in young Christians' faith (Harper 1988b: 4–5). Another zine, *Different Drummer*, published an essay that dismissed religious sectarianism while forwarding a similar path to salvation (Yambar 1989: 12–15).

Salvation occupied an important place in these young Christians' belief system, but the zines often defined their difference from the world through adherence to a strict personal code of conduct rather than through doctrine. The zines urged readers to exercise self-control and assured them they would find an improved state of satisfaction through religion; these behavioral norms mirrored the renunciatory tendencies of the secular straight edge movement, discussed in Chapter 4, that was viewed as a reaction to the nihilism of early punk. The zines were often quite specific in naming the kinds of temptation that young people needed to resist. For example, in an article entitled "Eternal Life," the *Rizzen Roxx* editor told readers that a convert needed to "take control" of his or her life by repenting from sin and following "righteousness" rather than "foolish desires of the flesh" such as "getting drunk, smoking dope, having sex outside marriage, cutting people down, and being a jerk" (Harper 1988a: 2). Another zine, *Gospel Metal*, tried to empathize directly with readers by offering situations—including parents' divorce, the end of a relationship, or a hangover from a party—and counseling them to avoid "Misery, Opposition, Remorse, and Emptiness" by opening their hearts to Jesus, reading the Bible, talking to God, and going to church (Day 1987: 32–4).

Most Christian zines devoted the bulk of their pages to delineating the path to salvation and dissecting the latest releases by Christian rock bands. While some remained focused on Christian audiences and Christian cultural trends, others positioned themselves and their readers for engagement with secular audiences and music. Engagement with popular culture made Christians more aware of the interests of their non-Christian friends and neighbors. Publications such as *Cutting Edge* and *CCM* occasionally reviewed the releases or concert performances of mainstream bands like U2, whose members included professed believers, in addition to its coverage of evangelical groups (Kennedy 1984: 1; Horne 1992: 35).

Even as many young evangelicals settled into the comfortable Christian youth subculture established by the previous generation, a sense of alienation—whether from the church or the world—remained prominent in Christian zines. Some Christian cultural products were intended to make young believers feel less alienated from society, but many Christian zines took an outsider's stance toward the world. As a means for marking their distance from the mainstream, zines embraced some of the conventions of punk. A "self-consciously oppositional genre of popular music and culture" (Abraham and Stewart 2017: 241), punk emerged in the mid-1970s in London and New York. To express their refusal to partake of mainstream norms and authority, punks have mobilized a range of oppositional rhetorical practices, archetypes, and symbols. The vulgar rhetoric of iconic, early British punk was "drenched in apocalypse," according to Dick Hebdige's (1979: 27–9) influential cultural analysis of the period.

The young American evangelicals who embraced punk did so out of a desire to express an otherness from the so-called "mainstream." Zine editors appropriated the punk subculture's propensity for defiantly adapting derogatory labels and mimicking the language of crisis that permeated British media in the 1970s. The titles epitomized this attitude: *Take a Stand, Radicals for Christ, Baptized Rebellion, Radically Saved, The Nonconformist, Against the Grain, Different Drummer,*

Knights in Messiah's Bold Radical Army (or *KIMBRA*), *Screams of Abel*, *Thieves and Prostitutes*, *Narrow Path*, and *Slaughter House*. However, the alienation that pervaded Christian punk was not a refusal to assimilate into the capitalist parent culture. Whereas secular punks embraced negative labels out of a sense of irony, or the language of crisis out of a sense of nihilism (Hebdige 1979: 112), Christian zines signified their "otherness" through their sense of moral righteousness. The zines that most thoroughly embraced the punk aesthetic, *Thieves and Prostitutes* and *Slaughter House*, affirmed strict religiosity among its young readers. Young evangelicals cited punk aesthetics and music as influences, but their demands also resembled elements of the "come-outer" tradition of Protestant sects that sought religious truth from a position outside established religious institutions.

Although young editors sought to proselytize among the unchurched, evangelical zines did not view their secular counterparts as allies, nor did they seek their good opinion. This was perhaps a good thing, since secular editors scoffed at the work of their Christian counterparts. In response, *Slaughter House* and *Thieves and Prostitutes* flaunted the negative reviews granted to them by secular zines. Even as Christian zines advocated personal rather than political revolution, Christian editors accused their counterparts of creating a normative standard for judging "punk" attitude.

The editors of *Thieves and Prostitutes* put a great deal of thought into their assertion that they were the authentic rebels of American society. The publication's main contributors, John DiDonna ("the thief") and Alexis Levy Neptune ("the prostitute"), were recent converts to Christianity; DiDonna claimed to have been a drug dealer and user, while Neptune was a convert from a nonobservant Jewish family who had dabbled in a number of religions and the occult. Unlike many Christian zine creators, who seemingly published primarily for Christian audiences and who were critical of secular music and culture, DiDonna and Neptune intended their publication to be used for evangelism (the zine was free) and candidly expressed admiration for secular bands like The Damned and novels like *Catcher in the Rye* (DiDonna and Neptune 1993: 7).

In an effort to establish its punk bona fides, *Thieves and Prostitutes* published a lengthy essay that traced a genealogy of punk showing the cultural and dispositional parallels between Christianity and punk. In an article entitled "Christian Punk?" Neptune (1993: 8–9) outlined her response to the question, "How can you be a Christian and be a punk at the same time?" For Neptune, the stances of punk and radical Christianity were not so different; indeed, she suggested, "If Jesus were here today ... punks would be just the people he would hang-out with and make disciples of." As described by Neptune, Christianity and punk were, at their root, reactions to stale aesthetics: early Christians rejected the hierarchies of organized religion, while punk shunned the pretensions of art and the music industry (1993).

Neptune knew her punk history. She noted that "the punk movement started as a reaction against mainstream methods of artistic expressions of the 70's and middle- or working-class youths rejecting the middle-class values and bourgeois status quo philosophy of mainstream culture." She added that the "punk aesthetic" helped punks separate themselves from society. Neptune also pointed to several New Testament verses—including the verse from Paul's second letter to the Corinthians that fundamentalists used to justify separation—to argue that Christians are called upon to remain separate from the world. Referring to the other contributors, all of whom were recent converts, Neptune stated, "As punks we were more willing to accept Jesus because we were already non-conformists so being accepted by the world didn't matter much to us." She concluded her analysis with a series of comparisons that elaborated the affinity between punk rock and Christianity: as Jesus "sought to make God accessible to the common man," so did punk try "to make art accessible to the average working class guy"; just as Jesus used uneducated fishermen and shepherds to spread his message, punk rock valued "untrained performers"; just as biblical figures like John the Baptist and Samson used clothes and hair to highlight their devotion to God, punks used clothes, hair, and jewelry to announce their stance toward the world. In this formulation, Christian punks claimed an identity based on their marginalization from both the established Christian church and mainstream society. Like the Jesus Movement before her, Neptune organized her understanding of religion around the figures of Jesus and a handful of iconoclastic, mostly New Testament, figures. The emphasis on the message of Jesus, rather than on a historical church, provided young people with a renewable inspiration for rebellion (Neptune 1993).

As formulated by Neptune, both punk and Christianity provided a radical reorientation of the self through nonconformity. Whereas many punks embraced individualistic negation, Christian punks channeled their new religious code into a moral crusade that did little to challenge economic structures while attacking the perceived permissiveness of liberalism. The outsider rhetoric proved to be a particular asset because it allowed Christian zine owners, like their predecessors in the Jesus Movement, to claim that they were the authentic exemplars of dissent in American culture.

Christian zines helped young people develop the boundary of their religious identity through concepts of salvation, fellowship, and personal morality. At the same time, however, the identity forged through their engagement with popular culture allowed young Christians to become more active speakers in cultural debates about values and beliefs. The zines occasionally printed articles that expressed a social gospel message, which tended to be identified with liberal and progressive Christianity. For example, in an interview commemorating his zine's one-hundredth issue, *Cutting Edge* editor Dan Kennedy (1992: 7) lamented that his denomination, the Southern Baptist Convention, was controlled by the conservative contingent that was "opposed to the idea of a social gospel." Although Christian punks emphasized their alienation from institutional and political Christianity, their beliefs often intersected with conservative evangelical activists. The attitudes of Christian zines regarding abortion demonstrate that a key component of Christian identity rested in one's relationship to the unregenerate world. The Christian punks at *Slaughter House* and *Thieves and Prostitutes* took the most extreme position, but other zines voiced similar antiabortion opinions.

Christian zines cited a number of beliefs that distanced them from the world, but the issue of abortion crystallized their approach to sin and social behavior. *Heaven's Metal* (1986) printed an ad reading "Abortion is murder!" that urged readers to take political action by contacting their representatives in Washington on the issue. Some zines tried to get readers tapped into grassroots organizations that opposed abortion, as when *The Burning Bush* printed an invitation for interested parties to attend a weekly Bible study and fellowship group in Kansas City that included a "pro-life branch" in addition to outreach to bands and concertgoers (Julian 1990). *Radically Saved* also featured a pro-life article titled "Abortion is Not the #1 Problem," linking the problem of abortion to general sexual immorality in America, since "the sin of abortion is really a follow-up sin to the sin of fornication" (Wilkerson 1989: 3–4). *Slaughter House* (1990), a free punk zine, worked its antiabortion message into a collage on its title page. Amid text and other drawings pasted at odd angles on a youth-oriented catalog, there was a drawing of an empty highchair on a slightly elevated platform; the chair was hooked up to electrical outlets, suggesting that it was an executioner's chair. The drawing's caption read, "A baby is a terrible thing to waste: Stop Abortion."

Conclusion

The Jesus Movement established spaces for young evangelicals to "Christianize" American culture within a youthful, outsider vernacular. Subsequent generations, especially within the Christian punk scene, drew upon these symbols and traditions as they continued their critique of mainstream churches and society. An alumni of the Jesus Movement, and editor and publisher of *CCM* magazine, John Styll (1991) told a new generation of readers that "your world today is different because of a major cultural revolution that began in [the 1960s]." He challenged "songwriters, artists, record industry executives and those in related fields" to undertake a similar mission. The new generation needed "to think in terms no smaller than starting a new revolution in popular culture. It happened in the '60s when some musicians captured the spirit of the age and led the way to a new reality. It's time for a new revolution, and followers of Christ are to lead it. Isn't that the essence of the Great Commission?" (Styll 1991). Rather than reversing changes of the 1960s, the leaders of the new "cultural revolution for Christ"—as one reader called it—believed that the 1960s provided the blueprint for a new movement (*CCM* 1991: 6). Even as Christian youth culture became big business, a subset of believers still thought the endeavor to be a rebellious and subversive act. This time around, they hoped, Jesus would be bigger than the Beatles.

2

"We're Not into Social Compliance": Sin and Prophetic Protest in Christian Punk

Eric Strother

Introduction

Punk rock emerged in the mid-1970s in a musical landscape that was more diverse than at any other time in history. Musically, it was an offshoot of the garage rock of the late 1960s. Its deliberate amateurishness and do-it-yourself (DIY) aesthetic were evidenced by its stripped-down performances and raw production style, standing in stark contrast with the virtuosity of heavy metal and the polished production of disco. Its brash tone and sometimes screamed vocal style were also decidedly different from the folk-influenced soft rock that filled radio programming lists. In spite of some short-lived commercial success, this was hardly music for the masses; instead punk was music for a subculture dissatisfied with what mainstream society offered.

Punk's emergent subculture generally believed that the values of the 1960s counterculture were being lost to an empty aesthetic—everyone had long hair, fringes, and flares. As Phil Strongman's (2007: 16–17) history of punk described it:

> The look that was "youth being a little extreme" in the last half of the sixties is all-encompassing now ... It is curiously enough, the uniform of an age of individuals ... Individual singers, and individual bands, sing individual songs. They sing about love, sex, romance, romantic disappointment, etc. ... and they wear the Uniform.

"Like trousers, like brain!" declared the Clash's Joe Strummer (Walsh and Perry 2017: 45), and the punk aesthetic, as journalist and punk chronicler Jon Savage (2008: xvi) described it, was a bricolage that "threw together almost every single youth-cult style, stuck them together with safety pins, and then proudly paraded around the results ... The effect was at once striking, hallucinatory, and threatening." Savage's description reveals an important understanding that moves beyond fashion: while punk is often viewed as a single movement, the truth is that there have been a wide range of manifestations of punk identity, unified by a few common threads.

One common thread that has bound the subculture together is the emphasis on individual autonomy, authenticity, and self-expression. Philip Lewin and J. Patrick Williams (2009) argue that ideals of self-expression and authenticity are foundational for punk. They root the quest for these ideals in the eighteenth-century writings of philosopher Jean Jacques Rousseau, who popularized the idea of "moral freedom," defined as submitting only to oneself and not allowing external influences to dictate one's life. According to Lewin and Williams, the quest for authenticity and self-expression by members of the punk subculture is "oriented toward self-discovery inspired by Romantic aesthetics and an effort to stabilize reality in the postmodern condition" (2009: 66). Punks are perceived to reject social norms, particularly in terms of appearance and acquiescence with authority, but many punks believe they are more authentically embodying the modern moral imperative to individuality than those who might more obviously claim to be living moral lives.

Another common thread has been the angst and frustration of working-class youth. In contrast to the typically middle-class youths of the 1960s counterculture, who experienced cultural alienation within conformist societies that refused them space for self-realization, the working-class youth of the 1960s and 1970s held no such ambitions. Rather, they experienced the same inequalities as their parents' generation, even fearing things might get worse (Clarke et al. 1976). Tricia Henry's (1989: xi) study of the birth of punk makes this clear, describing the economy of mid-1970s Britain as one in which

> the steadily rising cost of living exacerbated a mood of unrest and discontent among working class people forced to struggle for the basic necessities of existence ... the outlook for bettering their lot in life seemed bleak. In this atmosphere, when the English were exposed to the seminal punk-rock influences of the New York scene, the irony, pessimism, and amateur style of the music took on overt social and political implications.

In her study on hardcore in the United States, Susan Willis (1993: 375) makes the assertion that in the 1980s and early 1990s, when hardcore punk was in its ascendancy, economic conditions in the United States led to a "depreciation of middle-class standing" in conjunction with "an expansion in working-class consumption, making it appear that the two classes have merged in a common experience of a life-style." The frustrations over economic inequalities and the growing awareness of systemic racial (and eventually gender) inequalities coalesced within many punk scenes into a meta-ideology of anti-establishmentarianism based on the view that society is broken at a fundamental level and requires restructuring in order to function properly. This has typically been expressed by punks as "a desire to topple hierarchies and power structures that undermined their abilities to achieve self-realization," rather than through more conventional campaigns for social justice and equality (Lewin and Williams 2009: 72).

While self-expression and frustration have been a common underpinning for the punk subculture, punk's diversity has led to a wide variety of expressions within these perspectives. In Willis's (1993: 374) view, the ideologies circulating within hardcore function as "styles whose codes of meaning are manipulated and disputed," complimenting Stacy Thompson's (2004) view that punk in general is constituted by vague "desires" rather than specific rules. In contrast to more normative approaches, such as the theological analysis in Chapter 10, which may seek out punk's true moral center, the approaches discussed above are quite comfortable with the contested nature of punk. Discussing the sociology of youth culture, within which punk has been a topic of serious interest, Andy Bennett (2000: 11) notes that "rather than attempting to impose a singular discourse on the stylistic sensibilities of youth," sociology (and musicology for that matter) "remains receptive to the plurality of issues and circumstances that underpin the identity politics of contemporary youth cultures." One punk interviewed by Lewin and Williams (2009: 71) echoes all these scholarly views with the observation that "the punk scene has so many different facets … but everybody is rejecting the same thing."

One of the variations upon the themes of self-expression and frustration involved the emergence of bands in the early 1980s that blended the look, sound, and style of punk with evangelical Christianity. These bands maintained the nonconformist fashion choices, the DIY musical aesthetic, and the outspoken lyrical style while creating Christian-themed punk anthems that proclaimed, "God rules," "Jesus is number one with me," and "I'm into God." While much of the output of Christian punk bands in the 1980s and 1990s were songs of positive, spiritual encouragement of this variety, a number of these bands also maintained punk's desire to bring awareness of the dysfunctions of the current social order. Drawing on illustrative examples of American Christian punk lyrics from the 1980s and 1990s, this chapter explores the ways Christian punk bands approached social awareness and musical protest. The chapter will show that while Christian punk was not simply about personal spirituality, Christian bands' approach to social issues differed from their secular peers by primarily focusing on social issues through the lens of sin. In this way, we will see Christian punks taking on a "prophetic" role, using aggressive music to bring a discomforting message to American evangelicals living comfortable lives.

Punk, Protest, and Sin

Some of the most prominent early Christian punk bands, such as Lifesavors, Undercover, and Altar Boys, were associated with Calvary Chapel in Costa Mesa, California. Calvary Chapel came under the leadership of Chuck Smith in 1965 and developed a mission for evangelizing members of the hippie and surfer subcultures (Balmer 2004: 121), making it a focal point of the Jesus Movement in the 1970s, analyzed in Chapter 1. The Jesus Movement was a charismatic evangelical (Pentecostal) movement that sought to return to the principles of the early church, as depicted in the Acts of the Apostles, including in many cases communal living and an emphasis on "signs and wonders," such as faith healing and speaking in tongues. At its peak, the Jesus People, or the Jesus Freaks, as they were also known, "formed communes, fellowships, and coffeehouses; created their own Jesus Rock bands; and printed their own street papers to hand out on evangelistic forays" (Eskridge 2013: 4). The Jesus Movement also encouraged a countercultural political outlook, which not only helped to make it appealing to the hippie subculture but also provided a perfect breeding ground for Christian punks, who "found that the genre's righteous sense of alienation appealed to their sense of dispossession from mainstream American society" (Luhr 2010: 448).

By the early 1980s, the Jesus Movement had fragmented and been subsumed into the factions known as the "Christian right" and "Christian left," or as David Gushee (2008) more accurately labels them, acknowledging divisions between evangelicalism, mainline Protestantism, and Roman Catholicism, the "evangelical" right and left. The evangelical right has been led by figures like James Dobson, Jerry Falwell, Pat Robertson, and more recently, Jerry Falwell, Jr., and Franklin Graham. In their understanding, the evangelical right has taken up the cause of establishing the Kingdom of God on earth through legislation that promotes a morality rooted in a conservative reading of the Bible. Gushee describes this activism as "an effort to bring faith to bear on the world. It is rooted in a commitment to Christ and one particular understanding of what that commitment means for culture, law, and politics," and it is often couched in the language of "traditional American values" (2008: 44). Publicly, the evangelical right is known for its advocacy for abstinence-only sex education, antiabortion legislation, and prohibitions against same-sex marriage, as well as its championing of school prayer, public religious displays on government property, and the rights of Christian business owners to refuse service based on their religious beliefs.

The evangelical left, championed by people like Tony Campolo, Brian McLaren, Jesse Jackson, and Jim Wallis, has taken a different approach to bringing the Kingdom of God to earth. Through its focus on social justice in connection with the teachings of Jesus concerning the treatment of other people, the evangelical left has sought to live out the words of the Lord's Prayer, "Your kingdom come, your will be done on earth as it is in heaven" (Mt. 6:10). Gushee (2008: 59) describes their core beliefs as follows:

> Characteristically, the evangelical left argues that the teachings of the Bible, especially the prophets and Jesus, require Christians to be concerned about poverty, war, racism, sexism, and the environment. These are not the only salient issues ... but they are indeed at the center of their moral vision. They are most interested in pursuing peace and justice as these relate to race, class, and international conflict. They highlight issues that the evangelical right generally downplays (race and class and ecology) or takes an entirely different approach to (gender and war). They tend to downplay issues (abortion and homosexuality) that the evangelical right highlights.

While these two groups historically have been in conflict regarding what Christianity should look like in contemporary America, they tend to agree on one basic point: social problems are the result of sin.

The nature of sin, however, has been debated and contested throughout the history of Christianity. In Joy Ann MacDougall's (2011: 473) concise historical overview of the debate, sin is conceptualized as "a disordered or disrupted relationship to God," with theologians from Paul onward attempting to codify what this concept looks like in everyday life. For Augustine, sin was a matter of pride "in which human beings place their will above that of God's and, in so doing, assume God's place as ultimate judge" (MacDougall 2011). Augustine also formulated the doctrine of "original sin," the belief that Adam's refusal to obey God created a condition in humanity in which human beings are no longer capable of avoiding sin and choosing to pursue God's will on our own. Augustine believed this condition is transmitted from generation to generation through procreation, as if it is part of the genetic makeup of humanity, as well as through socialization. Martin Luther took this idea a step further by saying that Adam's sin changed the very nature of humanity to such a degree that the natural righteousness that existed in Adam and Eve before the Fall has become completely destroyed, and human nature now has a natural propensity toward exalting the self rather than exalting God. For these theologians, sin represents a universal condition manifested at an individual level that affects each individual equally.

Contemporaneously with the Jesus Movement, but quite separately, liberation theology emerged in the Americas in the 1960s and 1970s, discussed in Chapter 10, and challenged these traditional views of sin as "too individualistic and overly focused on the internal dynamics of the soul" (MacDougall 2011: 474). Instead, liberation theologians began to focus on sin as a structural element in society, manifested in "those systems that diminish human flourishing through oppression, domination, and exploitation of others," and as "a societal self-contradiction that manifests itself in unjust and oppressive relationships between genders, races, or classes" (MacDougall 2011: 474–5). Some groups of liberation theologians, including feminist theologians, take the argument further to say that aspects of the traditional view of sin are complicit in creating and perpetuating oppressive social structures, and individuals commit sin when they participate in, rather than resist, those systems and structures. For instance, the notion that all of humanity is on an equal footing because of our common sinful nature blurs the distinction between the oppressor and the oppressed. Furthermore, defining sin as pride or exalting one's own will above God's can be used as a means of social control by defining divergent views, particularly those held by oppressed or marginalized groups, as sinful and contrary to God's plan.

In *Hellfire Nation*, James Morone (2003: 4) argues that this tension, between addressing sin as a matter of personal piety and sin as a matter of a moral society, has established the framework through which "visions of vice and virtue define the American community." The history of evangelicalism, in particular, has been marked by the struggle to negotiate the middle grounds between the view of sin as a matter of personal piety and the view of sin as a matter of social injustice. Reflecting on this tension from a charismatic evangelical perspective, Terry Cross (2007: 101) argues for the necessity of "re-mapping sin in today's world," because it is difficult to effectively "speak the Good News to the world without understanding some of sin's permutations in our various contexts." He continues by arguing that in evangelical circles, "sin is usually preached about in ways that circulate around behaviors we find abhorrent," with the purpose of creating an atmosphere of guilt around those behaviors. Yet this is not always consistent. In an interview with the *Financial Times*, historian and Baptist minister Wayne Flynt criticizes his fellow American evangelicals for "mobilising against the sins they either do not want to commit (homosexual acts) or cannot commit (undergoing an abortion, in the case of men) [while t]hey turn a blind eye toward temptations such as adultery and divorce that interest them" (Silverman 2017). Cross (2007: 103) contrasts such an approach with the idea of a life transformed by the work of the Holy Spirit manifested in a love for others through "transforming the structures that oppress their very humanity."

Christian Punk and Personal Sin

Early Christian punk bands were born into this evangelical theological framework, and negotiated it through their lyrics. Most of these early bands defined themselves as ministries, or what Jay R. Howard and John M. Streck (1999: 49) refer to as "separational" bands, which "see the world in black and white, good and evil, right and wrong." They argue this separational evangelical view of popular music "attempts to reconcile the paradox of 'walking in two worlds' … by withdrawing into one world and out of the other as completely as possible" (Howard and Streck 1999). While the stated goal of many of these bands was evangelism, the reality was that they generally found themselves performing for audiences that were overwhelmingly composed of people who already believed their message. Therefore, bands focused on writing songs that encouraged and instructed evangelical believers in living out a Christian life.

For Christian punk bands, that often meant defining what living a Christian life looks like from a punk perspective. Secular bands like the Clash presented an image of militant resistance against the Establishment, and Christian bands followed their example and created a sort of "anti-world" militancy, in which "the world" represents the sinful values and attitudes of society and culture, antithetical to those of God. The concept comes from several New Testament passages, the most prominent being Rom. 12:2, in which Paul urges believers not to conform to the ways of the world. Altar Boys encapsulated this idea more than the other early bands by taking "the joy of three-chord punk and [marrying it] to a frenetic fist-in-the-air faith … fully co-opting the trappings of punk rock—from the clothes to the anti-establishment sentiments" (Thompson 2000: 121). The title track from *When You're a Rebel* (1985) includes the lines "When you're a rebel / The world is just so different from you," and "against this world we stand." Undercover's cover of the hymn "Holy, Holy, Holy," from the album

Boys and Girls Renounce the World (1984), includes the line "I fall down on my knees and I renounce the world / 'cause He's the one I want to please." One Bad Pig's first recording, *A Christian Banned* (1986), contained the song "Sleepin' with the World," while Crashdog's track "Voice of Defiance" expounded on this attitude of standing against the world's values by declaring "We're not into social compliance / 'cause we are the voice of defiance" (*Mud Angels*, 1994).

This anti-world position continued to resonate with the antiestablishment ideology of the punk subculture by proclaiming that the problems people faced were the result of a system that was inherently broken. Where the views diverged was the source of that brokenness. Antiestablishmentism placed the blame on dysfunctional institutions, such as corrupt governments and greedy corporations. The anti-world ideology, on the other hand, placed the blame at a deeper level: sin. For these Christian punks, and evangelicals in general, all the problems humanity faces are the result of the sinful nature of humanity. While secular punk bands were addressing social ills by calling out the governments and corporations they believed were contributing to the problems of society, Christian punk bands addressed them by calling out particular attitudes and actions they considered sinful. In their song "I Question It" (*Gut Level Music*, 1986), Altar Boys addresses the normalization and acceptance of sin as one of the problems facing the world today. Hardcore band Torn Flesh's song "World Pollution" (*Crux of the Mosh*, 1989) likened the attitudes and values of the world to a chemical spill that was destroying society from its foundations. In a clever piece of wordplay, the band put some of the blame on secular heavy metal bands and the values they were transmitting through their music: "The Poison in the music is a raucous Motley Crüe / The Venom of the White Snake will Slay yer Heart in two." In many cases, the anti-world position began to move away from a general avoidance of sin and the world and toward a position that was against particular sins, those "behaviors [they] find abhorrent" (Cross 2007: 101).

One prominent issue Christian bands addressed in the 1980s and 1990s was abortion. While there are numerous examples of both pro-choice and pro-life advocacy among secular punk bands, the Christian punk voice appears homogenously pro-life. Even bands that are more likely to be identified with the evangelical left, such as Crashdog, and tend to shy away from directly addressing abortion, still articulate a pro-life position when they do, as on the track "My God" (*Cashists, Fascists, and Other Fungus*, 1995). This is not surprising considering the relationship of Christian punk to American evangelicalism. Sociologists Andrew Greeley and Michael Hout (2006: 33) connect antiabortion activism to the overarching theme of religiously inspired activism in American history, noting "several of the great socioreligious movements in American history were driven by fervent religious enthusiasm—abolition, prohibition, civil rights. Perhaps the contemporary antiabortion, antihomosexuality, antipornography crusades represent the continuity in moral righteousness among the Conservative Protestants." The legalization of abortion in the United States after the 1974 *Rowe v. Wade* ruling made it a crucial issue for conservative churches, even uniting Catholics and evangelicals in their opposition. The prominence of abortion in Ronald Reagan's 1980 election campaign and the rise of Jerry Falwell's "Moral Majority" political action group made abortion a prominent issue for many evangelicals.

One thing that differed among Christian punk bands that did address abortion was the language they used. In "I Question It," Altar Boys sang, "Well the law says it's ok to kill an unborn baby / It's a mother's choice, throw the baby away" (*Gut Level Music*, 1986), which is slightly more direct than more mainstream Christian artists of the time. Hardcore punk bands tended to use even more graphic language. In "Silent Scream," the Crucified used lines like "From mother's womb to garbage can those little babies die … / The infants are sucked through a tube … / The saline salt's injected and the baby melts away" (*Take Up Your Cross*, 1986). Officer Negative's song "Human Garbage Can" includes the lines "It's not a fetus, not a blob, you're ripping her head off" (*Zombie Nation*, 1999). Some bands choose to address the issue by writing songs from the perspective of an aborted fetus, as in Dogwood's "In the Line of Fire," where the fetus laments the life it could have lived. "No one will ever hear me laugh or see my smile / I would have made my parents proud" (*Through Thick and Thin*, 1997). Regardless of the actual language used, each presents a clear antiabortion perspective in unapologetic terms using the in-your-face language common to punk.

In keeping with Greeley and Hout's (2006) analysis, sexual sins are also common targets for many of these bands. Given the audience of teenagers and young adults, the emphasis on extramarital sex is consistent with the evangelical push in the 1980s and 1990s for abstinence-only sex education and youth-focused "purity" groups such as the True Love Waits movement (Gardner 2011). As with abortion, Christian punk bands pull few punches when discussing sexual sins. One Bad Pig's "Sleepin' with the World" attacks a variety of sexual sin, including promiscuity ("Bill and Sue were out all night / They weren't sleepin' in that car"), prostitution ("There's women sleepin' for wages"), and molestation ("In the little house next door / Daddy's sleepin' with Tommy") (*A Christian Banned*, 1986). Dogwood's "Lapchild" rehashes the common Christian music trope of the teenage boy and girl who start off with innocent infatuation and end up becoming sexually involved, which led to an unplanned pregnancy and having their dreams derailed over "five minutes o' love," concluding with the moral lesson that "their foolish child games put them in a living hell" (*Good Ol' Daze*, 1996).

While some other bands tangentially addressed the issue of homosexuality under the umbrella of general sinfulness, hardcore band Torn Flesh addressed the issue outright in their song "Gay Rights" (*Crux of the Mosh*, 1989). The band begins by describing a world full of "men lusting men," with the chorus then enumerating a list of "gay rights," including "the right to repent" and "the right to heed Romans 1:26–30." But after the breakup of Torn Flesh, lead vocalist Greg Hudson seemed to have had a change of heart regarding homosexuality. In 2004, Hudson founded the Woobie Bear Music label to promote music within the bear community, a gay subculture. Woobie Bear Music released four compilation CDs (*Bear Tracks*, 2004–2006), and Hudson himself appeared on three of those using the name "Grecote" (Doyle 2007).

The discussion of Christian punk's treatment of sexual sin is incomplete without considering the output of the hardcore band Lust Control, which built its reputation on songs about sexuality and gender, as discussed in Chapter 6. The band's debut album, *This Is a Condom Nation* (1988), included the songs "Mad at the Girls" and "The Big M," and *We Are Not Ashamed* (1992) contained "Get Married" and "Virginity Disease." When "The Big M" came out in 1988, the subject of masturbation was still largely taboo in evangelical youth culture, so to have a song that screams "masturbation is artificial sex" was quite shocking. "The Big M" contrasts the argument that masturbation is a natural way to release sexual urges with the argument that it is using the body for sin, and quoting 1 Cor. 6:13, states that the body is not meant for sexual immortality (*This Is a Condom Nation*, 1988). "Mad at the Girls" addresses sexual temptations and lust through the lens of a male working at the mall watching girls walk around with their "sexy smiles" and their miniskirts. He eventually thinks about his own responsibility, saying, "I can't control my lust, my mind I cannot trust" and concludes that rather than being mad at the girls, he is actually mad at himself (*This Is a Condom Nation*, 1988). "Get Married" is a musical exposition of 1 Cor. 7:9, "if they cannot control themselves, they should marry," while "Virginity Disease" is about the stigma associated with remaining "sexually pure" (*We Are Not Ashamed*, 1992). Lust Control's songs dealt with issues of sex with frankness, but with a sometimes surprising level of maturity, given the satirical and "shock rock" image of the band, indicating a desire for their message to be taken seriously.

Christian Punk and Social Sin

Not every band used their music to crusade against the world and personal sin. Some bands saw the problems in the world less as a result of the church being insufficiently "anti-sin," but more as a result of it becoming too aggressively so, to the detriment of some of Christ's foundational teachings, namely to love one another and to care for "the least of these" (Mt. 25:40). These bands began to question the very definition of Christianity as it had been defined by the evangelical right. Altar Boys' album *Against the Grain* (1987) explores this idea. The band burst on the scene defining the idea of being a rebel for Christ as being different from the world (*When You're a Rebel*, 1985), but with this album, it seemed to imply that the true rebel for Christ was one whose life was marked by love, rather than condemnation. "Where's the compassion in people's lives today?" they asked on the title track. "Words mean nothing until you show you care" (*Against the Grain*, 1997). Hardcore band the Lead's song "Change the World" includes similar lines: "I said it's not what you say, it's what you do / That's how they know Him / They know Him by watching you" (*Burn This Record*, 1989).

Some of these Christian punk bands did not deviate as far from the ideals of their secular punk counterparts as we might assume, but instead used their music to speak out against the dominant institutions and values of society from a Christian-influenced perspective. One of punk's most commonly associated political values is anarchy, the freedom of the individual through the dissolution of centralized authority. In truth, punks' affinity for anarchy is more perception than reality. Some secular hardcore bands, notably Crass, discussed in Chapter 10, did openly promote anarchism, but most simply used the ideas as theater in the same way heavy metal bands have used the occult. In its own way, the specific anarcho-punk subgenre occupies as much a minority position in punk as Christianity does. Most Christian punk bands do not support this view of anarchy and freedom, but some have played with the idea in order to maintain an aesthetic continuity with the secular punk scene. For instance, Officer Negative's logo parodies the "Circle A" symbol, the most recognizable symbol of anarchism, by superimposing N over O with a horizontal line running through both letters.

As Francis Stewart (2017: 122) argues, "anarchism is not automatically atheistic or humanistic; rather, it is a fluid concept open to multiple interpretations united by common themes of rejection of coercive power." So some Christian punks do subscribe to the ideology of Christian anarchism, which shares the characteristics of other forms of anarchism in that it rejects the authority of the state, which

Christian anarchists view as a violent, deceitful, and potentially idolatrous institution. Rather than advocating for absolute individual freedom, Christian anarchism promotes the idea that God is the only authority to which humanity ultimately answers. While there is no indication that the members of One Bad Pig were actually Christian anarchists, these basic ideas are at the root of their song "Godarchy" (*Smash*, 1989), which portrays anarchy as the mere illusion of freedom, with true freedom as submitting to the rule of God. In some ways, the idea of Christian anarchy shares similarities with the concept of "populist traditionalism" coined by Tex Sample (1996) in his study of Christianity and country music, which is "a subversive relational individualism evincing strong distrust of the normative social institutions and practices of secular modernity" (Abraham 2017: 34).

Some early Christian punk bands actively mixed politics and social justice with the Christian themes in their music. The most prominent one, Crashdog, was one of the bands affiliated with Chicago's Jesus People USA intentional Christian community, best known as the organizers of the punk-friendly Cornerstone festival between 1984 and 2012, analyzed in Chapter 8. Unlike many of the Christian bands of their era, Crashdog was more closely aligned with the evangelical left than the evangelical right, which made its voice distinct in the world of Christian music. Mark Allan Powell (2002: 202) described the band as

> draw[ing] equally from the angry legacies of modern punkers and ancient prophets. Crashdog discerned their role as often being that of exposing sin in the government and in the church. Such sentiments took them outside the mainstream of contemporary Christian music, which usually either ignores political issues altogether, covers them with a veneer of spirituality, or addresses them in terms that are defined by and inoffensive to the religious right.

Their song "GOP" challenged the common notion promoted among American evangelicals that the platform of the Republican Party was more closely aligned with Christian values than the platform of the Democratic Party because "we're pro-life and squeaky clean" (*Cashists, Fascists, and Other Fungus*, 1995). The song challenges listeners to ask, "How much of Jesus do you find in their lovely party line?"

A summation of Crashdog's position is found in the song "My God," which repudiates the image of a God that was held by many conservative evangelicals of the era, a God who sent HIV to punish homosexuals, who called people to militantly oppose abortion, and who placed men in a superior position to women.

By contrast, the band presented what it believed was a more biblical view of a God who "lives to touch and heal and reconcile ... doesn't call his people to judge and kill ... doesn't hold man over woman" (*Cashists, Fascists, and Other Fungus,* 1995). Their song "Millstone Co." attacks corporate culture with what amounts to a Marxist-inspired critique of the nature of power and exploitation in capitalism, while "History Lesson #1" is a criticism of the nationalist desire to whitewash American history and forget that the ideals of freedom, democracy, and equality Americans espouse have been largely unrealized (*8 Years to Nowhere,* 1998). "Liberation" seems to encapsulate the philosophy and theology that drove their music. It contrasts the lived theology of many American churches that leads to comfort and prosperity, with the theology they find in the Gospels of caring for the poor and the needy. It is summed up in the chorus: "The Kingdom of God is in our midst, silently crouching, it sits waiting for its people to awake" (*Outer Crust,* 1997).

Crashdog went on "indefinite hiatus" in 1998, and several former members formed the Celtic folk-punk band Ballydowse, which espoused a more radical sociopolitical philosophy genuinely close to Christian anarchism, with songs focusing on human rights and social justice. "The Banshee Song" connects the Irish legend of the harbinger spirit to the imagined downfall of the power elite, with the twist that when the banshee is heard for them, there are no tears and no grief (*The Land, the Bread, and the People,* 1998). "Weapon of Mass Destruction" opens with a clip of a 1996 *60 Minutes* interview with then Secretary of State Madeline Albright, in which Secretary Albright stated that the administration believed that the 500,000 deaths of Iraqi children that were reportedly the result of economic sanctions against Iraq in the wake of the Gulf War was a price worth paying to ensure that Iraqi leader Saddam Hussein did not obtain weapons of mass destruction. The song condemns the actions taken against the country in terms of their effects on the innocent, including the citation of a report about a flock of sheep and the young shepherds tending the flock, killed as a result of "collateral damage" (*Out of the Fertile Crescent,* 2000).

The plight of Iraqis under US-led sanctions in the 1990s became a focal point for the band. Powell (2002: 65) relates an account of band members Andrew Mandell and Dan Kool being removed from a taping of *The Oprah Winfrey Show* after they asked then candidate George W. Bush if he would "continue the Democrats' policy of sanctions that kill 5,000 children a month in Iraq." *Out of the Fertile Crescent* focuses on several other international issues, including the effects of US policies on Guatemala ("Open the Records") and child prostitution in Thailand ("Sons and Daughters"). Even when Ballydowse touched on subjects that were more common to Christian music, like abstaining from alcohol, the impetus is rooted in social morality, rather than personal piety. The song "Bud Morris" urges listeners to avoid alcohol and tobacco, not because they are sinful vices but because alcohol and tobacco corporations prey upon the most vulnerable members of society (*The Land, the Bread, and the People*, 1998). This is clearly a departure from the approach taken by most of the band's contemporaries.

Conclusion

Like their secular counterparts, Christian punk bands in the 1980s and 1990s existed on the fringe of the Christian music industry. From that outsider position, many bands took up the mantle of modern prophets who boldly proclaimed the Word of God without being concerned with popularity and fame. It was a position that was perhaps easier for these bands to claim because they had chosen, even if tacitly, to embrace that separational ideal of Christian music and engage primarily with supposedly like-minded evangelical audiences. In the Bible, the role of the prophet is depicted as a complex one that combines various aspects of other public roles in the life of biblical Israel. What sets the prophet apart is what Paul Tarazi (1991: 4) terms the "aggressiveness" of God in prophetic discourse. Tarazi describes the role of the prophet as actively inserting God's voice into the life of a post-Egypt Israel that was settled and comfortable in its redemption. With that idea of aggressiveness in mind, it is easy to envision Christian punk bands fulfilling the prophetic role by taking a strong stand against sin, whether specific sins, or warning believers against the dangers of being enmeshed in a sinful social system.

The evangelical right has tended to focus on this public condemnatory aspect of the prophetic message, romanticizing Elijah and John the Baptist as crusaders against kings who epitomized the evil and godlessness of the world. In the context of Christian punk, as this chapter has shown, such an approach has taken the form of graphic denunciations of sinful American society, often focusing on personal, sexual sins. However, an examination of biblical prophets shows these proclamations of judgment over the entanglement with sin to occur within the context of drawing God's people into a redemptive and transformative relationship, often using indictments of particular sins as a means for raising awareness of more pervasive systemic sin. This understanding makes room under that prophetic mantle for the bands that fall more within the parameters of the evangelical left, bands such as Crashdog and Ballydowse, who urged their listeners to embrace the full implications of Christ's teachings by pursuing social justice. Regardless of their focus, these early Christian punk bands embraced the opportunity to live out the punk ideal of creating songs that confront complacency and complicity within contemporary American Christianity.

3

Fearless Men of God: Fighting Religious Stigma in Hardcore Punk

Amy D. McDowell

Introduction

In spite of the critical and commercial success enjoyed by many Christian hardcore and metalcore bands in the twenty-first century, Christian hardcore youth complain that it has been difficult for Christians to find acceptance in punk music scenes. In part this is because American hardcore punk, materializing in the late 1970s and early 1980s when the economic, political, and moral order of the United States was turning to the right, has a history of criticizing conservative religions like evangelical Christianity (Azerrad 2001; Moore 2004). During this time, hardcore youth moved punk from a "culture of deconstruction" to an underground "culture of authenticity" that resisted commercialism (Moore 2004: 307). In their efforts to define and achieve punk authenticity, hardcore punks developed a do-it-yourself (DIY) music subculture, including record labels and venues that "served as a forum for facilitating political critique and action" (Moore 2004: 308). Some hardcore punks were highly politically conscious and used their DIY music to rally against the right-wing political, religious, and corporate Establishment (Moore and Roberts 2009).

Bands like the Dead Kennedys were especially vocal in their opposition to religious and political conservatism. After the election of Ronald Reagan, the Dead Kennedys released *In God We Trust, Inc.* (1981), an album with tracks titled "Religious Vomit" and "Moral Majority," both of which denounce religious leaders as political conmen who profit from people's suffering. Hardcore critiques like these quickly caught the attention of conservative evangelicals, many of whom responded in one of either two ways: by condemning punk as the "devil's music" and promoting censorship laws (Kennedy 1990; Chastagner 1999) or by supporting a handful of early Christian punk bands, including those analyzed in Chapter 2.

Given the tumultuous relationship between Christianity and punk in the past, I was suspicious of Christianity in the hardcore punk scene when I started my research. Admittedly, my opinion about Christian hardcore stemmed from my own involvement in punk music in the 1990s. At the time, I was in charge of stocking the shelves of CRAMM music, the record store I opened with my father in Pensacola, Florida, in 1993. CRAMM was a cheap place in every sense of the term. Launched on a meager two-thousand-dollar budget, our inventory was decidedly low cost: used rock records and new emo records were our specialties. It was the place where kids came to pick up their Born Against and Unwound EPs for three dollars. Religion may have been intrinsic to some of the hardcore bands we carried at CRAMM, but the gospel of Jesus Christ was not salient in our inventory. Instead, most of the punk albums we stocked were dismissive, if not critical of religion. In those days, it seemed punk was a place for autonomous critical thinking that was (ideally) separate from the influence of conservative religious institutions like evangelical Christianity.

When I attended the Cornerstone Christian rock festival for the first time in 2008, my perspective on how Christianity fits in hardcore punk began to change. There to explore Christianity in underground music more broadly, I was stunned to find that hardcore, screamo, and metalcore bands were covering the festival grounds, as discussed in Chapter 8. Other festivalgoers also took note of their presence, some expressing that they were fed up with "screaming bands" and complaining that the festival organizers, Jesus People USA, needed to come up with ways to reduce the number and volume of hardcore bands.

In 2008, any band could bring an amp and play a show on a "generator stage," which meant setting up stage directly on the ground with a generator, and many new hardcore and metalcore bands were doing just that. Perhaps in response to this trend, when I attended Cornerstone again in 2010, punks told me that the festival had implemented new rules that addressed the explosion of hardcore bands on generator stages. To play a show at the festival, a band had to secure sponsorship from a record company or a ministry team that ran one of the red and white tents. If a group did not have a sponsor, the band had to pay an additional fee to perform. Nick, a festivalgoer and lead singer of a hardcore band, was pleased with the change: "I hated it. It was too much. There was too much music—too much going on. You couldn't hear anything. There were bands playing two feet from each other." Nick believed this new system ensured a higher quality of music at Cornerstone. He reasoned that if a band cannot afford to perform or is not sponsored, then they probably are not that good anyway. For him, the festival improved when it started privileging hardcore bands like his that play the Underground Stage.

The breadth of hardcore music at Cornerstone moved me to ask: How are Christian youth establishing themselves as legitimate members of hardcore punk scenes? How are they overcoming the stigma that comes with being an evangelical Christian in this subculture? Christian rockers have been making punk rock and metal music as early as the 1980s (Powell 2002; Luhr 2009), as noted in the Introduction and in Chapter 2, but this earlier take on defiant faith-based music did not make as many inroads into secular underground spaces as hardcore and metalcore bands do these days (Moberg 2015; Abraham 2017). Instead, this music was generally restricted to what my interviewees call a "Christian bubble" of Christian radio stations, festivals, and church youth groups. This bubble started to burst when Spirit-filled hardcore bands came onto the scene in the 1990s, with "one foot" in the secular hardcore punk scene and the other in Christian spaces like church and the Cornerstone festival (Abraham 2017: 39–40). By the turn of the millennium, many Christian bands were putting on live shows in churches, but they were also playing about half of their shows in secular venues (Abraham 2017). In the 2000s it was not unusual for Christian hardcore or metalcore groups to tour with secular groups (Moberg 2015), nor was it odd to see a Christian hardcore group top the Billboard charts or for a Christian band to headline a "non-Christian" show.

The integration of Christian punk into hardcore scenes is of interest because it reveals that American evangelicalism has made space for itself in some of the most resistant corners of American popular culture, as noted in Chapter 9, and at a time in which most Christian congregations are losing members, especially young white men and teenagers (McCaffree 2017: 213). Christian hardcore music is part of an evangelical belief that Christians should use rebellious music to bring the gospel to social outcasts, a tradition that the Jesus Movement institutionalized in the 1970s, analyzed in Chapter 1, with its adoption of rock music and countercultural styles (Luhr 2009; Stowe 2011). Like the Jesus Movement that preceded them, Christian hardcore youth are on a mission to integrate into a larger countercultural community. They believe that God made them punk so that they can minister to society's "black sheep," which they imagine as young white men who feel excluded by their church and mainstream society for being punk (McDowell 2018). Their focus on ministering to young white men is akin to other masculinized evangelical groups that try to make Christianity relevant to men in non-Christian spaces (Putney 2001; Greve 2014), discussed in Chapter 7. It also matches the demographic profile of the larger hardcore punk subculture, which is dominated by young, white, suburban men (Moore 2004; Haenfler 2006).

In this chapter, I show how Christian punks fight the "stigma" of being religious in the hypermasculine subculture of hardcore music. As Erving Goffman (1963: 3) theorized, although a stigmatized person is a "tainted, discounted" person, stigma is not a thing in itself; rather, it is a particular attribute that stigmatizes a person, such as evangelical Christianity in the case of punk. Furthermore, stigma is not constant or consistent, such that evangelicalism will not be discrediting in all settings, in all circumstances. Instead, it is our perception of who and how a person should be in a specific context that determines the stigma. Therefore, while American evangelicals are a powerful religious and political force in US society, evangelicals can nevertheless experience stigma on the basis of their religious identity in punk spaces, because they do not fit the profile of what most punks are or have been. Their task, then, is to convince other punks that they are authentic members of the subculture, combatting the notion that Christian punks are inauthentic punks.

My findings are based upon qualitative data collected largely between 2008 and 2012 in the United States, when Christian hardcore and metalcore were at the peak of their popularity. I spent my time at live music shows in churches, bars, and all-ages venues in Pennsylvania, camping out at the Cornerstone Christian rock festivals in Bushnell, Illinois, in 2008 and 2010 and attending two Unified Underground (UU) subcultural ministry conferences in Annapolis, Maryland, in 2008 and 2010. I purchased albums by bands who had played at Cornerstone (notably the Underground Stage), bands associated with the UU conference, and bands signed to Christian labels like Facedown Records, a prominent independent Christian hardcore and metalcore label. I performed twenty-three intensive one-on-one interviews and five informal group interviews, totaling forty interviewees, with Christian and secular band members and pastors supporting this music. Pseudonyms are used when referring to private interviews but the real names of research subjects are included when referencing statements made in public settings, such as on stage during concerts. The majority of musicians and fans I observed and interviewed were young white men between the ages of 18 and 30, which reflects the broader demographics of contemporary American punk (Leblanc 1999; Moore 2004; Haenfler 2006; Mullaney 2007).

The following section examines how Christian punks describe the resistance they face from some non-Christian punks, and how they use this resistance to define themselves as authentically punk and Christian. The subsequent sections show that some Christian punks are overcoming religious stigma in hardcore music by making noise about what makes them different. Firstly, by presenting themselves as "fearless" men of God who stand up for their faith and, secondly, by redirecting stigma to other Christians in the punk scene seeking to avoid religious controversy or conflict.

Fighting Religious Stigma

Christian musicians, show promoters, and subcultural ministry leaders recognize that it has been difficult, especially in the past, for Christian bands to find acceptance in the punk subculture. Paul, the lead singer of a straight edge Christian band in Florida, says that most of the resistance comes from what he and others term "anti-Christian" punks who do not like Christians or want to be affiliated with them. These punks, Paul tells me, are narrow-minded and sometimes outright rude, which is no longer necessarily one of the "commonly accepted punk social conventions" (Bestley 2015: 121). "We are told that we're close minded because we believe that Christ is the way and he's the only way. But in the same way, they're close minded in the sense that they never want to hear our side—why we believe what we believe." Melinda, who organizes Bible studies at a Christian tattoo shop in Pittsburgh, also thinks Christian punks are more tolerant of different views than non-Christian punks. In an interview with me, she describes a situation in which her husband, Isaac, opened for one of his favorite secular bands. During a friendly exchange, Isaac gave one of the band members his band's T-shirt. When he later found out that he was wearing a Christian band T-shirt, he reportedly got angry and called Isaac a "phony." Melinda concludes that this secular punk musician is "anti-Christian." He rejects the presence of Christianity in punk and does not want to be mistaken for a Christian.

Anti-Christian punks may hinder Christian hardcore acceptance, but they also help Christians legitimate their membership in hardcore scenes. When Melinda and Paul criticize anti-Christian punks for being unreasonable or rude, they bolster punk authenticity against a negative reference group "who are unlike them, who actively serve in their minds as models for what they do *not* believe, what they do *not* want to become, and how they do *not* want to act" (Smith 1998: 105). In referring to what anti-Christians do, Christian punks like Paul and Melinda establish that they are the ones who genuinely embrace the idea that punk is a space for radical self-expression. Being Christian in punk is radical, they imply, because it breaks the mold of what others think punk is or should be. Consequently, the "anti-Christian" punks who try to shut them up, they reason, are not genuinely punk when they try to censor how other punks express themselves. Hence, Christian punks are achieving punk authenticity by shifting references to what is "real" or "fake," a move that underscores that stigma, like authenticity, is defined, negotiated, and redefined in social interactions (Weninger and Williams 2017; Fuist and McDowell 2019).

Indeed, Christian Smith (1998: 88) has argued that evangelicalism has thrived not because evangelicals have "built a protective shield" around themselves, but because they are engaging with the forces that seem to oppose them. Christian hardcore punks exemplify this evangelical spirit of active engagement and dissent, as further evidenced in Chapter 7. Yet unlike the evangelicals that Smith studies, Christian hardcore youth are not solely engaging those who may oppose them only to shore up their own particular subcultural identity. Instead, they engage nonreligious and even anti-Christian punks, because they want to be part of hardcore scenes and have an influence on hardcore music. They want to tear down the walls that separate them from non-Christian punks, which is why hardcore Christians think it is important that Christians tour with secular bands and set up secular shows.

Brandon, a vocalist in a Christian metalcore band, takes pride in the fact that he regularly tours with big-name secular groups. He likes that "a lot of Christian bands are branching out" and "getting to a market that they need to reach instead of just playing the same old Christian church venues." Brandon insists that integrating into secular hardcore is healthy for the Christian mission, as well as for Christian record and ticket sales. Besides, he asks rhetorically, "What's the point in playing shows that are just for Christians?" He thinks that when Christian bands only do Christian tours like *Scream the Prayer*, a Christian hardcore and metalcore tour, they fail at sharing the gospel with non-Christian punks. Brad admits that it is not easy to convince these punks that they need Christ, and he does not expect kids to accept Jesus into their hearts at one of his shows. However, he does believe that his music can inspire punk and metal kids to form a relationship with Jesus.

Reflecting on, and perhaps justifying, his decision to be on a secular tour, Brandon states:

> Secular tours draw more secular fans, and when there's a Christian band on it, those secular fans that wouldn't go to a Christian tour might go to that Christian tour next time … Maybe only five or ten [out of 400] will take something from [our music] when they leave that night. But that's five or ten that wouldn't have taken it if you only did Christian tours.

Like so many others in the Christian hardcore scene, Brandon claims that he feels the presence of God at secular shows because that is where he "plants the seed" for Jesus. If he were to cover up his faith or only do Christian tours, he might not be as excited about doing ministry.

Paul also thinks if Christians want to be accepted as hardcore, they must tour with secular groups. He explains:

> The hardcore scene wasn't made for Christians! Like, it wasn't a Christian organization! So who are we to seclude ourselves and be like, "Oh, Christian bands play together now, We're better than non-Christian bands." No! We stepped into a scene that was started by other leaders. So you know we wanted to fellowship with them. We wanted to just love on them. We didn't want to just tell them that they needed to change their lives or whatever … We wanted to give a message outside of the typical anger, hate, and depression that you hear in a lot of hardcore music. It just seems like so many of the bands are broken so we wanted to share a message of, "Hey, we were broken and this is where we found our completion." This is where we found our healing and if it's something that interests you, we're here for you.

According to Paul, he and his band have experienced all kinds of backlash at hardcore shows. Audiences have told him to "go drown in holy water," cursed him out, and thrown beer bottles at him while he was on stage. Yet despite these tough experiences, Paul maintains that most hardcore youth accept him for who he is and are open to touring with and befriending a Christian band. For Paul, this is no accident. Nonreligious punks include him because he "does not shove it [religion] down their throat," as Paul and other Christian punks put it. Instead, he exhibits pride in his faith and he thinks this helps secular youth respect him for his beliefs, even if they never accept Jesus at one of his shows.

Performing as Fearless Men of God

Christian hardcore punks commonly say that Christianity is "better integrated" into secular tours and shows because bands are being more "fearless". Indeed, "fearless" is the catchphrase that leaps to mind when I think of Christian hardcore music. On T-shirts, album covers, and on stage, hardcore Christians stress the importance of being fearless men of God who are unapologetic about their faith. This emphasis on fearless faith is unmistakable in Christian hardcore lyrics, which include thrilling accounts of divine annihilation. Take, for instance, the title track "There Will Be Violence!" by the metalcore group Impending Doom, a song that depicts their God as omnipotent and ready for revenge: "For the unbelievers / Who try to retain their 'faith in humanity' / I promise there will be violence! / There will be violence!" (*There Will Be Violence!*, 2010). Interviewees claim that lyrics like these set Christians apart from everybody else. Dan, who is part of the Christian metalcore scene, does not want to keep making music about the "same old things." He wants to create music that is fearless, music that has "realness" and "substance" to it. For many of these youth, a song is "real" when it addresses how "afraid" and "weak" people feel when, as War of Ages (2012) sings on their track "Redeemer," they turn their backs on God (*Return to Life*, 2012). Through God, these artists propose, they find strength and courage to live and fight for Christ. They are not afraid of anything—death, eternal damnation, or Satan.

While Christian hardcore punks do put a biblical spin on their music, offering a distinctive perspective within the genre, they also follow well-established punk and metal norms when they sing about violence and fearlessness (Kahn-Harris 2007; Laing 2015; Moberg 2015). In fact, it is through such songs about personal suffering and even obliteration that Christian hardcore punks are able to establish themselves as part of the larger hardcore and metalcore scenes. While Christian bands replicate foundational genre norms in general terms, some Christian bands with the most explicitly biblical and apocalyptic lyrics gravitate to the metalcore subgenre, which is known for its "unintelligible vocal style" (Abraham 2017: 49), which may smother some of the more obvious or obscure religious differences in a wall of sound, passion, and musical aggression.

Christian punks also present themselves as fearless men of God because they can lose their status as authentic hardcore men more easily than can their non-Christian peers. Through masculine signifiers like violence, death, and aggression, Christian hardcore men establish themselves as punk, which involves first establishing their status as men (Mullaney 2007; McDowell 2017). This is because in punk, "the presence of Christians serves, for some, as analogous to the presence of women; for some punks, both are litmus tests for how far punk has shifted from what they view as authentic punk culture" (Abraham 2017: 50). This struggle to be seen as men explains why they make so much noise about fearlessness—they do not want to be mistaken as too soft or too weak for hardcore, and they know that they need other punk men to validate their performance of manhood if they want to be part of this community (McDowell 2017).

The members of For Today, a Billboard Hard Rock chart-topping Christian band, are widely celebrated among Christian hardcore fans for representing what it means to be fearless men of God. The group exclusively makes biblically themed music, and their first three albums were released on Facedown Records, a label that pursues bands that "want to glorify God through the music that they play, and at the same time, break stereotypes of what people thought of Christians to be" (Sciarretto 2010). Most of their music is about spiritual warfare, the afterlife, and not being ashamed of being Christian. Some songs, however, seem to support Christian nationalism, the belief that the United States' future rests on evangelical Christianity (Gorski 2017). For example, the track "Under God" (*Immortal*, 2012) imagines Christians "under a flag of freedom ... painted with stars and stripes" so that they "can turn this nation from its path," if they are willing to "pay the price." Whether addressing immortality, war, or Christian nationalism, For Today returns to fearlessness, informing audiences that if they accept Jesus into their hearts they will no longer fear life or death, because in Christ, "Death will hold no power!" as they declare on "Isaiah (The Willing)" (*Portraits*, 2009). They even released a single called "Fearless" about God protecting Christians from fear itself (*Immortal*, 2012). The chorus of the song repeats, "We will not, we will not, we will not be afraid" before the singer roars: "We are Fearless! Fearless!"

For many young people in the Christian hardcore scene, For Today symbolizes a fearless faith because they preach on stage, even in secular venues. The lead singer of For Today, Mattie Montgomery, is the real rock star of fearlessness. As many Christian punks put it to me during interviews, "he is bold in his witness." When For Today performed at the 2012 Warped Tour in West Palm Beach, Florida, Montgomery did not hold back on the gospel. Instead, he delivered a two-minute sermon about the saving grace of Jesus before directing the crowd to form an enormous circle pit. This is what he shouted as he stood in the hot sun in a sleeveless T-shirt, tattoos, and beads of sweat:

> It's my honor and my privilege to be able to stand here today! And to be able to say that I'm not just some broken kid, not that I'm an addict like I used to be. Not that I'm suicidal like I used to be. Not that I'm depressed [*audience cheering*] and hopeless and alone and broken like I used to be! I get to stand here today in front of all of you people that I consider friends and family. People that I would lay my life down for [*audience cheering*]. That because of the blood of my King Jesus [*audience cheering louder*], I've been set free! I've been made me! And I've been set back on my own two feet again!

By this point in the performance, the audience cheered so loudly that it was difficult to discern what Montgomery was saying, even as he shouted in a microphone. He then screamed, "Listen! I know that there's a lot of messages that bands will stand on a stage like this and preach. I know there's a lot of stigma around who Jesus really is." Montgomery paces back and forth on stage before telling his audience that he knows some of "you" may think Jesus is "some vindictive, hateful, angry person who just hates you because you're not perfect." "Well," he continues, "no one is perfect, and Jesus does not expect perfection. He loved us so much that he took our price on that cross!" His voice becomes louder, more aggressive, as he tells the audience that Jesus did this because he wants to save them from hell, because he wants to rescue them from depression, drugs, and suicidal thoughts. Then, Montgomery shouts that he is a "free man" because of his King. He repeats, "I will never shut up about that! I will never shut up about that! I will never shut up about that! I will never shut up about that!" Once again, Montgomery proved that he is not ashamed of his beliefs and that he, as his fans describe him, is courageous in his faith.

Christian punks are not the only ones who think Christian bands are more accepted when they are explicit about their faith. Non-Christian punks I met at Christian hardcore shows also point out that they appreciate Christian bands who are up front about their beliefs. Sean, a self-proclaimed agonistic who I met at a For Today show in Pittsburgh, says he respects Christians "who stand up for what they believe." For him, preaching bands like For Today are "genuine" in their faith—they "feel convicted to tell people what they believe." He, like many other hardcore musicians and audience members I interviewed, thinks that Christians have a right to be involved in this music, and that some Christian bands are making some of the best music because they are passionate about hardcore.

Indeed, Sean's description of hardcore as passionate music that forms unity and community resonates with what other Christian and non-Christian punks say about this music (Haenfler 2006; Abraham 2017). Take, for instance, a conversation I had with Cliff, a young straight edge Christian hardcore punk who organizes shows and holds a Bible study in his house. After explaining that hardcore shows are something meaningful and fun to do that does not involve drinking and drugs, Cliff clarifies that he likes the "anger, and passion, and aggression" that defines hardcore. For him, hardcore is a place where you are "able to share your opinions and ideals … in an open forum," and he thinks that openness is vital to his Christian mission. It encourages him to profess his beliefs proudly but in a way that does not make others feel that he is trying to "shove religion down their throats." His remarks underscore the thread that binds Christianity and punk. When Christians are forthright about their faith, they personify hardcore passion and in doing so legitimize their membership in the subculture.

In this section, I have shown how Christian hardcore punks combat religious stigma by being outspoken about their faith and preaching from stage. When they come out boldly as Christian, these young men position themselves as fearless men of God who dare to talk about their beliefs in spaces where Christians have not always felt welcome. Like other hardcore punks who describe punk as a fundamentally passionate subculture, hardcore Christians insist that they are hardcore because they are steadfast about what they believe in. If they were quiet about their faith, they would not be hardcore.

Redirecting Stigma

Performing as fearless men of God is not the only way Christian hardcore punks defeat stigma in this music. Criticizing other Christians for not being up front about their faith is another way they take honor in their "spoiled" identity as Christians (Goffman 1963). In this section, I show how hardcore Christians redirect stigma to other Christians for "playing it safe." There are two different groups of Christians that they accuse of this: "Christians in a band" and "Sunday Christians" or "mainstream Christians."

Musicians who identify as being part of a "Christian band," also referred to as a "preaching band," argue that "Christians in a band," Christian musicians who do not call themselves a "Christian band," are insincere because they keep quiet about their Christianity. Paul, the straight edge musician who calls some punks "anti-Christian," maintains that Christians should be outspoken about what makes them different because it sets conversations about Christ in motion. Paul asserts, "We would share our message on stage not with the expectation that hundreds of people were going to come up and be like [in a sarcastic tone] 'Oh can I get a CD and can you baptize me in the Holy Spirit? I'm such a sinner!'" Paul thinks it is rare for conversion to happen overnight at a live music show, but still feels that explicit talk about Jesus is essential to the process of saving souls. He argues that he preached from stage, not because he thought people would come up to him and accept Christ at his merchandise booth, but for two interconnected reasons: he wanted to show his pride in Jesus; and he thought that being direct about Jesus was his way of exhibiting hardcore integrity. He explains his performance of Christian identity on- and offstage:

We would be like, this is what we stand for, if you're interested, please come up and we'd love to talk to you. Even if you just want to come up to us and tell us that we're idiots for believing what we believe, we just want to chat with you guys. If you need prayer, we'll pray with you.

From his perspective, once the audience knows that a band is Christian, true acceptance begins.

Some Christian bands will publicly ridicule Christians in a band for playing it safe. In a YouTube video, one member of the metalcore band Demon Hunter nods his head and moves closer toward the camera to announce, "We're definitely a Christian band. We're definitely all Christians. We're all believers" (*Is Demon Hunter a Christian Band?*, n.d.). Immediately after him, another band member claims, "From the minute we started saying that, we got more respect and even from those other bands, you know, so it was exciting. Now we make no bones about it." Another member remarks, "if you stick to your guns" and proclaim Christ, non-Christian youth will respect you (*Is Demon Hunter a Christian Band?*, n.d.). Reflecting on the significance of this Demon Hunter video, one Christian metalcore musician I interviewed at Cornerstone explained that the group was simply making the point that "there's no shame" in pronouncing their Christianity. He concluded that a lot of bands stay quiet about their faith because they want to "fit in." He thinks it is wrong for a Christian to be "embarrassed of it" and that so-called "Christians in a band" are too soft for hardcore. If they were passionate about their faith and about hardcore, they would not be scared to stand up for it.

Contrary to most Christian bands, Christians in a band think that preaching reinforces a wall between Christian and non-Christian youth, creating a roadblock to full acceptance. Clint, a punk ministry leader and hardcore enthusiast, told me:

I think a lot of secular hardcore kids, like they're open to the idea of Christianity or ... any kind of religion, or faith, or worldview, but you can't get too preachy about it. And I feel like a lot of the bands right now are too preachy and they automatically shut people off and people are just turned off before they'll even listen to what they're saying.

Similarly, Melinda, introduced earlier in the chapter, says:

I think some bands—I don't want to call out somebody in particular—you know, some bands think they are supposed to do certain things. And that's fine. That's between them and God. But if there's a Christian band playing with non-Christian bands and they're up there preaching, I think that turns people off.

Melinda feels that her husband's band is a model of Christian ministry because they put friendships first. She says:

> They hang out with people. They get to know people. And that's how conversations are opened up about what people are going through, their beliefs and stuff ... I think that's a little bit more comfortable for people than someone who is just like "I'm a Christian, I believe in this and you should too or you're going to hell." It's less threatening.

A few interviewees suggest that Christian bands openly define themselves as Christian just to make money. One Christian folk-punk musician told me that a band who "prays for people at their merchandise booth" is not doing the work of God; they are selling T-shirts. He, like other punks invested in underground DIY culture, implies that punk music should not be lucrative and that popular bands are inauthentic sellouts (Moore 2007; Force 2011). Christians in a band also insist that "preaching bands" only reach young Christians who are looking for a harder, faster version of what they get in a typical evangelical church service: music and male-led sermons about Jesus, salvation, and heaven and hell. These speculations about Christian bands are not ungrounded. Members of the Christian bands I interviewed admit that the Christian hardcore and metalcore market is relatively stable and that there are some perks to performing as a Christian band such as securing free tour vans from churches or getting a solid record deal from a Christian label. Plus, there are plenty of Christian parents who prefer to buy Christian music for their teenagers (Hendershot 2004; Luhr 2009). Despite these perks, Christian bands protest the idea that they have it easier than Christians in a band. When they come out as Christian or preach from stage, they take the risk of being ridiculed by the punks that they call anti-Christians. Christians in a band do not take chances and therefore, members of Christian bands claim, do not exhibit hardcore integrity.

Christian bands and Christians in a band do not agree on how Christians should define themselves to others in subcultural settings. Some argue that Christians who are bold about their faith are most respected by non-Christian youth. Others argue that explicit talk about Jesus separates Christians from the culture. In the end, both factions face the challenge of fitting into the larger subcultural community without compromising their religious beliefs. But it is the self-identified Christian bands that appear to be most concerned with overcoming Christian stigma, a stigma that they attempt to deflect by being up front about their beliefs and by calling out others, the Christians in a band, who they say do not approach hardcore ministry as boldly as they do.

Christian hardcore punks also attempt to redirect stigma to those they label "mainstream" or "Sunday Christians," and they use these other Christians to symbolize what they are not like and what they do not represent. They characterize mainstream Christians as Christians who are not punk because they do not support their music or their ministry. In their opinion, mainstream Christians give Christianity a bad reputation because they make all Christians look like judgmental bigots. Christian hardcore punks often describe these mainstream Christians as insincere Sunday Christians, who attend church on Sunday mornings but do not practice the love and grace of Jesus in their everyday lives. Some even go so far as to claim that the mainstream "kills" Christianity because it encourages people to follow the herd and allow a leader to guide their relationship with Jesus (McDowell 2014).

Hardcore Christians distance themselves from Sunday Christians because they are cognizant of the fact that evangelical Christians have been major critics of punk in the past. Hardcore Christians deflect their stigma as Christian by pointing out that most Christians do not behave like Jesus commands them to and that they have also been "burned" and "rejected" by the mainstream church for being and thinking different than the status quo (McDowell 2018). At the same time, Christian punks also point out that it's unfair for punks to assume that all Christians are the same or to dismiss them as insincere religious monsters. Christian punks, they contend, are nothing like the mainstream "hypocrites" who look down on those who are not like them.

Critiques of mainstream or Sunday Christianity were widespread at the UU meetings, a gathering that brings together punk, hardcore, and goth Christians for a weekend of music ministry workshops, spiritual speakers, and live music. Like a goth Martin Luther, David from UU feels that the "mainstream church" corrupts people's relationship with God because it "doesn't motivate people to think for themselves, act for themselves and be responsible for themselves." Rather, he says, the church teaches young people to attribute their spirituality "to some leader that they're paying." According to David, church is not a "pew facing forward." It should be egalitarian, like a "circle" that everyone participates in. He, like others at the UU conference, concludes that if young people want to get closer to God, they should break away from the Sunday church model and support underground Christian music. In this music, he and other UU participants suggest, young people are "being church" (McDowell 2018) in underground settings and against mainstream Christians. They are punk because they love it, they counter, not because they think punk needs to be fixed.

Conclusion

Studying how Christian youth fight religious stigma in punk is crucial for understanding how an evangelical mission is carried out in spaces that are not always friendly toward Christians (Moberg 2015; Abraham 2017). Previous research shows that some Christian musicians, especially "crossover" bands, manage stigmas by distancing themselves from the "Christian band" label and by blending into the mainstream secular music industry with "watered-down" music that does not call attention to their faith (Hendershot 2004: 58). Other studies, like the ones in this book, offer a different picture of Christianity in alternative music genres such as punk and metal. These studies show that Christian punk is successfully integrating into these music genres (McDowell 2014; Abraham 2017). In this chapter I have argued that integration is successful because Christian punks are distancing themselves from those they label "mainstream Christians," being outspoken about their faith, and redirecting religious stigma to other, less "fearless" Christian punks. Put another way, Christian hardcore punks are exhibiting a core value of punk: they are wearing their difference like a badge of honor. In doing so, they are defining what it means to be authentically punk on their terms, proving that punk authenticity can be constructed and achieved in various ways (Force 2011; Fuist and McDowell 2019).

As I have shown in this chapter, Christian hardcore youth want to be part of the larger hardcore community, but they realize the scene has been suspicious of Christians in the past. To overcome their "tribal stigma" (Goffman 1963) as Christians, hardcore Christians present themselves as fearless men of God who are not afraid to preach about what they believe, even if secular audiences mock and berate them at live shows. This is because, from their perspective, Christians who are unapologetic about their faith help combat the stereotype that Christian men are passive and weak, and that Christians cannot play good hardcore music. Hardcore Christian punks generally argue that young people need to be open about their faith and even preach from stage. There are others, however, who disagree with this tactic. Rather than preach from stage, they argue that Christians should make personal connections with audiences and raise the issue of Jesus when the time feels right, not by preaching. Besides, they reason, preaching can go too far and turn some audiences away from the message. The Christian bands who have achieved the most prominence for their outspokenness in the hardcore and metalcore scenes tend to disagree.

They believe that fearlessness includes preaching or praying from stage, or at least being direct with their audience about their Christian identity; to do otherwise, Christian bands argue, feeds into the stereotype that Christians are "fakes." If Christians want to save the nation, surmised one interviewee, they "must be willing to take the heat for their faith," symbolically, socially, and physically.

4

Straight Edge Evangelicalism
and DIY Spirituality

Ibrahim Abraham
and Francis Stewart

Introduction

Emerging in the American hardcore punk scene in the early 1980s as a secular humanist ideology advocating abstinence from intoxication, the straight edge movement was in direct conflict with the conventional morality of late capitalist society in general and with the conventional morality of the punk subculture in particular. Drawing on fieldwork in the punk scenes of Australia, the UK, and the United States, this chapter critically analyzes two key religious trends in straight edge, which also tell us a great deal about how belief is articulated in punk in general and in contemporary Western society more broadly: firstly, evangelical Christianity, the most prominent expression of religion within the global punk subculture, which often takes a Pentecostal form. Secondly, the diverse and discordant spiritual subjectivities circulating within punk scenes we have called "DIY spirituality" (Abraham and Stewart 2017: 249–50).

The idea of spirituality, embodying "the deepest values and meanings by which people seek to live" (Sheldrake 2007: 1–2), has become detached from conventional religious language and diffused throughout Western society in myriad ways (Holmes 2007; Sheldrake 2007). Building upon the idea of punk's self-reliant, do-it-yourself (DIY) ethic, and Paul Heelas's (1996) definition of New Age religion as "self-spirituality," the concept of DIY spirituality also finds affinity with Nicholas Hookway's (2018: 108) theory of "do-it-yourself morality," an ethical system emphasizing "the authority of the self, choice and ideals of authenticity." We will find that in spite of obvious differences between straight edge evangelicalism and straight edge DIY spirituality, in both cases belief is articulated in a highly personal manner, in keeping with the general "subjective turn" in Western culture, as analyzed in philosopher Charles Taylor's (1989, 2007) cultural histories and as theorized in the empirical research of sociologists Paul Heelas and Linda Woodhead (2005).

The interactions between straight edge and religion within the broader punk subculture have been shaped by these attitudinal changes. As the former head of the Anglican Communion, Rowan Williams (2018: 51), has observed, "Religion today is often understood, from within and without, as having a lot to do with what moral philosophers call 'heteronomy'—that is, the imposition of law, convention, norms from outside, from the 'other.'" The anxiety around outside control or coercion has been foundational in the shaping of the punk ethic, a combination of DIY anticorporate antagonism and expressive individualism (Abraham 2017: 37–50; Abraham and Stewart 2017). While many of the pioneering punk bands of the 1970s were enthusiastic participants in the commercial music industry, the creative limitations this imposed lead to an ongoing antipathy toward the culture industry that exists to this day (Tschmuck 2006: 143–5). Punk's second decade, the 1980s, saw the development of sophisticated underground cultural infrastructure; amateur musicians, small record labels, volunteer promoters, and collectively run, squatted, or borrowed performance spaces created a culture of autonomous self-expression (Moore 2007). As suggested in Chapter 2, rather than any single radical ideology, it is this value of individual authenticity and creative expression that is foundational to contemporary punk (Lewin and Williams 2009).

This privileging of personal and subcultural autonomy has produced a general suspicion toward religion in most punk scenes, at least in the West. Punk is a normatively secular form of self-expression; even though a variety of religious beliefs and expressions do circulate in local punk scenes, religious values are rarely given deference. In spite of this, in the 1990s and 2000s, the straight edge label was adopted and finessed by many Christians in the punk scene. Christian hardcore bands, such as xDeathstarx, xDISCIPLEx A.D., and xLooking Forwardx, incorporate a straight edge synecdoche in their names, the "X" once drawn on the hands of underage patrons at bars and nightclubs forbidden from purchasing alcohol transformed from a legal necessity to a symbol of subcultural virtue (Haenfler 2006: 7–8). Although not all Christians in the punk scene who adhere to straight edge prohibitions consciously identify with the movement, for many the values of Christianity, punk, and straight edge are complimentary; some of xLooking Forwardx's tracks, such as "For Those Who Believe," overlay or fuse these identities (*The Path We Tread*, 2005).

Straight edge adherents have also explored "Eastern" religions. The Hare Krishna movement, a youth-focused form of missionary Hinduism gaining countercultural prominence in the 1960s, was present in the American East Coast hardcore scene in the form of "Krishnacore," and various strands of Buddhism have circulated on America's West Coast (Luhr 2010; Abraham and Stewart 2017; Stewart 2017: 50–7). While some straight edgers wrestled with the rigidity of life in an urban ashram, and others traveled to India to further their religious knowledge (Lahickey 1997: 25–36, 129–35; Peterson 2009: 109–53), the majority of punks who have embraced Eastern religions have done so in a more selective and individualistic manner. This is in keeping with trends in religion in the West over the past half century. Rather than responding to the frustrations of modern life by sacralizing a close-knit faith community, as the Hare Krishna movement did, the sacralization of the individual self has been far more common (Bromley 2012), placing personal autonomy and self-care at the center of spiritual practice.

This chapter will explore precisely how this process of religious individualization manifests in straight edge punk by drawing on a blended sample of interviews from the authors' research projects, carried out between 2009 and 2015 in the punk scenes of Australia, the UK, and the United States. With straight edge being a "hidden identity" not quantified in any sources, and with religiously or spiritually engaged straight edge being a floating, conceivably "third-order subculture" (Christopher, Bartkowski, and Haverda 2018), with differently defined borders, constructing a representative or random sample is impossible. So while the chapter's findings cannot be generalized in the sense of being standardized, we believe they can be generalized in the sense of enlightening experiences that broadly hold within the assigned categories across the data. The methodologies informing this chapter are unexceptional and rather unadventurous within qualitative social scientific studies of religion: a combination of semi-structured interviews, focus groups, participant observations, and content analysis.

This chapter will begin with an overview of straight edge values, recognizing the tensions that have developed between different expressions of the movement. The chapter will then analyze the process of individualization in contemporary Western religious and spiritual practice, noting how this has manifested among some straight edge punks, emphasizing an ethic of self-reliance. By contrast, the chapter will then analyze the beliefs of evangelical straight edge adherents who, while similarly expressing individualized convictions, differ by authenticating their faith via something other than themselves.

The Spirit of Straight Edge

The compatibilities and conflicts between spiritual expressions and straight edge values become apparent through exploring the core beliefs of the movement, which began as a response to the hedonistic tendencies in punk's first decade. Straight edge was an act of subcultural self-reflection that sought to differently embody punk's oppositional ideology, disavowing the notion of punk as "all about debauchery and self-destruction" (Adams 2002: 354). Straight edge's ideology of sobriety and self-control was first outlined in the songs of Minor Threat, key protagonists in the early 1980s Washington DC hardcore scene, discussed in Chapter 10. "Out of Step" summarizes straight edge's prohibitions on alcohol, drugs, and casual sex: "I don't drink / I don't smoke / I don't fuck" (*Minor Threat*, 1984). Teenage vocalist Ian MacKaye intended these songs to express his personal beliefs and criticize his peers; "Always gonna stay in touch / Never wanna use a crutch / I've got the straight edge" declared the movement's eponymous anthem (*Minor Threat*, 1984). Although MacKaye did not intend to start a social movement, or even a subcultural "schism" (Wood 2000), straight edge became a term that a number of individuals and bands came to self-identify with, promoting the movement through recordings, zines, and tours. Quantifying straight edge is impractical, we have noted, but we conservatively estimate the number of self-identified adherents to be in the low tens of thousands worldwide.

Despite its entanglements with religion, noted above, and subcultural and scholarly claims of a religious asceticism animating straight edge (Blush 2001: 26–9; Haenfler 2006: 10), the movement developed as a strictly secular one. The straight edge rejection of intoxicants, and what it considers destructive sexualities, with its corresponding praise of addressing life's challenges with stoic sobriety, echoes Charles Taylor's (2007: 9) description of the ideologies of modern reason, "contemplating the world and human life without illusion, and of acting lucidly for the best in the interests of human flourishing." Like conventional religions, there is room for reforming, syncretizing, and personalizing straight edge. While abstinence is the core straight edge practice, and the key indicator of commitment and identity, there are a series of secondary and tertiary commitments of spiraling intensity. Adherents often interpret the prohibition on casual sex differently, many adopt vegetarian or vegan diets and lifestyles, and some even avoid caffeine and nonprescription medicine. Some also seek careers connected to straight edge values or the punk scene, as tattoo artists, drug and alcohol counselors, or other careers in the caring or creative professions.

Straight edge is generally characterized by individual commitment to self-improvement, and only rarely is it interpreted as a systematic policy to be imposed upon a local punk scene, let alone wider society. Nevertheless, violent attempts to impose the movement's thou-shalt-nots are not unheard of, especially in the United States, amplifying the aggressive masculinist undercurrents present in hardcore (Haenfler 2006: 81–101; Stewart 2017: 39–42). Laura, from New York, represents the general view of straight edgers in denouncing the "fucking assholes giving us all a bad name" by bullying non-straight edgers in the punk scene; "it is supposed to be a positive individual thing not a fucking gang."

However, as Ian MacKaye mused, "for people with a tendency to veer towards fundamentalism, straight edge is a perfect vehicle" (Blush 2001: 28). Part of the problem is that one can more easily profess than perform an identity, especially an identity based on the self-denial of personal pleasures and especially if those pleasures are also rejected by one's peers. So it is that straight edge reached its violent peak around the turn of the millennium in Salt Lake City, the orderly heart of the Mormon world, where a "mutant Brady Bunch" of straight edge youth used violence to differentiate themselves from their Latter-day Saint neighbors who were annoyingly rejecting the same vices (Lopez 1999). Steven, from San Francisco, witnessed these straight edgers at a show in Utah, "stalking the edge of the [mosh] pit" looking to attack anyone with a beer or a cigarette in their hand. Another extreme example was the adoption of radical environmentalism by a small faction of "hardline" straight edgers, which included the bands Earth Crisis and Vegan Reich—briefly renamed Vegan Jihad after its founder converted to Islam—which epitomized the violent posturing and often patriarchal attitudes of the tendency. Ironically, these "fundamentalist" straight edgers are the most likely to "sell out" their values, as they discover militancy and maturity are a difficult combination, and compromise is often necessary (Haenfler 2006: 204).

Sheila Is a Punk Rocker

It could be argued that the process of religious individualization is all about compromise. In the late capitalist West, the precise adoption and replication of inherited creeds, whether conventional religions or youth subcultures, run contrary to the dominant related ideologies of liberalism and expressive individualism. In the case of punk, Azerrad (2007) observed a subjective and introspective turn in punk's third and fourth decades; the commercial success of grunge and emo was the most obvious example of inward turns toward personal angst and away from radical politics. The study of punk and related music-based youth subcultures took a contemporaneous turn away from the Marxian studies of the collective politics of youth subcultures of the 1970s, to focus on individual meaning-making through consumerism in the 1990s (Bennett 2011; Abraham 2017: 25–9). In the case of religion, on the other hand, the process of individualization, and the turn away from established religious institutions and ideologies, came to be embodied by a young woman named Sheila.

In the important study *Habits of the Heart* (Bellah et al. 1985: 219–49), the individualization of American religion, beginning with emerging evangelical norms around personal conviction in the colonial period, coupled with a growing culture of self-reliance, culminates in the 1980s with "Sheilaism," the self-defined faith of a research participant given the name Sheila Larsen. Described by Sheila as "just my own little voice," and by the researchers as an attempt to extract "internal meaning" from a history of external conformism, the key tenets of Sheilaism are "just try to love yourself and be gentle with yourself. You know, I guess, take care of each other" (Bellah et al. 1985: 221, 235). Sheilaism is a "perfectly natural expression of current American religious life," the authors argue. Many Americans would, like Sheila, reject any faith prescribing anything more onerous than this basic ethic of self-care and reciprocal decency (Bellah et al. 1985).

A generation later, Christian Smith demonstrated persuasively via the National Study of Youth and Religion that a close denominational relation of Sheilaism, which he labeled "moral therapeutic deism," had become the default belief system of American youth (Smith and Denton 2005: 162–70; Smith 2010). Its basic moral teachings, that the "central goal of life is to be happy and to feel good about oneself" and that salvation exists for all those who follow God's general desire for us to take care of each other, as Sheila would say, emphasize the therapeutic nature of contemporary spirituality, focused on creating subjective well-being and managing interpersonal relationships (Smith and Denton 2005: 163–4). On the one hand, such "therapeutic individualism" is a way to "rescue some sense of individual uniqueness, spontaneity, and meaningful emotion in the face of a massive, proceduralistic, mechanistic, and alienating public sphere," but it is hardly incidental that this ideology reflects normative consumer-capitalist values "by constituting people as self-fulfillment-oriented consumers subject to advertising's influence on their subjective feelings" (Smith and Denton 2005: 174).

This therapeutic culture of self-realization offers a broad normative template for spiritualties incorporating an array of ideas from diverse religious traditions, curated for contemporary Western consumers in the way noted above, but also strongly shaped by one's peers (Hammer 2010). The DIY spirituality circulating within punk incorporates diverse cultural and personal references, therefore, but whether one's orientation is liberal and individualistic, or more politically radical, as discussed in Chapter 10 in the case of punk musician Tomas Squip, the authority of the self is always central. For Taylor (1989, 2007), this dominant contemporary approach to religion is part of the subjective turn in Western culture, tracing itself back (in the modern era at least) to Romanticism's emphasis on the inner life of the individual. Truth comes to be thought of as something found within, rather than received from without in the form of religious tradition.

Ever since the baby boomers came of age in the 1960s, it is arguable that a low-intensity spiritual "quest" has become the typical religious form in America and proximate societies (Roof 1999), even if these are the quests of tourists rather than pilgrims. A similar analogy is used by Wuthnow (1998: 8), arguing that "faith is no longer something people inherit but something for which they strive." The former system implies permanence and perhaps subordination within an existing institution, while the latter implies impermanence and individual agency. In some cases this may amount to little more than the contemporary spiritual marketplace telling you to be yourself, *"only better"* (Heelas 2008: 61–2), but for Wuthnow (1998: 48) the cultural shift promises something more profound: being on your own "with no direction home," as he quotes Bob Dylan's "Like a Rolling Stone" (*Highway 61 Revisited*, 1965).

The counterculture of the 1960s and 1970s was an extreme example of this religious seeking; pursuing seemingly uncorrupted belief systems from the East and from the occult margins of the West, the movement eventually moderated in suburbia into more stable and consumable "New Age" forms. Described as a reaction "against the head-dominated, cold, calculating qualities of the rational," it made sense that alongside New Age spirituality, the Pentecostalism of the Jesus Movement also found a home in the counterculture and its later conservative suburban expressions, as both could be described in the therapeutic vein as "religions of self-help" (Bouma 2006: 91–3). Within this emerging normative culture of religious individualism, what Bellah et al. (1985: 55) call "the nervous search for the true self," in which the individual can only be held back by society, develops into the anxiety over heteronomy Williams (2018: 51) identifies in this chapter's introduction. Watts's (2018: 352) study of "spiritual-but-not-religious" millennials explains the hegemonic logic in all this: "If what guides an individual's day-to-day decisions is the cumulative total of their personal experiences—unique to them—then no one, nor any institution, is as fit to govern their beliefs, thoughts and actions as they are."

It is therefore hardly surprising that the conventionally irreligious straight edge research participants Stewart has interviewed hold rather rigid views of religion, especially Christianity, and that they make no attempt to demonstrate awareness of its diversity. These rigid views emerge from generalizations of their individual experiences, combined with a sometimes starkly unequivocal moral outlook, reminiscent not just of Watts's analysis, above, but also the countercultural view of the West as utterly corrupt. As Malott's (2009) study of secularist punk opposition to Christianity illustrates, a fear of the reversal of the secularization process, or a fear that the West simply never has been secularized and religion still plays a dominant heteronomous role, is the key source of anti-religious subcultural suspicion. While we have never encountered evidence of individual Christians or Christian bands under church control in the punk scene, and churches are at best ambivalent supporters of Christian alternative music (Abraham 2017: 135–53), the notion that conservative Christians desire complete control—or at least the right of censure—over creative expression does have an historical basis. Like most other music genres, punk endured a period of attempted censorship from the religious right (Shuker 2001: 217–26), and while some now view censorship as a preoccupation of the secular left (Bestley 2015: 121–2), the hostility of conservative Christianity to punk, metal, and hip hop in the 1980s and 1990s has remained in the subcultural subconscious.

Straight edge adherents of DIY spirituality therefore make a clear distinction between religion and spirituality, illustrating Sheldrake's (2016: 17) point that such a distinction "frequently depends on a reductionist view of religion." Lucy, a former hardcore drummer from California, who was involved with a Dharma Punx study group in San Francisco (Stewart 2015; Abraham and Stewart 2017: 248–9), articulates this distinction by invoking punk's DIY approach to music:

> I have an eclectic approach to my spirituality. I am part of the Dharma Punx here and really value it, but they are not a religion for me. I am not a religious person, I am a spiritual person. I consider my spirituality to be Dharma Punx, yoga, praying, crystals, straight edge, my addiction support group and increasingly an interest in Wicca. These things are all very, what's the word, fluid. If they were to be a religion then someone or something would stop that [fluidity], rules would be put in place, it would all be out of my control. How would that be any different than a big record label buying up the independents or signing punk bands just to make money from them?

Hans, from nearby Berkeley, made a similar distinction by describing religion "as the churches or mosques or temples," with an ethic of "sit down, shut up, and we will tell you what to do." Spirituality, on the other hand, "is what you do day to day, what you choose to do, how you find your answers. It has nothing to do with any institution, any leader. It can't be controlled."

What is central here is the authority of the individual and the fear of the individual losing that authority. Just as Minor Threat viewed drugs and alcohol as "a crutch" in their song "Straight Edge" (*Minor Threat*, 1984), Watts's (2018: 351–2) spiritual-but-not-religious millennials also view religion as "a crutch" because it is "a form of negative dependency that keeps the individual from being truly independent, free and self-reliant." This emphasis on self-reliance is also a feature of Hookway's (2018: 108) concept of "DIY morality," within which morality "is not sourced from religion, tradition or similar but is understood as rooted in choice, personal responsibility and self-creation."

While the rhetoric of DIY spirituality and DIY morality certainly emphasizes the individual's responsibility for constructing their own systems of meaning and challenging received wisdom, this does not happen in a vacuum. As Rowan Williams (2001: 4) puts it, morality "is not made by a will operating in the abstract, but by someone who is used to thinking and imagining in a certain way." Taylor's (2007: 473–86) later work on expressive individualism came to emphasize the role of popular culture and consumerism in this process of moral formation, recognizing that cultural "styles" play a more important role for many young people than religious or political groups. He therefore judges us to be "co-determiners" of our beliefs and identities along with the culture industry (2007: 481). However, as Watts (2018: 358–9) observes, citing successful secular pop-punk acts Avril Lavigne and Sum 41 along the way, the discourse of what we are calling DIY spirituality is so thoroughly diffused throughout commercial popular culture that it has become hegemonic to the point of invisibility. One cannot point to specific instances of being evangelized by DIY spirituality as one can in the case of a Christian punk band preaching on stage between songs.

Even if we think of morality as merely a matter of doing what we want, a pertinent formulation in the context of DIY morality and spirituality, Williams (2001: 4–5) argues we still need to identify what precisely it is that we want and the social forces forming our desires. Following Durkheim's view that whatever is foundational to a society takes on a sense of the sacred, Houtman and Aupers (2010: 14) argue that the dominance of what we are calling DIY spirituality in late capitalist society simply reflects the sacralization of individualism. This can be viewed positively, as a process that "sacralizes human dignity"

(Watts 2018: 357), and contemporary popular discourses of spirituality can also address public morality and social justice (Sheldrake 2007), but most analysis of DIY spirituality sees conformist consumerism where its adherents see personal autonomy. Carrette and King (2005), representatively, argue there is no net gain in liberty if Christian hegemony is replaced by capitalist hegemony. Scholars of DIY spirituality often express similar value judgments, implicitly or explicitly grounded in normative religious or political critiques (Woodhead 2010). While recognized as a product of late capitalist culture, DIY spirituality is also often looked down upon as superficial and self-centered, undermining traditional ideas of a dichotomy between the sacred and the profane by focusing unashamedly on individual well-being and embedding itself within the mundanity of everyday capitalist life (Heelas 2008). A number of female straight edgers were annoyed that "spirituality" or "faith" is not granted the same seriousness as "religion," therefore, while simultaneously insisting upon its individualized nature and worldly, pragmatic focus.

So although there is nothing exceptional about the circulation of DIY spirituality within straight edge—these punks are following in the footsteps of the baby boomers, whether they like it or not—punk and straight edge values mitigate many of the individualistic and consumeristic features of DIY spirituality. The foundation of straight edge in prohibitions on certain personal pleasures, as well as the networks and identities that straight edgers are embedded within, gives straight edge DIY spirituality a social anchoring and ethical discipline absent from other DIY moralities and spiritualities. Rather than being another example of the individualistic moralities critiqued by social theorists focused on moral decline in late capitalism (Hookway 2015), straight edge DIY spirituality is often mobilized in conspicuous opposition to elements of individualistic morality—especially if personal pleasure is seen to entail exploitation of people or the environment.

To this end, straight edge lyrics often promote the notion of a coherent, but gendered, community, invoking the language of "brotherhood," "family," and "unity." A symbolic community is created through shared symbols, notably the "X" that features in tattoos, band names, and merchandise. Live shows embody these values in the mosh pit through stage-diving and crowd-surfing, in which straight edgers set aside their individualistic tendencies to rely on their "family" to keep them from falling on the floor. Straight edge also continues the punk tradition of breaking down barriers between performers and audience members, sharing the microphone between vocalists and fans. Furthermore, although there is no single agreed-upon way to "be edge," nor is there any straight edge leadership or hierarchy, the subculture certainly judges those who claim membership and holds members to collective standards, even if these are imprecise or inconsistent standards. A relatedly ubiquitous feature of straight edge culture is the celebration of those who "stay true" and dismay at those who "sell out." "So tired of mangled and broken convictions / Your will stands as weak as your addictions," xDeathstarx complain on "Die to Remain" (*The Triumph*, 2008).

While the overwhelming majority of straight edgers reject the idea of imposing the movement's prohibitions on others, as discussed, there is still hope that the positive behavior of straight edge individuals can become the locus of collective change. "Our approach to chang[ing] the world is by living our life and being proud to say we are straight edge," said Gail, from Leeds. Similarly, while the rituals and symbols of straight edge solidarity are less significant for older adherents who are no longer active in their local punk scene, when straight edge becomes a "personal lifestyle," commitment to subjectively embodying the objective disciplines of the movement takes on even more importance (Haenfler 2013).

Straight Edge Evangelicalism

As the individualization discussed in the previous section has affected the West as a whole, normative understandings of religion have changed for everyone, Christians included. It is certainly not the case that a moral elite craft DIY spiritualities while the conventionally religious repeat thoughtless rituals. As Bellah et al. (1985: 236) noted, comparing religious individualists like Sheila Larsen and more conventional born-again religious conservatives, both conceive of their choices as providing the "basis for genuine personal autonomy," because both choices can conceivably liberate individuals from unwanted external pressures. One can also find "spiritual eclecticism" across the spectrum of Christianity (Sheldrake 2016: 18). Wilcox (2002: 498) observed forms of "Sheilaism" among progressive Christians, creating forms of "spiritual bricolage" on mainline Protestantism's pastel-colored margins. Most significantly, perhaps, what Greeley (2004: 78) refers to as "selective Catholicism" has become the dominant expression of faith for Roman Catholics in the West, illustrating Taylor's (2007: 727) theory of our "post-Durkheimian world" in which religion no longer regulates public behavior or belonging. Michael, a straight edge musician and activist from Oakland, explained that he "walked away from the Catholic

Church" because he disagreed with official teachings on gender and abortion, but many Catholics still within the church would agree with him. Drawing on congregational surveys, Dixon (2014) observes that only one in five frequent churchgoing Australian Catholics claims adherence to all the church's official teachings and practices, and barely one in twenty of Australia's self-identifying Catholics meets this criteria overall. Pope Francis in fact acknowledges that Catholicism can be lived in a plurality of "deep and sincere" ways that might exclude conventional practices (Dixon 2014: 271).

It is worth emphasizing the importance of individual experience in evangelicalism, and especially Pentecostalism, in this context. There is a general ontology of "feeling right" in evangelicalism, emerging from the emphasis placed on personal revelatory experience as confirmation of belief (Flory and Miller 2008). Within Pentecostalism, moreover, the exaggerated emphasis on personal experience has a "radically laicizing" tendency (Wright 2002: 253). Because the ecstatic experiences foundational to Pentecostalism occur regardless of rank, in what has been called a culture of "spiritual democracy" (Sheldrake 2007: 203), Pentecostalism can promote a "do-it-yourself ecclesiology," which devalues ministerial training, undermining institutional authority, especially the authority of the bookish theological education predominating in mainline churches (Wright 2002: 257–8). Tomas, the former vocalist of a Florida-based Christian hardcore band, and later a church pastor, noted the similarity between his vocations. "It was just like being in the band," he said of his church. "Setting up all your equipment then breaking it down afterwards. We were meeting in movie theatres, rented facilities, homes; it was very similar, very DIY." Young evangelicals finding fellowship outside of organized churches, in the Christian punk scene (McDowell 2018), is therefore a surprisingly logical development.

Encountering a diversity of individual beliefs and institutional doctrines within even American evangelicalism is therefore a given for touring Christian punk bands. Jeff, a former grunge musician and later a church pastor in Nashville, described conflict over conflicting messages from touring Christian musicians, the church hosting them, and parents supporting youth ministry, as "basic church drama 101." Various controversies were bubbling under the surface of the evangelical churches in the United States, and elsewhere, supporting touring punk and metal bands in the 2010s, included debates over what is commonly called the Prosperity Gospel—the belief that Christians can be empowered to achieve worldly wealth, health, and success—and over the influence of the New Calvinism movement associated with Mark Driscoll, analyzed in Chapter 6. Some Christian punk bands alleviated their anxiety around predictably unpredictable theological differences by removing all but the most basic and positive religious messages from lyrics and onstage statements. This approach is analogous to a trend in evangelical worship music in which simplicity or ambiguity in lyrics allows songs to be utilized by a variety of churches, and subjectively interpreted by a variety of individuals, with conceivably contradictory beliefs (Abraham 2018).

These changes in religious practice are reflected in Christian approaches to straight edge ethics and identity. In interviews, straight edge Christians typically employed experiential or relational language, and only rarely was more traditional expository language used, extracting straight edge ethics in a rational way from scripture. While Christians usually identify with straight edge for personal and experiential reasons, the Christian straight edgers Abraham interviewed were less likely to have personally experienced the kinds of addictions or deprivations found among Stewart's research participants. Their experiences were more about a sense of alienation with the hedonism of late capitalism and a desire to disassociate from that culture, rather than a desire to disassociate from their past.

Two broad positions on straight edge are to be found among Christian punks. A positive view is commonly taken that the straight edge movement is compatible or even complimentary with Christian belief and identity. Matthew, a teenage Christian straight edger interviewed by Haenfler (2006: 185), describes Christianity as focused on his inner spiritual well-being and straight edge as focused on his physical outer well-being. Ty, an American punk musician and pastor living in the UK, described straight edge as allowing punks to legitimately embrace a more "traditional" morality—"not that I think Christianity is always associated with being traditional," he hastily added—but in any case making it legitimate to be punk without having to "go the whole gamut of more permissive ethics which often comes with punk." Straight edge is also recognized as a possible bridge to non-Christians in the punk scene interested in exploring different spiritual and ethical ways of living. Tomas, the former hardcore vocalist and pastor of the "very DIY" church, recognized that the presence of straight edge in punk gives Christianity "one foot in the door," even if his band ultimately rejected the label.

A negative view also circulates, arguing that straight edge's constitutive prohibitions on casual sex, drug use, and at least excessive alcohol consumption are already present within Christian ethics, but that straight edge values are inferior insofar as they lack any religious anchoring. Some Christians also struggle with absolutely repudiating alcohol, even if they themselves are teetotal, since wine is so ubiquitous in biblical language and Christian tradition. "Grape on the vine / We've been alone a long time / Grape on the vine / Why not be crushed to make wine?" drone mewithoutYou, a Sufism-infused Christian post-hardcore band, on "Son of a Widow" (*Catch for Us the Foxes*, 2004). Similar to Wood's (2006: 134–6) analysis of straight edge Krishnacore punks' desires to embrace a "higher" set of beliefs and practices, belief in Christianity's sufficiency on lifestyle matters can make straight edge an unnecessary label and perhaps even an illegitimate one.

Jono, a Christian hardcore musician and zine editor in his early twenties from the British Midlands, who described himself as "straight edge and almost vegan," explained the development in his thinking and his identity in a rather typical experiential way. The son of a Church of England Minister, Jono had an awakening sense of personal identity and social justice as he transitioned into adulthood:

> Originally I was just thinking, "don't get drunk," because that's not scripture, that's not right. But now I see how alcohol companies try to push alcohol on younger people and how particularly, I think, in the UK more than anywhere else, there's such a heavy binge-drinking culture and to separate myself from that is important to me. I don't want to be a part of a culture that works 9–5 and wastes away their weekends. I want to be a part of a culture that lives every day with a clear head and is living every day to the absolute fullest for Jesus Christ.

Such a statement seems at odds with the rhetoric of individual autonomy found within straight edge DIY spirituality. The idea of living for a supernatural being runs counter to the emphasis on self-reliance in DIY spirituality and morality, as well as the desacralization and materialization of salvation in straight edge we have analyzed elsewhere (Abraham and Stewart 2014).

Despite the clear dissimilarities with straight edge DIY spirituality, for Jono and other Christians, straight edge can be individually adapted for strengthening their spirituality and for performing their identity. Mark, a Christian musician in a secular hardcore band, argued that straight edge sets Christians an ethical challenge that can remedy what he believes is the "abuse of God's forgiveness" by those who "use Christianity as a safety net rather than a way to make the world a better place." Furthermore, in recognizing the culture of accountability in straight edge, Mark recognized that, as in the case of DIY spirituality, straight edge can address the permissive tendencies within contemporary Christianity that are largely a result of the general process of religious individualization and the shift toward the therapeutic that this chapter has analyzed. "Straight edge keeps people more honest. It's much less forgiving than Christianity is," he said.

In a few cases, Christian straight edgers articulated a more "traditional" rational and expository approach. Suvi, the female vocalist in an Australian Christian metalcore band, explained her straight edge commitment as a logical application of biblical teaching, applied to her prominent position as one of the few female vocalists in the Australian punk and metal scene:

> In the Bible it talks about not having anything in excess, and not doing anything that will cloud your vision or cloud your relationship with God. The main reason why I chose to take that [straight edge] label, and not just not do those things, is because I believe I'm in a leadership role, and when I get up on stage and the kids see that I'm edge, they know straightaway what I don't do—they know I live a life not involving drugs, casual sex, or alcohol. I believe there are Christians out there who are living lukewarm lives and they're saying alcohol, and drugs, and sexual desires aren't pulling them down, and they're just living lukewarm. I don't wanna be like that; I wanna live a life of purity and sobriety for God.

In addition to hinting at the particular pressures placed on female Christian musicians, this statement embodies quite clearly what sociologist and Anglican priest Gary Bouma (2006: 89, 101) calls the rational "know-it-all" God of modern Christianity, "providing the structure to all of life through rules and regulations," as laid out in the Bible and observable in the natural world. As a charismatic Christian, Suvi does not live entirely according to all the strictures of this form of religious life; personal religious experiences and revelations are a vital part of her spirituality, but her statement demonstrates how grounding in scripture and tradition—even for a nondenominational charismatic—sets Christianity quite apart from DIY spirituality.

Given that this model of Christian straight edge identity is concerned in no small measure with embodying what is believed to be God's will, even those who do not openly identify as straight edge can locate themselves within its logic. Tim, a hardcore guitarist from the British Midlands, who does not identify as straight edge, quoted Minor Threat in explaining that both Christianity and straight edge call their adherents to live "out of step" with the morals of broader society (*Minor Threat*, 1984). Tim articulated this in familiar evangelical language that disavows the idea of imposed religious regulations and emphasizes what Bramadat (2000: 10) suggests is "perhaps the definitive clement of contemporary evangelicalism … the emphasis on having a 'personal relationship' with Jesus Christ." Tim argued that Christianity is "not about a bunch of rules and regulations; it's a relationship, isn't it? So it's sort of saying; I'm giving up this because I'm devoting myself to what God created me to be. He didn't create me to go and drink myself stupid." In contrast to the straight edge

DIY spirituality, this straight edge-like behavior emerges from interpellation into a preexisting religious subjectivity, albeit one conceived of relationally.

This emphasis on one's relationship with God is also foundational to anti-straight edge attitudes found among Christians in the punk scene. These negative approaches to straight edge recognize the importance of self-reliance and individualism within straight edge ethics, just as straight edge adherents of DIY spirituality do, but they find this reason to disassociate from the label. Tomas explained that his band decided to disassociate itself from the straight edge label on the basis that "we felt the straight edge movement was something that's done because of self ... we weren't positive for self; we were positive for the life and teachings of Jesus Christ." The risk, from this perspective, is conceiving of a path to salvation that is not only wholly material but wholly individual. Suvi, the Australian metalcore vocalist, refers to this as the danger that "straight edge becomes an idol." Within evangelicalism in general, a vast number of activities or cultural forms are conceivably potentially idolatrous by providing a source of identity and commitment that undermines one's relationship with God (Abraham 2017: 121–2).

Conclusion

Rather than conceiving of punk as inherently and consistently politically radical, it has been suggested that it is rather more accurate to recognize the desire for individual expression as foundational to punk practices (Lewin and Williams 2009). In this way, even if straight edge abstinence runs counter to conventional liberal capitalism, punk has perhaps been more attuned to the dominant ideologies of the West than its protagonists would probably be comfortable in admitting. In the case of religion, this includes a familiar commitment to individualized spirituality or to more conventional religion expressed in thoroughly subjective language. Punk's attunement to the dominant ideologies of the day is also reflected in the wariness toward heteronomy identified by Rowan Williams (2018) and found in most punk scenes in the West.

While recognizing that the process of religious individualization has impacted Western society in general, Christians and non-Christians alike, this chapter has demonstrated key points of differentiation between straight edge DIY spirituality and the evangelicalism that dominate conventional expressions of religion in punk. From the perspective of straight edge DIY spirituality, Christianity's grounding of moral and religious authority outside of the self undermines the authenticity of its beliefs, even if one accepts that the choice to place one's faith outside of one's self is freely determined. On the other hand, it is precisely the insistence upon individualism and self-reliance within straight edge ethics that undermines its legitimacy in the view of a minority of Christians in the punk scene, concerned with maintaining a conspicuous difference from conceivably rival moral systems. As this chapter has illustrated, the common criticism of DIY spirituality and morality as individualistic consumerism is undermined by the cultivation of collective identity and self-discipline within straight edge. Punk does not simply mirror its parent society, therefore; even when reflecting the broader social process of individualization, punk's DIY values are arrayed against consumerism such that it creates communities of authenticity and accountability.

5

"Grow a Beard and Be Somebody": Disavowal and Vector Space at Rocketown, Nashville

Joshua Kalin Busman

Introduction

In spring 2003, Rocketown opened its doors in downtown Nashville, Tennessee. On any night thereafter, one could see a myriad of punks, goths, skaters, and emo kids—including a late adolescent version of myself—hanging around the coffee bar, arcade, skate park, or the large basement venue that hosted four or five live music shows each week. Younger teenagers were particularly drawn to the venue, which always offered all-ages shows and provided a tightly controlled environment that forbade the use of drugs, alcohol, and even profanity from the stage. While there is a strong tradition of this kind of ascetic practice within straight edge punk, analyzed in Chapter 4, Rocketown's ethos comes primarily from the fact that the venue is owned and operated by Christian pop musician and longtime Nashville resident, Michael W. Smith. However, Smith's ownership is not prominently advertised anywhere in the space, and the venue seems to go out of its way to avoid any explicitly Christian language or imagery in its branding. And in the early 2000s, they also tended to be one of the few venues to reliably book young punk and metal acts coming through town. So on any given night, part of the audience might be teenage members of the local hardcore scene looking for whichever venue had the best show that night, others were fans of the specifically Christian bands who often played the venue, and still others were simply Christian youth from Nashville and the surrounding region whose parents felt comfortable sending them to the venue because of its connection to a prominent Christian recording artist.

I attended my first show at Rocketown as a 17-year-old high school senior in the spring of 2005. Although I was raised in a Southern Baptist church in East Tennessee and the son of a pastor, my parents were not particularly averse to my love for punk rock, hardcore, and metal music (as much as that would have probably delighted me at the time), so I didn't choose Rocketown as a safer or more palatable alternative to other venues. My frequent trips to Rocketown, especially after moving to the Nashville area to attend college, were most often spurred by the fact that the bands I wanted to see—like those nominally Christian bands on the Tooth & Nail label—would almost always play there when passing through Tennessee. For that first Rocketown show back in 2005, my impetus was a headlining set by the Christian metalcore band Underoath, who had just released their breakthrough album *They're Only Chasing Safety* the previous summer. That album had provided the soundtrack to months of social occasions with my friends, even eventually serving as the score for a skateboarding parody video called "Lords of K-Town" that my friends and I shot and edited in the months immediately following our Rocketown trip.

We arrived at the venue with a fair amount of anticipation after the two-and-a-half-hour drive from Knoxville and found ourselves close to the front of the line when the doors eventually opened. As the headliners, Underoath wouldn't actually take the stage until much later in the evening, but upon entering the venue, we still pushed as close to the stage as we could get. As we waited for the space to fill up, we began chatting with the fans around us and discovered that many of them were there primarily to hear one of the earlier bands on the bill. Opening the show were Underoath's labelmates The Chariot, another Christian-identifying metalcore band from the American South and one with which my friends and I were at least passingly familiar. However, the other two bands on the bill—These Arms Are Snakes and Scary Kids Scaring Kids—were completely unknown to us. This was partly because both bands were from the West, rather than the South, but primarily because neither of them shared the Christian identification and affiliation of Underoath and The Chariot. Similarly, the fans of These Arms Are Snakes or Scary Kids Scaring Kids we engaged were almost completely unfamiliar with either Underoath or The Chariot. We discussed our mutual fandoms as we waited for the show to start, and as the evening unfolded, I remember exchanging many eager glances as we each experienced for the first time music that was already so meaningful to the other.

During my time attending shows there in the mid-2000s, Rocketown had a special penchant for hosting mixed-bill shows featuring Christian and non-Christian acts, allowing for more fluid "opener" and "headliner" roles for bands on stage and in advertising, mixing artists from different genres or subgenres, and placing local and touring acts together. Add these myriad opportunities for comingling to the powerful forces of Christian formation and the inchoate adolescent masculinity that dominates punk scenes worldwide, and Rocketown was bound to be a powerful venue for a kind of self-discovery and self-actualization among its patrons. In a 2005 documentary interview, James Smith, a rhythm guitarist for Underoath, joked that the central challenge for both the band and its fans was to figure out how to "grow a beard and be somebody" (*Underoath: They're Only Chasing Safety*, 2005). To my friends and I, this two-step program seemed to open up a kind of radical futurity and these two "goals" help me thematize the identity struggles encircled by Rocketown and the music that animated it. First, how does one grow into sexual maturity with an outwardly legible masculinity, and second, how does one live a life of value? Underoath addresses these questions not with clear or definitive answers but by intentionally opening spaces for the play of multiple simultaneous selves, especially among their predominantly adolescent male fan base.

In this chapter, I will explore these issues by focusing on two studio albums made by Underoath, *They're Only Chasing Safety* (2005) and *Define the Great Line* (2006), as well as the DVD documentaries that accompanied "special editions" of each album. Focusing on the release and promotion of these two albums will serve a twofold purpose. First, it will allow me to explore the connections between the broader phenomenon I describe and my own personal experiences as a teenage fan. Between 2005 and 2007, I saw Underoath play at least a half-dozen times, including three different shows at Rocketown in support of both albums. Second, these two albums represented a significant inflection point in the success of Underoath as a band and the visibility of Christian metalcore more generally. Although *They're Only Chasing Safety* was Underoath's fourth full-length album release, it was their first with a new lineup in which drummer Aaron Gillespie was the only remaining founding member and Spencer Chamberlain was added as a new lead vocalist. Additionally, *They're Only Chasing Safety* was a seismic shift for Underoath in terms of commercial success. While their first two albums sold approximately 2,000 and 3,000 copies, respectively, on a tiny independent label, *They're Only Chasing Safety* sold nearly 100,000 copies in its first week of release and was ultimately certified gold less than a year after its release. *They're Only Chasing Safety* and its follow-up, *Define the Great Line*, delivered independent Christian label Tooth & Nail Records their first two RIAA Gold certifications. Additionally, *Define the Great Line*'s debut at No. 2 on the Billboard 200 album chart is still unmatched in the label's output.

These two albums represent the beginnings of Underoath navigating the recording and touring process as a genuine musical brand, and this provides an additional layer of interest to the questions of self-actualization that this chapter considers. Through close analysis of these two albums and my own experiences surrounding them, I will demonstrate the ways that Underoath uses gestures of disavowal to open up what I call "vector space" on their records and in concert at a place like Rocketown.

Rocketown as Vector Space

In the years since I moved away from the Nashville area in 2009, I have come to describe of Rocketown as a vector space, borrowing the term from Euclidean geometry in which a "vector" is a mathematical object defined by both magnitude (velocity and acceleration) and direction. Vector space is a multidimensional plane whose parameters are defined by the existence of any particular collection of individual vectors and the possibility of their interactions through addition and multiplication. These interactions can create new vectors, which further populate the vector space. In the vector space of Rocketown, one similarly finds a wide variety of participants traveling through the space with radically different velocity and acceleration and often traveling in fundamentally different directions. And yet, the space is opened by the existence of this collection of vectors and the conditions of their interactions. Vector spaces are typically finite since they are limited by the possibilities of those vectors present and the axial limits of mathematical permutation, and they often have clear boundaries or fixed starting points that give them shape. For me, understanding Rocketown as a kind of vector space provides a potent metaphor for the complex mix of boundedness and seemingly endless reconfiguration that characterizes any venue and its interaction with a local musical scene.

The idea of vector space also helps to make sense of the degree to which the sharedness of the space at Rocketown does not translate to any sort of unity or uniformity existing outside of the live show itself. In this way, the concept has some similarity with Maffesoli's (1996) theory of the "neo-tribe" in which "spontaneous emotional connections" predominate over structural ones based on shared social backgrounds or beliefs (Bennett 1999; Abraham 2017: 28). Kiri Miller has observed a similar phenomenon in the context of Sacred Harp convention singing, a lively and harmonically distinctive tradition of hymn-singing that flourished in North America during the eighteenth and nineteenth centuries—and which The Chariot sample at length on their album *The Fiancée*

(2007). Although originally practiced through a grassroots rural network of church-sponsored "singing schools," in recent years the music has attracted more and more participants who are interested in the music's status as an "authentic" lineage of American folk culture, or the kinds of neo-tribal connections discussed above, rather than its exhortations to a life of Christian piety (Warner 2008). In discussing tensions that occasionally arise between diverse attendants of Sacred Harp conventions, Miller (2008: 208) argues, "The undeniably forceful feelings engendered by singing encourage singers to discount apparent conflicts and marks of difference. A group of people with sharply different political ideologies can occupy the same space because singing keeps them from talking and talking reminds them of how different they feel when they're singing." As in so many musical encounters, it is precisely the inexactitude of group singing over against group speech—and thus its ability to simultaneously accommodate such a variety of individual interpretations—that allows for the creation of a sense of community in the first place. But this sense of community does not collapse or erase the profound differences that separate those participants who gather nor does it guarantee that all participants are even having the same experience in the moments of singing itself.

Underoath is able to occupy these vector spaces in particularly complex ways, thanks to gestures of disavowal that were a standard feature of their public presentation during the period considered. The defense mechanism of disavowal was first identified by Sigmund Freud as a kind of split in the ego, such that the person simultaneously acknowledges and denies some kind of traumatic reality, often oscillating between the two states. Philosopher and psychoanalyst Slavoj Žižek (2007: 29–30) has described this oscillation as a transferred or "disowned" belief that is ultimately constitutive of the symbolic order:

> We go through the ritual of Santa Claus, since our children (are supposed to) believe in it and we do not want to disappoint them; they pretend to believe not to disappoint us and our belief in their naivety (and to get presents, of course) … In an uncanny way, some beliefs always seem to function at a distance: in order for the belief to function, there has to be some ultimate guarantor of it, some true believer, yet this guarantor is always deferred, displaced, never present in persona … The point, of course, is that, for the belief to be operative, the subject who directly believes need not to exist at all: it is enough precisely to presuppose his existence, to *believe* in it.

For Žižek, disavowal is a kind of game played by and for the benefit of multiple actors; it is a perichoretic movement that ultimately constitutes a vector space with an empty center. By presupposing a "true believer" somewhere else as a guarantor of meaning, we are able to fully inhabit two opposing selves: according ourselves the benefits of our naïve beliefs while simultaneously shielding ourselves from the trauma of their inevitable puncture.

If strategies of disavowal can open up complex vector spaces constituted by internal antagonisms, they can also serve as a safety valve that helps to keep antagonistic systems functioning smoothly. This "safety valve" is something that Žižek (2009) sees as endemic to so many ideological structures in late capitalism. As an example, he observes that when employees gather at the pub after work to complain about their boss or the oppressive corporate culture, they often believe that their complaining is a subversive act, reclaiming power that has been denied them during the workday and ultimately undermining the boss's authority. Yet as Žižek contends, this collective act of blowing off steam actually enables them to come back to work the next day. Without a safety valve such as this, the workers might actually rise up against the oppressive work conditions. It is precisely because of these seeming violations of the social hierarchy that the hierarchy is able to continue unabated.

For Underoath, disavowal manifests as a kind of double move in which the band is able to simultaneously engage with both Christian and secular ideas and receive credit from fans for both patterns of engagement. In my own experience, these strategies of disavowal did not simply open up space for multiple subjective experiences of the band by the diverse attendees of their shows, but allowed for me to experience Underoath in multiple ways within my own subjectivity and to oscillate between these multiple experiences and interpretations depending on the context. I might understand or explain Underoath as a "Christian" band in some contexts, a "Christian metalcore" band in other contexts, or simply a "metalcore" band in still others. Strategies of disavowal allow and even encourage participants to occupy these vector spaces as their multiple selves and to use the music as a means to explore this subjective diversity. Underoath's use of disavowal or their complex navigation of these vector spaces is not unique among punk and metal acts. In fact, this model of vector space is probably the norm for punk and metal music and maybe even for popular music more generally. But although their Christianity does not make this phenomenon distinctive among metalcore bands, it is nevertheless crucial because they so often use Christianity as a kind of crowbar to pry open these complex vector spaces for their audiences. Underoath is distinctive not because they occupy a space separate from the rest of the metalcore scene but simply because they have one extra and particularly potent tool in their kit.

Baptized in the Mainstream

In the predominantly Southern Baptist cultural spaces that defined my childhood, there was particular attention paid to questions of "crossover," whereby a Christian-identifying artist or entertainer would achieve some success in mainstream secular culture or vice versa. Music journalist Andrew Beaujon (2006: 155–6) has noted evangelicals' "odd relationship with celebrity" by joking that "there may be a good deal of carping when a Christian band makes a run at the mainstream, but if one has any measure of success, it is feted like Napoleon returning from Egypt … Likewise, when a celebrity converts to Christianity, all sense of perspective seems to go out the window." As a result, my generation of Christians was handed down stories about crossover artists with increasing suspicion. Especially growing up during a time when this pop- and rock-styled music was establishing a permanent foothold in Sunday morning worship through the "praise and worship" movement, the entire crossover ethos seemed too often to function as an elaborate bait-and-switch operation. One either aimed to lure in fans with sounds that mimicked mainstream popular music and then tricked them into hearing an explicitly Christian message or else one was writing vaguely Christian songs that dropped just enough breadcrumbs to maintain a public reputation for your band as "secretly Christian." Ultimately, neither of these approaches is truly the outwardly facing evangelism it purports, but rather an elaborate internal posturing of the type described by Žižek, taking place entirely within the Christian subculture and maintained through a constant evocation of both real and imagined audiences.

Christian metalcore is not strictly part of this crossover tendency in the broader industry of contemporary Christian music (CCM), as Underoath and their ilk belong instead to a parallel tradition of Spirit-filled hardcore, which developed organically in the mid-1990s out of church kids participating in their local hardcore scenes (Abraham 2017: 38–41). However, this crossover paradigm was still crucial to my own reception of this music and that of many of my friends. As a teenager, I felt somewhat trapped between two paradigms: crossover on the one hand and praise and worship on the other. As a pastor's kid growing up in the American South, my central challenge was to find ways to publicly live out my Christian faith without separating myself from the secular world, but also without needing to constantly confront that world on behalf of the Christian message. These two fears are, in some ways, epitomized by the two poles of CCM identified by Howard and Streck (1999). On the one hand, "separational CCM" attempts to remain separate from the mainstream secular music world, creating music by and for evangelicals. At the opposite end of the spectrum, "integrational CCM" is epitomized by the crossover artists discussed above, designed to integrate Christian artists, producers, and songwriters into the broader music industry.

Following theologian H. Richard Niebuhr (1975) who helps to frame these two poles, Howard and Streck (1999) identify a third "transformational" category of CCM in which aesthetic concerns about the music's status as "art" override concerns with the "insider" or "outsider" group dynamics of American evangelicalism. Undoubtedly, these pervading concerns about making "good art" are expressed by the members of Underoath in explicit terms. In describing the recording process for *Define the Great Line*, lead guitarist and songwriter Tim McTeague said:

> We're in a situation where we're in this poppy, produced, fake, substanceless music scene where every band sounds the same, and we're trying to do something and keep the same mindset we had when we were recording *They're Only Chasing Safety*, and that's to just keep pushing the limits, to put something in kids' hands that is unexpected, that's going to make them look outside of their genre-specific pop-screamo CD collection. And so that's why we're doing things the way we are now. (*Making of Define the Great Line*, 2006)

Here, artistic vision and experimentation are put forward as the band's guiding values, and by contrasting themselves against the "poppy, produced, fake, substanceless music" of the metalcore scene, these guiding values are put forward in implicitly masculinist, "rockist" terms (Sanneh 2004). However, the transformational understanding of CCM posited by Howard and Streck (1999) is ultimately predicated on a degree of aesthetic myopia that is simply not a characteristic of hardcore music or twenty-first-century American evangelicalism. Instead, Underoath ultimately creates a vector space for the comingling of their Christian and hardcore identities through gestures in which tropes of evangelicalism and tropes of popular music are knowingly acknowledged precisely so they can be disavowed.

At the end of each show, Spencer Chamberlain, the lead singer of Underoath, would typically move to the front edge of the stage and inform the audience that the reason they were playing the show that evening was because of their Christian faith. "I just wanted to let you guys know that we do everything we do in the name of Jesus Christ [*crowd cheers*]. And we don't do that for a cheer and we don't do that to make you uncomfortable. That's just who we are and we love and respect all you guys for who you are" (*Underoath: They're Only Chasing Safety*, 2005). Chamberlain would always take great pains to clarify that while Jesus was a motivating factor for the band members themselves, they did not have any expectations that the audience would share their feelings. In this case, the band has taken a standard trope of separational CCM, an altar call or evangelical pitch that would end a religious gathering, but by removing the expectation or even actively discouraging audience members from responding through conversion, they disavow this evangelical gesture and allow it to function in multiple ways. Chamberlain's evangelical gesture is accompanied by a loud cheer from the audience as well as an immediate and explicit disavowal of that cheer by Chamberlain himself. Thus, the gesture can be simultaneously understood by fans as an authentic expression of their evangelical Christianity and a marker of their fundamental difference from evangelical Christianity.

In the documentary film *Underoath: They're Only Chasing Safety* (2005), one also sees this strategy with particular clarity through the band's interactions with its Jewish manager Randy Nichols. The opening scene of the film shows Underoath and crew at a cookout hosted by the band's A&R representative from Tooth & Nail Records, Chad Johnson. In a cutaway interview, Nichols leans forward to reveal his yarmulke and jokingly refers to himself as "the first Jew of Christian rock," which is followed immediately by a shot of Johnson yelling, "Hey Randy, these are kosher, bro," while standing over the grill tending some sausages. Nichols continues his cutaway interview by talking about how much he respects the "passion" and "raw emotion" that the band brings to their songwriting and live performances, which is again followed immediately with a cut back to the cookout at which Johnson is offering a Christian prayer to bless the food they are about to eat. Later in the documentary, Johnson provides a passionate defense of Chamberlain's deployment of their Christian faith on stage, saying, "They make it clear to everyone that it's their personal faith and they feel it's the right way, but they're not trying to beat you over the head and sell you" (*Underoath: They're Only Chasing Safety*, 2005). Throughout the documentary, religious others—whether Nichols or one of the myriad secular bands with which Underoath is seen touring and hanging out—serve as guarantors of their disavowal of evangelical gestures. They want the documentary to clearly demonstrate all the ways that they are living out their Christian faith in a public way through their band while simultaneously taking great pains to show that they are not "those kind of Christians" and not "that kind of band."

A perfect example of how they accomplish this in sound is in the track "Sálmarnir" (*Define the Great Line*, 2006). The track's title comes from the Icelandic word for "psalms" and the song features the text of Ps. 50:1-6 read meditatively in Russian over an ambient backdrop. About halfway through the two-and-a-half-minute track, a quieter track enters with keyboardist Chris Dudley reading the same text in English and adopting the exuberant style of a televangelist accompanied by thunderous applause from a crowd. This track becomes an almost-perfect cypher for fans and critics regarding the band's relationship to traditions of heavy metal music and to Christianity. Some critics point to the track as emblematic of the dramatic new "post-metal ambience" (Burgess 2006) added to the band's sonic repertoire and note clear influences from Nordic bands like Sigur Rós (Kern County Kid 2006). Other critics saw the track as a reverent, even monastic expression of their faith (Monger 2006), and the review on the *Jesus Freak Hideout* website interpreted the placement of the track in the center of an unrelentingly heavy album as a poignant reminder that "God's presence is never factored out of the equation no matter how rough things get" (Taylor 2006). Additionally, the inclusion of the televangelist reading of the text underneath seems to cut potentially both ways: either evidence of their sincerity through a loving send-up of the rural evangelical preaching with which many of the band members were raised or evidence of their disdain through a biting satire of American Christianity.

Even the band's explicit rejection of Christianity with their most recent record, *Erase Me* (2018), is ultimately enmeshed with gestures of disavowal. In dozens of interviews to promote the record and the band's reunification, band members discussed the shifting status of their faith identities. In one particularly potent interview with *Alternative Press* billed as their "last words on Christianity," Chamberlain and Gillespie lay out the history of their interactions with the Christian subculture and how it led to frustrations and eventually to their decision to break from a Christian identity (Trapp 2018). However, all of their criticisms, while trenchant, are carefully centered around their frustration with the ultimate inauthenticity of contemporary American evangelicals. Although these interviews were widely covered as a repudiation of their earlier professions of faith, any inspection of the video reveals that both of Underoath's frontman still have nothing but positive things to say about the person of Jesus and even about the tenets of Christianity itself. Instead, they express their frustrations that most Christians do not seem to practice a version of the faith that is "authentically" rooted in the revolutionary ideals of the New Testament.

In framing their critique this way, Gillespie and Chamberlain may gain renewed credibility among secular fans for disavowing the faith that made them potentially problematic, but also score points with Christian fans for being such deep students of Christianity's histories and doctrines. Andrew

Mall (2015a: 107) has documented the ways that the subcultural rhetoric surrounding evangelicalism itself facilitates particularly easy transferal to youth subculture formation. Christian youth subcultures are often "resistant to both dangerously secular mainstream culture as well as to those of previous generations of Christians," using their "resistant identities" in ways that unite evangelical and alternative music subcultures in a single complex vector space (Mall 2015a). The reception of Gillespie and Chamberlain's comments on the British website *Christian Today* demonstrates the effectiveness of this strategy, with the author even going out of his way to praise Chamberlain's honesty and the hard truths it reveals to contemporary evangelical culture (Saunders 2018). The precise terms of Chamberlain's ultimate departure from the faith also serve as a guarantor to the depth and authenticity with which it was undertaken.

Just a Bunch of Kids

When I was attending shows at Rocketown, I was a straight, white man in my late teens and I was very much the norm. Whether in the mosh pit, the skate park, or even on the stage, Rocketown and venues like it serve as powerful crucibles for adolescent white masculinity. And to narrate and catalyze this intense process of self-actualization, metalcore music like Underoath is a common choice for white male teenagers in music scenes all over the world. Deena Weinstein (2000: 105) has observed that "heavy metal music celebrates the very qualities that boys must sacrifice in order to become adult members of society." Unfortunately, we have seen far too many times that "boys" are not actually asked to sacrifice their adolescent behavior as they move into adulthood and that this adolescent "grace period" actually helps to solidify many of the patriarchal norms that characterize their later adult lives (Walser 1993: 108–36). But Weinstein's point still holds in that the animating energy at many shows seems to be a kind of youthful energy that is explicitly contrasted to adult "responsibility."

When examining the documentary *Underoath: They're Only Chasing Safety* (2005), one is immediately struck by the band's constant use of the word "kid" to describe one another, a common term especially in hardcore punk. They reminisce about starting the band "when we were kids," opine about the difficulties being in a successful band when "we're still just kids," and describe the changing band lineup as the addition of a "new kid" or "good kid" here and there. Throughout the documentary, the band's status as "kids" is further reinforced through interviews with the "adults" who surround them, especially their manager Randy Nichols and their label's A&R representative Chad Johnson. The film is replete with examples of their boyishness, from their inability to perform tasks of basic hygiene like remembering to shower, shave, or wash their clothes to a penchant for destructive and violent games in hotels and tour buses, and ultimately through constant demonstrations of their raucous and bumbling homosocial relationships.

At one point, the documentary shows a tense exchange between the band and an unnamed rock journalist who repeatedly insinuates that the band must really enjoy "partying." Aaron Gillespie responds in a later interview saying, "We're not the kind of dudes who hang out and sleep around and stuff. Do you know what I mean? We're just kids." Although punk musicians have often made pains to distance themselves from the standard excesses of the rock 'n' roll mythos (Thomson 2004), using the band's youth as the distancing mechanism is striking because it takes on precisely the opposite valence one might expect. In other contexts, one could easily imagine Gillespie using "we're just kids" as a defense of precisely the kinds of bad behavior he is claiming it excludes them from. Ross Haenfler's (2006) book on straight edge punk, dedicated to "positive straight edge kids," similarly invokes the standard hardcore label "kid" as the generic term for everyone in the scene, even (or especially) older participants who choose continued abstinence from tobacco, alcohol, or casual sex despite being of appropriate age. Similar to Underoath's use of the term, the word "kid" seems to help straight edge participants to sketch the contours of an alternative masculinity beyond the most common tropes of rock 'n' roll debauchery and hypermasculine excess.

Underoath's disavowal strategies around sexual attention occur at several other interesting junctures in the documentaries (*Underoath: They're Only Chasing Safety*, 2005; *Making of Define the Great Line*, 2006). In one shot, guitarist Tim McTeague is showing off his orthodontic braces—also an interesting visual cue of adolescent immaturity—to the camera and pulls down his lower lip with the index and middle finger of his left hand. He extends his tongue at the camera before realizing that he has inadvertently made a vulgar pantomime of oral sex and he quickly shouts, "No! No! I didn't mean it! I didn't mean it!" Of course, including such a moment in the final cut of the documentary assumes that the band expects their audience will understand the joke he wasn't trying to make: using disavowal to bank credit for both the making of the joke and not meaning it.

The most forceful disavowal of this trope of sexual virility as a marker of rock stardom comes courtesy of rhythm guitar player James Smith. In one of his interviews, keyboard player Chris Dudley jokes, "Yeah, the ladies like [James]. He's *that guy* in our band." An awkward scene unfolds as Dudley heads back to the tour bus after a show holding a pink bra on which someone, presumably a young female fan, has written "James Smith U Rock XOXO." He enters the bus and proudly announces, "James Smith, you got your first bra!," which engenders a smattering of applause and encouragement from the other members of the band on the bus. Smith's response to the bra, however, is to throw his hands up into the air as if to indicate his innocence in the whole matter and to back away from Dudley. When Dudley eventually drops the bra onto his lap, Smith quickly brushes it off of himself and onto the floor without ever actually touching the bra with his hands. Again, Underoath's disavowal allows them to have it both ways: gaining credibility because a female fan would favor them with sexual attention and because they steadfastly refuse such attention.

Musically and lyrically, these strategies of disavowal are captured best in the track "A Boy Brushed Red Living in Black and White" (*They're Only Chasing Safety*, 2005). The song begins with a nervous eighth-note pulse on lightly distorted guitars with Aaron Gillespie singing in a clean pop-punk style: "Can you feel your heartbeat racing? / Can you taste the fear in her sweat? / You've done this wrong. / It's too far gone. These sheets tell of regret." These opening lyrics in the second person create an accusatory tone right from the start and frame the anxious sexual encounter described as a kind of cautionary tale. Immediately following this, Gillespie introduces first-person language with the line "I admit that I'm just a fool for you," which repeats three times and suddenly the musical texture smashes into overdrive. Spencer Chamberlain enters with a blistering screamed vocal on the lyric "here is where we both go wrong" over a flurry of distorted guitars. Depending upon one's reading of the lyrics, this song comes across either as a kind of moralistic anthem of sexual abstinence—though notably one told from the perspective of someone with sexual experience—or as simply the story of one particular relationship gone wrong. Again, there is the desire to disavow a kind of shallow sexual attention while at the same time capitalizing on the appeal it might have to an adolescent male audience. Is this particular encounter the place we "both go wrong" because of this particular girl or because of the dangers inherent in sexual encounters outside of marriage? Underoath again allows their fans to occupy either or both of these subject positions simultaneously, here further reinforced by the duality between Gillespie's melodic vocals and Chamberlain's metal growl.

Guitarist James Smith's joking connection between masculinity and facial hair in the quote that gives this chapter its title—with the "beard" as a kind of metonym for the idealized hypermasculine—is perhaps more telling and more subversive than one might initially suspect. Obviously, the term "beard" has a long history within queer subcultures as a way to describe a kind of public presentation that obscures or covers over an underlying queerness (Baker 2004: 80). While I certainly don't mean to suggest that Underoath is intentionally referencing that queer usage of the term, if one places Smith's comment within the broader scope of the documentary *Underoath: They're Only Chasing Safety* (2005), the connection of masculinity to facial hair seems to suggest masculinity as a kind of play. Because so many of the band members are still in the late phases of adolescence, facial hair is a frequent topic of conversation throughout the documentary and usually framed as a kind of ongoing self-discovery or self-actualization.

In one scene, band members compare their mustaches and comically chide Gillespie for his three days of growth that could easily be mistaken for a clean-shaven face. One particularly interesting sequence shows guitarist Tim McTeague, possessor of the most fully realized beard in the group, surrounded by his bandmates and holding a pair of electric shears. Over the course of the sequence, McTeague slowly shaves off his beard stopping at different configurations and commenting on how he looks by comparing himself to several fixed masculine archetypes. He ends the sequence with only a large bushy mustache that, combined with his asymmetrical unwashed hair and his bare chest, leads into an elaborate pantomime of McTeague submitting himself to arrest as if on the television show *Cops*. The joke here, made both explicitly and implicitly in this sequence, is that simply shaving off his facial hair into a particular pattern instantly transforms McTeague from a hipster metalcore guitarist into a rural white-trash outlaw.

Underlying all discussions of facial hair throughout the documentary, particularly this sequence, is a sense that the beard is a symbol of masculinity precisely because of its superficiality and malleability. Similar to the ethos of so-called "genderfuck" in drag performances, which uses ambiguous or transgressive performance as a way to call attention to the mutability of any gender attribution (Taylor 2012: 83–116), the connection of masculinity to facial hair, especially by a notably baby-faced guitarist like Smith, seems to suggest a similarly ambivalent relationship to questions of masculinity. Growing a beard (or not) helps to constitute "kid" masculinity as a process of ongoing experimentation in which multiple selves can be tried, assessed, and ultimately discarded with a flick of a razor.

Collapse of Vector Space

In the spring of 2016, Underoath announced a thirty-city reunion tour to celebrate the tenth anniversary of the release of *Define the Great Line*. The band had formally broken up following a series of tours to support their 2010 album *Ø (Disambiguation)* and the departure of drummer/vocalist Aaron Gillespie who went on to pursue a solo career with his band The Almost. The appropriately titled "Rebirth Tour" would not only bring the band's most successful configuration back together for the first time in five years, it would also feature the band playing their two most acclaimed records, *They're Only Chasing Safety* and *Define the Great Line*, back-to-back in their entireties at each show. On April 11, the tour stopped in Nashville and, perhaps not surprisingly, the band opted to play at Rocketown. Although identical in name, the venue that hosted this show is a completely new building to the one that I frequented more than a decade ago. Opened in the summer of 2010, the new Rocketown is a sprawling and top-of-the-line 40,000-square-foot entertainment facility several blocks from the original site.

The venue was packed and as the band launched into the first few songs of *They're Only Chasing Safety*, the audience came alive and enthusiastic fans began to crowd-surf toward the stage. When they reached the front of the room, however, they were promptly greeted by Rocketown security who threw them out of the show citing the venue's new and very strict policy against crowd-surfing. As the band became aware of the situation, they were visibly frustrated and began to ask the security guards from the stage not to throw people out of the venue. By the time they reached the end of their set, guitarist Tim McTeague was actively encouraging members of the crowd to rush the stage, even saying, "There are 1,200 of us and six of them. They can't kick us all out." Before their final song of the night, McTeague vowed the band would never again play at Rocketown and once again expressed frustration with the rules saying, "This is an Underoath show, not a Rocketown show, and nobody tells us what to do."

In the end, the carefully constructed vector spaces and ambiguous multiplicities opened up and maintained by Underoath and Rocketown are always in danger of collapse. In this case, the band was asked to choose sides between the expected civility of the venue and the expected raucousness of a metalcore fan base, and they definitively chose the latter. Vectors are defined by motion—direction, acceleration, velocity—so vector spaces are necessarily a dynamic proposition. But when they can be opened and occupied, they provide unparalleled opportunities for young music fans to experience and experiment with new trajectories and emerge with new insights about how to properly grow a beard and how to be somebody (or somebodies).

6

"A Heterosexual Male Backlash": Punk Rock Christianity and Missional Living at Mars Hill Church, Seattle

Maren Haynes Marchesini

Introduction

In the early 1990s, recent college graduate Mark Driscoll arrived in Seattle with a mission to innovate in ministry, motivated by three core goals: to "preach the Gospel, plant churches, and train men" (Worthen 2009). He envisioned "planting an urban church for an emerging postmodern generation in one of the least churched cities in the US," to channel and ease the creeping ennui and burnout faced by his Gen-X cohort, particularly targeting young men who felt alienated from the church and society (Driscoll 2000b). Together with several ministerial colleagues, Driscoll launched Mars Hill Fellowship in October 1996, meeting in a stuffy upstairs room in a North Seattle church (Mars Hill Fellowship 2015). This new church, populated by "college students and indie rockers," held weekly evening services with around 10–20 people in attendance (Driscoll 2000b). Conducting worship in dark spaces decorated with fabric and dozens of candles accompanied by a band playing sludgy, earnest worship music, the new church quickly established a reputation as a youth-oriented church for Seattle's artists and musicians.

Once a fairly obscure city known for fishing fleets, Microsoft computers, and Boeing airplanes, Seattle found itself at the center of American popular culture in the early 1990s following the unexpected success of grunge music, a post-punk genre that kindled in the city's underground music scene. Seattle-based grunge bands such as Nirvana established Seattle's reputation as the hub for the burgeoning "alternative" music scene, supplying the soundtrack to the lives of a generation of American youth portrayed as simultaneously angry, alienated, and apathetic. By the mid-1990s, the city supported a flourishing independent music scene encompassing punk rock, hardcore, grunge, and indie rock.

In its early years, Mars Hill Fellowship met many of these young Seattle punk and post-punk musicians in the felt tension between their Christian identity and artistic passions. In an interview with the author, John, a punk musician well known in the Seattle scene, described the church as a haven that bridged two seemingly disconnected attributes of his identity:

> Simultaneously being into punk rock and skateboarding about the time I was 13, and being a Christian, I was always *not Christian enough* for the Christians and *too Christian* for the non-Christians. So I grew up in this tension. So when I moved to the city, finally there's this church of people [who] were creative and understood culture, and were more or less embracing the fact that I was somebody who made what I made in culture, there was a great amount of solidarity and comfort in that community.

Driscoll encouraged artists like John to serve in church leadership by writing new music for worship in punk and post-punk styles.

Under Driscoll's charismatic but controversial leadership, Mars Hill became one of the fastest-growing multisite megachurches in the United States (Graham 2014). At its peak in early 2014, the church boasted fifteen locations across five states attracting 14,000 weekly attendees. Throughout Mars Hill's expansion, the ministry staff continued to draw upon the Pacific Northwest's youth culture to hone a young, hip aesthetic and music ministry. The church's adoption of punk and post-punk crucially aided in growing the fledgling house church into a successful megachurch, and continued to influence the church's identity, brand, and sound until the church's eventual collapse amid scandals, permanently closing its doors on January 1, 2015.

This chapter details the role of punk and post-punk music and subculture in the formation of Mars Hill Church in its early years from 1996 to 2005, showing how elements of punk's cultural politics influenced the church's institutional identity and structure. I begin by exploring the theological underpinnings of Mars Hill's embrace of punk and post-punk music, rooted in a theology of "missional living," situating this theology in the historical context of twentieth-century Christianity. I interrogate the intersecting class, race, and gender dynamics within the cultural formations of Seattle punk and post-punk to show how Mars Hill leaders intentionally appealed to a narrow constituency of primarily white, working-class young men. I then show how Mars Hill's interactions with the punk scene allowed the church to accrue subcultural capital by building a distinctive identity at the intersection of Seattle's underground music culture and evangelical Christianity while simultaneously differentiating Mars Hill as a "masculine" religious movement.

Music, Enculturation, and Missional Living

In the mid-1990s, Mark Driscoll attended a leadership network conference in Seattle where George Hunsberger, a Presbyterian pastor and cofounder of the Gospel and Our Culture Network (GOCN), spoke about evangelization and culture in contemporary American society (Driscoll 2006: 108–9). From Hunsberger's address, Driscoll recognized a resonance between Mars Hill's unique approach to music and worship, rooted in local music styles, and broader discourses pertaining to mission, culture, and outreach. Drawing from language utilized by GOCN, Driscoll began to understand Mars Hill's ecclesiology as a twofold strategy, saying, "the church has two simultaneous missions: going out into culture (missional ministry), and bringing people into God's kingdom, of which the church is an outpost (attractional ministry)" (Driscoll 2006: 109).

Mars Hill's leaders conceived of their embrace of punk rock through the lens of missional ministry. As Chris, a former Mars Hill music leader, explained:

> We started using the term "missional worship," trying to have the mindset of a missionary, or in some ways, a missiologist, as musicians and worship leaders, as well. And that is, we live in a particular place and time and so the most appropriate response of how God is initiating amongst us particular people in this place and time will probably come from within that people rather than from without. This is how I saw it.

At Mars Hill, he continued, "We're steeped in the indie rock culture of Seattle [but] you can be ethnically and culturally a lot of different things while being a faithful follower of Jesus." Mars Hill's staff characterized youth music as an indigenous practice analogous to other worldwide musical traditions (Driscoll 2006: 108).

This adoption of missional language linked Mars Hill with a global ecumenical movement in the field of missions that interrogated historical Christian doctrine pertaining to the relationship between orthodoxy (right belief) and orthopraxy (right practices). In the twentieth century, initiated by Christian leadership in the two-thirds world and concurring broadly with global postcolonial political revolutions and social reforms, the church began to renegotiate the "appropriateness" of using aspects of secular culture in worship, inclusive of musical styles, vernacular languages, and styles of dress. This reorientation pertained especially to the practices of non-European cultures. Framed as a reorientation toward God's mission on earth, a large number of scholars and church leaders in Western Europe and North America, including Karl Barth, David Bosch, and Jürgen Moltmann, began the process of decoupling Western cultural norms and practices from Christian orthodoxy. This broadly ecumenical movement sought to reform Western missionaries' relationship to subaltern cultures and Christianities in a post-Christendom and postcolonial context. It also played an important role in transforming attitudes toward popular music, now deemed appropriate for use in worship.

In the Roman Catholic church, the Second Vatican Council (Vatican II, 1962–1965) initiated new paths to evangelism, especially with regard to the meaning and value of cultures, and processes of liturgical adaptation and inculturation. Shifting from a centralized model, Vatican II established missions as a primary duty of local churches and bishops to be "witnesses of solidarity and partnership, and as expressions of mutual encounter, exchange, and enrichment" (Bosch 1991: 380). By foregrounding localization and mutual relationships, this position affirmed "a fundamentally new interpretation of the purpose of mission and the role of missionaries and mission agencies" based on ecumenical dialogue and aimed toward human flourishing (Bosch 1991).

In a papal decree, *Ad Gentes*, Pope Paul VI (1965) challenged the imperialist outcomes of the doctrine of inculturation, which understood Christianity as a universalized culture and Christian conversion as a process of cultural conformity. Instead, *Ad Gentes* affirmed cultural diversity, promoting a Christianity that manifested in diverse, culturally specific ways. Pedro Arrupe (1978), Father General of the Jesuit Order, championed a renewed approach to inculturation as "the 'incarnation' of the Christian life and of the Christian message in a particular cultural context, in such a way that this experience ... finds expression through elements proper to the culture in question," reversing nearly 500 years of Jesuit missionary practices.

Out of this renewed understanding, the Constitution on Sacred Liturgy emerged from the Second Vatican Council, allowing translation of the Mass into both vernacular languages and musical genres, unleashing a burst in new artistic approaches to Catholic worship. In the United States and Europe, young Catholics adapted the Mass into folk, rock, and other popular musical styles, an approach to worship music that would influence evangelicals (Canedo 2009: 7). Indeed, Powell (2002: 751) names Ray Repp's (1966) *Mass for Young*

Americans, written in response to Vatican II (and predating the evangelical Jesus Movement), as the first form of the folk mass and a precursor to the Christian rock music industry.

A similar reckoning took place among Protestants in the following decades, initiated by Church of Scotland bishop Lesslie Newbigin. A missionary to India from 1936 until 1974, Newbigin initially conflated the spreading of Western values and culture with the promotion of the gospel. He soon recognized the inadequacies of this view, and adopted and advocated for a model of mission predicated on forming relationships and encouraging culturally rooted forms of Christian practice. According to Newbigin (1985: 235), when he returned to Britain in the 1970s, he encountered a post-Christian, postmodern youth culture and found that evangelizing to these young people proved "much harder than anything I met in India." He began to apply his foreign missionary principles to the youth he encountered, viewing Britain's young people as a "mission field" (Gordon 2012: 99).

Influenced by Newbigin, evangelicals convened the first of a series of conferences to evaluate the function and strategy of Christian mission and its orientation to culture. Initiated by a committee headed by Billy Graham, the 1974 International Congress on World Evangelization in Lausanne, Switzerland, drew more than 2,300 loosely networked evangelical leaders from 150 countries. The Congress's resulting covenant affirmed a commitment to the task of evangelizing every continent, but it also affirmed that "the gospel does not presuppose the superiority of any culture to another, but evaluates all cultures according to its own criteria of truth and righteousness, and insists on moral absolutes in every culture" (Lausanne Movement 1974). The covenant calls for "imaginative pioneering methods" in evangelism, resulting in the rise of churches that embraced local and indigenous forms of music, art, and other aspects of cultural expression (Lausanne Movement 1974).

The *Willowbank Report* proceeded from the next gathering of the Lausanne Committee for World Evangelization and called for a "radical concept of indigenous church life" by which "each church may discover and express its selfhood as the body of Christ within its own culture" (Lausanne Committee for World Evangelization 1978). Thus the report celebrated the rights of congregations to "'sing and dance' the gospel in [their] own cultural medium" as a "multi-racial, multi-national, multi-ethnic" universal church community (Lausanne Committee for World Evangelization 1978). The *Willowbank Report* also raised complications in approaching "cultural elements which either are evil or have evil associations." The report offers that "if the evil is in the association only … we believe it is right to seek to 'baptize' it into Christ" (Lausanne Committee for World Evangelization 1978). This authorized the process by which "evil" popular music genres like rock could conceivably be Christianized. Although intended to reform Western postures toward global cultures in the mission field, an auxiliary outgrowth of this reorientation included a shift toward sanctifying American youth culture, conceived as its own form of "indigenous" cultural expression.

In the mid-1980s, GOCN, the organization that influenced Driscoll's embrace of missions as a theological framework for music, sought to formalize Newbigin's orientation toward youth culture. Considered "a progressive research network in the field of missiology" (Nikolajsen 2013: 258), GOCN introduced the use of a new term to describe this local focus: "missional". Missional churches and practices ideally challenge conventional theological discourse such that the missionary movement "appeals to all peoples irrespective of their cultural, ethnic or political borders" (Congdon 2015: 506). This movement introduced the concept of "radical contextuality," an orientation toward centering local cultures (Congdon 2015: 507–8). Although theorists of missional living argue that a missional orientation is rooted in an intercultural hermeneutic (Congdon 2015: 506), the coherence of this argument is complicated by the co-optation of *missional living* language by majority-white congregations that defined their place in the movement primarily by their use of alternative musical styles beyond the typical pop and rock of contemporary Christian music (Mall 2012: 212).

Missional Outreach: The Paradox Music Venue

From its earliest days, Mars Hill's leadership attracted well-known punk and grunge musicians into the church who led worship music in punk and post-punk styles, an element of their attractional ministry strategy. The church also began to embody their missional ministry goal of "going out into culture" in 1999 when Mars Hill elder Leif Moi purchased one of Seattle's oldest theaters located in the heart of the city, near the University of Washington, renaming it the Paradox. Moi's acquisition of this theater occurred near-simultaneously with the shuttering of Seattle's only all-ages music venues, RKCNDY and the Velvet Elvis, the result of a restrictive citywide Teen Dance Ordinance intended to regulate illegal activity at several Seattle-area clubs (Brunner 2002). The Ordinance undermined the for-profit all-ages music scene but offered an exception for nonprofit entities like churches. Although Moi purchased the building for use as a Sunday worship space, John and other Mars Hill musicians saw the Paradox as an opportunity to expand the church's missional outreach into the Seattle community, filling a gaping hole in the all-ages scene. John called this "the church of immaculate loophole" (Brunner 2002). Mars Hill members began volunteering their time to host punk rock, hardcore, grunge, and indie rock shows open to the public. Mars Hill's new building soon operated as a church on Sunday mornings and a popular all-ages music venue during the weekdays and weekends (Driscoll 2000b).

Former leaders of Mars Hill's music ministry, such as Chris, emphasized in interviews how the Paradox exemplified the church's emphasis on missional living, reaching out to the music community of Seattle with an attitude of openness and acceptance. Mars Hill's staff sought to equally welcome bands popular in Christian alternative music circles, as well as those that played "clearly satanic speed metal," according to Andy, discouraging church members and staff from using these shows as an opportunity to advertise for the church or promote its doctrines. Staging queer straight edge, angsty hardcore, weepy emo, and, once, a Japanese punk band that got naked during a show, the Paradox proudly professed an explicit welcome to everyone who attended the popular all-ages venue (Mars Hill Church 2011). Mars Hill Church successfully demonstrated its openness to local youth culture by allowing it to flourish on its own terms within the walls of the church building.

Over time, the Paradox secured Mars Hill's long-standing relationship with the broader punk, grunge, and indie rock scene in Seattle. For three years, the University District Paradox hosted a nearly constant stream of local alternative music shows, featuring local and national punk rock, hardcore, grunge, and indie rock bands. The venue closed briefly as Mars Hill Church relocated to a new flagship location in Seattle's Ballard neighborhood, but reopened with a dedicated space in their newly remodeled warehouse. The Paradox's (2005) website boasted the following list of bands the venue "had the pleasure of working with":

A Life Once Lost, Alkaline Trio, Bane, Bleeding Through, The Blood Brothers, Botch, Brand New, Bright Eyes, Cex, Champion, Converge, Cursive, Damien Jurado, Dead to Fall, Death Cab for Cutie, Deerhoof, Denali, Desaparecidos, Dolour, The Divorce, From Autumn to Ashes, Gatsby's American Dream, Give up the Ghost, The Good Life, Himsa, The Hoods, Hope Conspiracy, Hot Hot Heat, Ida, Inked in Blood, IQU, Damien Jurado, Kane Hodder, The Long Winters, Low, Minus the Bear, Misery Signals, Most Precious Blood, Norma Jean, Officer Negative, Pedro the Lion, The Pale, Q and not U, Rasputina, The

Red Chord, Rilo Kiley, Rufio, The Six Parts Seven, Starflyer 59, Static Lullaby, Taking Back Sunday, Rosie Thomas, Trial, Underoath, Unearth, Velvet Teen, Vendetta Red, Rocky Votolato, Jason Webley, Where Eagles Dare, Xui Xui [*sic*], Zao and many, many more.

Some of these bands, while fairly obscure at the time, eventually garnered enormous audiences.

The Seattle arts community responded enthusiastically to the Paradox. Seattle's local alternative arts newspaper *The Stranger* celebrated the venue, dedicating a regular column to all-ages music with the Paradox at its center, calling it a "mecca for smaller local bands to get their stage bearings, as well as playing host to national acts" (Seling 2002). Music journalist for *The Stranger* Megan Seling regularly attended, promoted, and reviewed concerts, and even occasionally dedicated her column to nonmusical issues like Paradox employee profiles and renovations. Meanwhile, Mars Hill's pastors maintained a distance from the Paradox, allowing it to operate as a space for local youth music to thrive, rather than as an explicit tool of evangelism (Mars Hill Church 2011).

Although Mars Hill members and leaders primarily claimed the Paradox was a missional outreach to serve local youth, the venue secured Mars Hill's relationship to the punk and post-punk scene in a way that in turn proved useful to the church's growth. Although it was not conceived as an explicitly attractional ministry, interviews with church members showed how the venue solidified an enduring bond between Mars Hill Church and the broader music community in Seattle, inspiring fans and other musicians to check out the church. Many people I interviewed cited the venue as their entry point for becoming involved in Mars Hill. For instance, Josh, a Seattle-based musician, recalled, "I used to go to shows at The Paradox, and I played in bands and knew people in bands, and eventually a lot of the people I knew in bands were going to [Mars Hill]." The Paradox served as the initial attraction, but each of these fans and musicians grew very active in Mars Hill's music ministry, all of them forming worship bands to play at the church.

Over time, Mars Hill's music ministry grew increasingly populated by members of the broader Seattle music scene. Most worship leaders also played in local bands. Several standout musicians such as songwriter Dustin Kensrue, drummers Matt Johnson and James McAlister, guitarist Jessica Dobson, and engineer/multi-instrumentalist Brian Eichelberger worked and toured with national acts including Thrice, The Shins, Rocky Votolato, Spoon, Beck, Pedro the Lion, Sufjan Stevens, Rufus Wainwright, and Jeff Buckley. In this way, the sounds of punk, grunge, and indie rock crossed over from band members' nonchurch projects into the church's unique approach to music ministry. These intersections thoroughly shaped the sounds of Mars Hill's music.

Masculinizing American Christianity through Punk Rock

Mars Hill's association with punk and post-punk also served to distinguish it from other contemporary evangelical churches, particularly as Driscoll sought to intentionally build a church for young men. Beginning around 2000, Driscoll's perspectives around gender and Christianity began to spill out through pseudonymous posts on a closed online message board for church members. Under the pseudonym "William Wallace II" Driscoll (2000a) posted a lengthy rant decrying the perceived feminization, or "pussification," of American culture and Christianity:

> We live in a completely pussified nation. We could get every man, real man as opposed to pussified James Dobson knock-off crying Promise Keeping homoerotic worship loving mama's boy sensitive emasculated neutered exact male replica evangellyfish, and have a conference in a phone booth. It all began with Adam, the first of the pussified nation, who kept his mouth shut and watched everything fall headlong down the slippery slide of hell/feminism when he shut his mouth and listened to his wife who thought Satan was a good theologian when he should have lead her and exercised his delegated authority as king of the planet.

He attacked femininity in the abstract, but also directed his ire at the power and agency of women and "non-manly" men within evangelical Christianity.

In public and away from the anonymity of a message board, Driscoll tamed the language of this crude rant, instead articulating systematic theological views on gender in many of his writings and sermons. In a sermon entitled "Men and Masculinity," Driscoll (2001) argued that in a "Christian church, you should see masculinity, you should see men who are masculine. Not just male, biologically male, but actually masculine in their essence and in their conduct." He contended that churches across the liberal and conservative spectrum presented a feminized Christianity that Mars Hill sought to oppose. In his memoir, he proclaimed, "I fashion myself as the self-appointed leader of a heterosexual male backlash," simultaneously opposing Seattle's gay-friendly culture and the perceived feminization of American Christianity (Driscoll 2006: 147). Thus, a core objective in Driscoll's vision for Mars Hill involved not only attracting young men but masculinizing Christians whose gendered identities and performances he perceived as hyper-feminized.

Driscoll, not himself a musician or even a very informed or dedicated music fan, understood punk rock and its surrounding culture through a fairly flattened and stereotyped version of the genre that served his broader aspirations of building a church for "manly men." Driscoll (2001) derived exemplary masculine Christianity from his "blue-collar, hardworking, union family." He drew sermon exemplars from rural "rednecks," suburban union laborers, soldiers, and mixed martial arts fighters—identities that, taken together, celebrated a masculinity emerging from the white, working class—comparing biblical figures like Noah, John the Baptist, and Jesus to NASCAR fans, Grizzly Adams–like mountain men, and fight club members (Driscoll 2001, 2005). Punk, described in its early British form as working-class protest music typified by an aggressive aesthetic and accessible playing style (Dancis 1978), and in its later American hardcore form as typified by youthful white male belligerence (Willis 1993: 373), fits with these loosely defined white masculine tropes.

Punk's masculine codes suited Mars Hill's image as a scrappy, adversarial church built for young, tough, working-class men. Its belligerent attitude also worked in tandem with the "New Calvinist" tendencies in Driscoll's theology, emphasizing authority and a return to tradition in contrast to engagements with postmodernity in "emerging" evangelicalism (Hansen 2008: 135–52) and relishing the church's outsider status (Worthen 2009). While histories of punk often celebrate all-female bands, egalitarian gender relationships, and queer performances, punk scholar Lauraine Leblanc's ethnography of women in the punk scene reveals the felt ways punk established itself as a majority-male subculture. She situates punk's performative norms within working-class masculinity, citing "the cool pose, the sexual objectification of women, the disdain for the feminine world of learning, and the valorization of violence" (Leblanc 1999: 108). Drawing from James W. Messerschmidt's studies in masculinity, she emphasizes that working-class masculinities, by comparison to middle-class masculinities, emphasize attributes of "toughness, coolness, and aggressiveness" (Leblanc 1999). "By the 1980s," Leblanc claimed, "punk had become resolutely masculine" (Leblanc 1999), a regression in gender politics, according to Thompson (2004: 40–2), toward a hegemonic aggressive masculinity, away from the subversive aspects of early punk.

Assimilating a Christian version of punk into Mars Hill Church also proved expedient in part because of the church's intimate proximity to Christian alternative record label Tooth & Nail. Brandon Ebel, former employee of the

Christian label Word Records, launched Tooth & Nail in 1993 to explicitly promote Christian punk rock, hardcore, grunge, electropop, shoegaze, and thrash metal, and moved the label to Seattle in 1994. Many Tooth & Nail musicians hailed from Seattle and participated actively in Mars Hill's music ministry, including Matt Johnson of Starflyer 59, Emery, Blenderhead, Roadside Monument (among many other bands), Jeff "Suffering" Bettger of Ninety-Pound Wuss, Matt Carter and Toby Morrell of Emery, and Jon Dunn of Demon Hunter, who became the label's A&R director. Ebel, too, counted himself as a Mars Hill member (Driscoll 2013).

The church's multifaceted proximity to punk and post-punk music thus served to perform a distinctively masculine music ministry, especially by contrast to the broader evangelical praise and worship music that Mars Hill leaders and members alike disdained. Matt, a church music leader, explained that Driscoll and musicians involved early on "really couldn't stand Christian music in general. They felt it was a half-assed knockoff of other music, trying to imitate music and use music only for its value to communicate 'Truth.'" For instance, he recalled how different Mars Hill's music sounded by comparison to the evangelical praise and worship music he performed in his previous church, saying, "The first thing I noticed right off the bat was the music. And I didn't hate it. Cause, you know, coming from the church where I was, every time I played a song, I died a little inside. Way back then, it was 'Shine, Jesus, Shine,' and 'Open the Eyes of My Heart, Lord.'" The songs he names are famous tokens of mainstream evangelical aesthetics, characterized by Mars Hill's music leaders as phony, and opportunistically and inauthentically appropriating and imitating popular music styles in order to attract the masses.

Driscoll and other Mars Hill leaders lampooned the music, but also the perceived femininity of evangelical music leaders, with Driscoll describing them as "weepy worship dudes" and "effeminate anatomically male" musicians who "seem to be very in touch with their feelings and exceedingly chickified from playing too much acoustic guitar and singing prom songs to Jesus while channeling Michael Bolton and flipping their hair" (Driscoll 2006: 146; Worthen 2009; Murashko 2011). Driscoll's focus on worship leaders' feminized performances of gender extended to the evangelical praise and worship music's intimate, vaguely erotic language, also perceived as a component of this effeminacy. John, a Mars Hill musician, recalled, "Mark [Driscoll] kept belittling people who would write about Jesus as lover." He described how Mars Hill pastors ridiculed evangelical mass culture together saying, "We mocked it and made fun of [evangelical culture] because it said [things like] 'Jesus, come inside me,' like, 'you grow bigger and bigger inside me,'" parodying the pseudo-sexual lyrics in these songs.

Mars Hill's punk rock music ministry performed a multifaceted opposition to the evangelical mainstream, constructed in a manner coherent with Sarah Thornton's (1995: 115) study of electronic dance music subcultures, marking off Mars Hill's music as a differentiated and privileged subjective category:

Us	Them
Alternative	Mainstream
Hip/cool	Straight/square
Independent	Commercial
Authentic	False/phony
Rebellious/radical	Conformist/conservative
Insider knowledge	Easily accessible information
Minority	Majority
Heterogeneous	Homogenous
Youth	Family/middle-aged
Classless	Classed
Masculine culture	Feminine culture

Whether punk or the evangelical mainstream in actuality resembled such monolithic and opposed cultures mattered less than the emic discourses that framed these oppositional attitudes. As Thornton emphasizes, monolithic constructions of the mainstream serve as useful ways to mark an alternate or subaltern identity. As Thornton writes, "For many youthful imaginations, the mainstream is a powerful way to put themselves in the bigger picture, imagine their social world, assert their cultural worth, claim their subcultural capital. As such, the mainstream is a trope which betrays how beliefs and tastes which ensue from a complex social structure, in turn, determine the shape of social life" (Thornton 1995). The discursive formation described by Thornton surfaced at Mars Hill to successfully position Mars Hill as a masculine outsider against the feminine Christian mainstream.

Masculine Worship Music at Mars Hill

Under Driscoll's leadership, Mars Hill adopted a variety of performative modes to assert their distinctively masculine, white working-class evangelical identity through music. For instance, Mars Hill's Sunday worship services featured very few of the popular praise and worship songs circulating in other evangelical churches in the late 1990s and early 2000s. Mars Hill's leaders proudly touted their distance from Christian Copyright Licensing International (CCLI), a Christian music copyright service that allowed churches to purchase access to a large repertoire of songs for use in worship. Music leader Chris explained, "We really hated a lot of modern Christian worship music. [So] we almost had kind of as a badge of honor that we didn't have a CCLI license. [We] were pretty committed to not playing anything that was on CCLI." Eschewing what he called the "trite, simple worship choruses" then typical of American praise and worship music, Mars Hill's musicians focused instead on performing old hymns no longer bound by copyright, considering these superior for their complexity, depth, and hip alterity or writing original music for use in worship.

Proudly avoiding CCLI, the church also encouraged its artists not to pursue copyright licensing of their own original music. Mars Hill musicians licensed their songs under the Creative Commons Attribution Non-Commercial 3.0 License, allowing free use of sharing and adaptation, according to Chris. Mars Hill also provided free song downloads and lead sheets of the many original songs written by church volunteers on its website. This limited artists' access to statistics tracking the use of their music and also precluded collecting royalties for original creations.

Around 2000, Mars Hill also decided to abandon the organizational "worship team" model typical in evangelical churches in favor of a "band model" more congruent with organizational structures in the secular music scene. According to Andy, a musician at Mars Hill, the worship team model featured "a conglomeration of random musicians that happen to be scheduled because they're available that week." In a worship team model, musicians share a common repertoire of songs and conform to a middle-of-the-road aesthetic capable of substituting different players while retaining the same general sound. Chris described the worship team model as limited because "you have to keep things more homogenous, you have to keep the arrangements more standardized." While the worship team model did offer expediency—Andy mentioned that Mars Hill occasionally used this model when necessary—to Mars Hill's staff and music personnel, it represented the conventions of evangelical mass culture's over-homogenization and simplification.

Mars Hill's music ministers, most of whom were members of bands in Seattle, viewed a heterogeneous band model as preferable. Mars Hill musicians thus began to form bands comprised of fixed members who rehearsed together to form a cohesive, recognizable sound with original songs and unique arrangements.

Andy described this formation as arising from the Seattle music scene where bands came together as "friends that we play music with." He continued, "We know each other, we understand each other musically, and we have relationship and we have a common language." Because each Mars Hill campus supported several bands that rotated the responsibility for leading worship each week, the band model created heterogeneous, multiplex, and highly differentiated aesthetic experiences from band to band, even as they cohered to a common formation of Mars Hill's identity by performing some iteration of punk or post-punk worship music.

Two of Mars Hill's early bands, Team Strike Force (*Tension,* 2001) and the Mars Hillbillies, exemplified distinctive approaches to genre and composition that both solidly represented the church's white, working-class, masculine identity performed through punk and post-punk genres. Team Strike Force, described by one former church member as "doing their best Nirvana impression with deep and heartfelt Christian lyrics (no Jesus is my boyfriend lyrics)" (Yetman 2014), represented the Pacific Northwest evangelical underground, performing boundary-pushing original songs. The band's members—Luke Abrams, Jeff "Suffering" Bettger, Matt Johnson, Rose Johnson, Andy Garcia, and Andy Myers—played in Seattle-based bands, including Supine to Sit, Suffering and the Hideous Thieves, Roadside Monument, Starflyer 59, Ninety Pound Wuss, and Raft of Dead Monkeys. Although described as "punk rock" by Driscoll in 2006, Team Strike Force seems to draw most of its associations with punk from the outside projects of its members. The band's music features the spare avant-indie guitar rock sound of bands like the Velvet Underground, Pavement, Dinosaur Jr., and Seattle's Modest Mouse.

With standard instrumentation of dry electric guitar, bass, drums, and occasional keyboard, instruments and vocals occupy distinct and separate sonic space. Chord progressions and instrumental arrangements are largely straightforward and simple; on this basic palate, their rotating cast of lead vocalists sing in a mumbling, nasal, and flat voice with inexact intonation and hazy diction. These elements conjure the punk "everyman" aesthetic of the unsophisticated novice. When Rose Johnson enters with backup vocals, they feel only variously rehearsed, sometimes achieving a lazy harmony, sometimes doubling the lead singer's pitches. Thus, the band's musical vocabulary, rooted in punk's everyman simplicities and grunge's ironic posture, forged a distinctive cross-genre Pacific Northwest–based style.

Lyrically, Team Strike Force pushed boundaries, foregrounding violent and aggressive religious images, deemed too inflammatory for the middle-of-the-road Christian music industry. For instance, their song "I Will Not Bow Down" (*Tension*, 2001) theologizes acts of suffering and violence: "If I receive what I deserve / Surely I would be cast into / Consuming fire, burning sulfur / Eternal distance from my Father." Similarly, the song "Promise Breakers" (*Tension*, 2001) describes an execution: "I am a promise breaker / Hanging in the gallows." Team Strike Force's lyrics depict a God consistent with Driscoll's aggressive, masculine images. For the members of the band, however, these images were not always earnest, but pushed boundaries into ironic extremes consistent with the spirit of grunge music, where the literal and exaggerated intertwine (Larsen 2008: 4).

By contrast, the Mars Hillbillies, an "old rootsy" band active at Mars Hill in the early 2000s, situated its sound in the alt-country genre. The band drew simultaneously from the throwback soundtrack to the Cohen Brothers' film *O Brother, Where Art Thou?* (2000) and *No Depression*, a Seattle-based alt-country and roots rock magazine and music named for the Carter Family's (1936) "No Depression in Heaven," the band Uncle Tupelo's album of the same name (*No Depression*, 1990), and a 1990s AOL message board (Barr 2005). Conjuring old country greats, the Hillbillies drew most of their repertoire from country hymns by the Carter Family, Hank Williams, and Allison Krauss and Gillian Welch's "I'll Fly Away" from the *O Brother, Where Art Thou?* (2000) film soundtrack. The Hillbillies also performed punk-inflected covers and reinterpretations of classic songs from American hymnody, including the revival-era hymn "Wondrous Love" from 1811, "When I Survey the Wondrous Cross" from 1707, and "When the Roll Is Called Up Yonder" from 1893, staples of the nineteenth-century Sankey and Moody hymnals.

Alt-country is defined by "a rhetoric of taste, ties to community tradition, and the cultivation of a contemporary, discerning community of liberal-minded fans distinct from the audience for mainstream country music" (Ching and Fox 2008: 4). Pioneers like Uncle Tupelo posited a nostalgic reclamation of the "raw violence, despair, and excess" of country greats like George Jones, Johnny Cash, and Merle Haggard (Ching and Fox 2008: 18), yet the genre claims its "alt-" prefix simultaneously from alignment with punk values. Uncle Tupelo cite influences from gritty, acoustic country music, and from punk bands like the Minutemen, "kicking up the volume, picking up the beat," and selectively centering vintage sonic markers of country music like slide guitar, accordion, and fiddle (Ching and Fox 2008: 19). Alt-country primarily aligns with punk in critiquing the centralization, commodification, and homogenization of country music, perceived as employing conservative stylistic boundaries to appeal to broad market tastes. Instead, alt-country musicians posit that a do-it-yourself production ethic secures artistic autonomy and thus stylistic diversification (Ching and Fox 2008: 6). It positions itself as marginal to the country music mainstream via both aesthetics and capital: an unfettered, hip, pure, authentic alternative to mass-mediated country (Ching and Fox 2008: 18).

Even when the Mars Hillbillies played a variety of hymns, they interpreted these as gritty, high-energy covers, a clear nod to alt-country's punk influences. Their version of the Carter Family's "No Depression" runs at a pop punk-like speed of 145 BPM, nearly twice the 80 BPM tempo of the Carter Family original. It is also significantly faster than Uncle Tupelo's 1990 version at 120 BPM. On the Carter Family's version vocals are accompanied by an acoustic guitar, featuring the Carter picking style with bass notes on the main beats and the upper string chords strummed on the offbeats. Replicating the offbeat chords, the Hillbillies forwarded snare-centered drums, with steady, loud hits doubling the rhythm guitar's offbeat strums. Furthermore, the version employs a large dynamic range, achieved largely through textural density—spare verses set drum and lead guitar against solo vocals, while the choruses feature three-part harmonies, countermelodies in the slide guitar, and doubled harmonies in the honkytonk-style piano playing and on the Hammond organ.

Through curation of repertoire, the "band model" organizational structure, aggressive lyrics, and other aspects of musical genre, Mars Hill's worship leaders performed self-conscious opposition to the evangelical mainstream through a use of punk and post-punk. These genres proved ideal extant cultural formations through which to assert Mars Hill's masculinized iteration of Christian music ministry. To Mars Hill's leaders and members alike, the church created a comparatively "authentic," missional Seattle-based music ministry in self-conscious contradistinction to the evangelical mainstream.

Conclusion

From its earliest days, Mark Driscoll and the music ministry team at Mars Hill built an institutional identity around Gen-X youth culture, creating a unique music ministry firmly rooted in the punk and post-punk music characteristic of Seattle-area subculture, conceived as an integral element of the church's missional theology. As the church grew, its identity as a youth-oriented, hypermasculine religious movement for "manly men" grew ever more central to Mars Hill's brand and message, and punk rock, an aggressive and "authentic" contrast to the "feminine" evangelical music industry, served to perform Christian masculinity.

As Mars Hill grew over eighteen years, music remained a central component of the church's brand and identity, branching out into a wide variety of Pacific Northwest–based post-punk styles that mirrored regional trends in indie rock.

Attributes of this identity persisted in the rhetoric and identity of Mars Hill Church until its last years. In 2011, Mark Driscoll poached former Tooth & Nail A&R director Jon Dunn, tasking him with founding a church-based record label called *Mars Hill Music*. In a promotional launch video, Driscoll proudly announced, "[We're] trying to take over Christian radio and give an alternative to prom songs for Jesus leading the march," a statement reiterating his critiques of Christian music and describing the label as a sort of militarized invasion of the industry (Driscoll and Dunn 2012). Attempting to blunt the long-standing conflict between Mars Hill and broader evangelical culture, Dunn described the launch somewhat differently:

> The first thing people often think of when they hear Mars Hill Music is that we're a group of punk rock Calvinists who hate the modern worship movement. Mars Hill Music is setting out to change that perception. Our music is not an expression against anything but instead an outgrowth of our theology, who we are, and the communities our churches are in. (Murashko 2012)

Dunn sought to recant Mars Hill's decades-long adversarial relationship to the Christian music mainstream and instead focused tacitly on the missional aspects of the church's community-based musical focus. These tensions never fully resolved. Two years later, the label folded, and Tooth & Nail Records imprint BEC Recordings absorbed Mars Hill's most popular bands, including Kings Kaleidoscope, Citizens & Saints, Ghost Ship, and Dustin Kensrue.

Meanwhile, Mark Driscoll's hypermasculine approach to Christianity, predicated on aggressive images and white, working-class tropes, persisted throughout the church's life span. This aggression bled into his leadership style, critiqued by many former employees as cruel, power-hungry, and abusive (Graham 2014). In 2014, coincident with a host of other scandals at the church, dozens of former members, employees, and pastors—including numerous music personnel—leveled formal charges of abuse and bullying against Driscoll (Throckmorton 2014). This culminated in a movement to remove Driscoll from the pulpit. The church hemorrhaged members, prompting Driscoll's resignation. He preached his last sermon in August of that year and, absent this charismatic, if controversial, founding leader, the church closed on January 1, 2015.

7

Todd and Becky: Authenticity, Dissent, and Gender in Christian Punk and Metal

Nathan Myrick

Introduction

Due to the simultaneously personal and communal value that unifies it, Christian popular music is a complex and at times contradictory activity (Romanowski 2000). One particular site of conflict in Christian music is gender, a conflict compounded by the understanding that contemporary Christian music (CCM) is marketed to a gendered individual code-named "Becky." Often positioning themselves against the "mainstream" pop sensibilities of CCM, there are perhaps no more contentious forms of Christian popular music than the various subgenres of Christian punk and metal. Notwithstanding the commercial success of Christian pop-punk bands such as MxPx and metalcore bands such as Underoath, August Burns Red, and The Devil Wears Prada, Christian punk and metal scenes reside on the margins of social and religious cultures, inhabiting the liminal overlap between rebellion and conformity (Moberg 2015). In such paradoxical contexts, contention and dissent are normative attitudes and postures.

Inhabiting such marginalized ideological, aesthetic, and physical spaces invites conflict from all quarters, including one's own. Both Abraham (2017) and Moberg (2015) agree that, to the surprise of many, the vast majority of those involved as consumers and producers of Christian punk and metal identify as evangelical (or "recovering evangelical") Christians. This religious identification presents still another site for conflicts to emerge, as the values most commonly associated with evangelicals in North America, such as personal piety, social conservatism, and traditional gender roles, contradict those associated with secular punk and metal cultures, such as hedonism, anarchism, and individualism (Walser 1993; Weinstein 2000; Kahn-Harris 2007). It is no surprise, then, that aficionados of Christian punk and metal are often in conflict with other evangelical Christians, including on matters concerning gender. As such, the persona of "Todd" has emerged among some industry insiders as a marketing designation for the consumer of Christian punk, in oppositional response to CCM's Becky.

The plethora of sites for conflict suggested above point to something that I believe is inherent in American evangelicalism that has been underemphasized in scholarship: what I wish to call the value of dissent. It is not only true that Christian punk and metal scenes value dissent but also that dissent is a common and perhaps ironically unifying thread across the evangelical left, right, and center (Gushee 2008), defined in Chapter 2. Dissent is present in the emergence of what we now call evangelicalism during the late nineteenth and early twentieth centuries, evidenced principally in the watershed writings of the movement published in the 1910s, *The Fundamentals* (Torrey and Dixon 1984), and it has characterized evangelicalism throughout its history. James Barr's (1977) classic *Fundamentalism* argued that evangelicalism considers itself inherently dissenting in sinful societies, while Christian Smith (1998: 89) argues that evangelicalism thrives on social conflicts that strengthen the identity of the "saved." Adding color to this palette, ethnographic studies show that while young evangelicals agree in principle with what I am calling dissent, they are sometimes disinclined to enact this dissent in everyday life (Magolda and Gross 2009; Abraham 2017). Yet as I suggest below, there are multiple postures of dissent, and many possible impulses to be dissented from; sometimes Christian punks dissent against the expectations of who Christians are.

Although it is beyond the scope of this chapter to provide a comprehensive history of dissent as a characteristic, or even to illustrate how the characteristic became a value, it is within the scope of this chapter to give evidence of how dissent is valued in discrete ways within Christian punk scenes. Thinking alongside Luhr's (2009) and Abraham's (2017) examination of "counter-countercultures" in evangelical youth culture, I wish to highlight how the value of dissent is manifest in relation to gender and gender ideals in Christian punk rock, hardcore, and metalcore. This, in turn, reveals how Christian punk and metal adhere to the basic tenets of evangelicalism while expressing those tenets in a wide variety of reflexive postures.

The scenes and networks of Christian punk and metal are, despite attestations to the contrary from some performers, held together by the various constituent institutions that comprise the Christian music industry. These festivals, concerts, radio stations, websites, fanzines, and—importantly—record companies provide the "scapes" for cultural flows to occur (Appadurai 1996). As such, much of my focus in this chapter is on the ways that the Christian music industry capitalizes on notions of gender to promote and distribute music to consumers across diverse contexts, and what effects those efforts have on audiences. Through analysis of published literature, interviews, and conversations with fans, musicians, and industry professionals, I show how gender ideals manifest themselves in ways that both capitalize on and construct desire for a kind of masculinity within Christian punk and metal scenes. Such desires, it will be shown, are forms of dissent from a perceived "feminization" of evangelicalism, as well as dissent from mainstream popular culture's embrace of gender equality, even if fans, artists, and industry professionals themselves may not share this perspective, exhibiting them instead as latent tendencies (Rademacher 2015). However, it will also be suggested that many subculturalists may now be dissenting from the masculine values that were ostensibly espoused by earlier Christian punk bands from the 1980s and 1990s such as One Bad Pig and Lust Control. Moreover, owing to the self-reflexive nature of the dissent inherent in Christian punk and metal scenes, contemporary affirmations of gender equality may be understood as a self-reflexive response to the overt patriarchal masculinity of some popular evangelical leaders.

While this chapter draws on my academic studies and professional experience in Christian punk and metal scenes, I am not a "fan-researcher," in that I do not intend to promote or advocate for the music and scene under consideration. Instead, my intent is to bring out latencies of value and activity that often pass unobserved by outsiders or are assumed a priori and therefore accepted without evaluation by insiders. But more than either of these, I hope that by picking out such a strand as dissent in relation to gender, I am able to offer something that reveals one of the threads of commonality between the various manifestations of evangelical Christianity in order to make no faction so foreign as to be rendered an "other."

A word of self-disclosure is necessary, even though I agree with Abraham (2017: 12) that scholarly self-reflection can turn into lint-ridden navel-gazing. I grew up in the 1980s and 1990s attending an evangelical church in northern Minnesota and was thoroughly immersed in evangelical culture in my youth. I experienced many conflicts over music—for both worship and personal entertainment—and as such I bring my own memory of the events and ideologies described by other scholars to bear on my research. Additionally, I experienced and indeed internalized much of the rhetoric used to describe the "feminization" of the mainstream evangelical church, and there is an element of confession in the attitudes I describe. For instance, I remember being especially intrigued by a series of sermons my pastor preached called, "Why Men Hate Going to Church," suspecting that there was some nefarious plot to make Christian men more feminine and therefore controllable. I remember my intrigue turning to anger upon discovering the existence of Becky, concluding that the nefarious plot emanated from "Gnashville." I remember attending a pair of Promise Keepers rallies with my father and other men from my church, concurring with one keynote speaker who bemoaned Canada's legalization of public breastfeeding, and having the tune to "Rise Up, O Men of God" ringing in my head for days afterward. I remember being intrigued by the anti-"pussification" espoused by Mark Driscoll and the Acts 29 network of churches, analyzed in Chapter 6. I also clearly remember how my suspicions and anger turned to despair when I realized that I had drawn the wrong conclusions about gender equality and patriarchal domination.

I experienced evangelical anti-feminization as part of a larger movement within conservative evangelicalism, reflected in the many "Christian living" books I read during my formative years. For instance, Eric Ludy's (2003) *God's Gift to Women* encouraged men to reclaim the lost greatness of masculinity. John Eldredge's (2001) *Wild at Heart* encouraged men to embrace their inner need for adventure and freedom, promising better and more fulfilling relationships as a consequence. It sold over a million copies (Donadio 2004). Countless other books were published making similar claims and encouraging a reclamation of "biblical manhood" in the face of feminization: evangelical analogues of the "mythopoetic" men's movement (Schwalbe 1996). McDowell's (2017) research on masculinity in Christian hardcore and Greve's (2014) research on masculinity in Christian mixed martial arts resonate with my own experiences of American evangelical masculinity during this time.

I have experienced, and at times still do experience, shame at the absurdity of the things I believed and championed. That said, even if my relationship to evangelicalism is far more complicated now than it was a few years ago, and I do not wish to implicate myself with the strand of evangelicalism that considers evangelicals "the only Christians" (Moberg 2015: 26), I am still a practicing Christian. I also still believe there is a malaise afflicting evangelicals in North America: it just is not feminism or Becky.

Dissent in Christian Punk and Metal

"So, if you had to describe the theology of Christian heavy music, what would it be?" I asked, leaning forward in my office chair to be sure the microphone captured my question clearly. I was speaking with David Stagg, the owner and editor-in-chief of *HM Magazine*, about the relationship between metal music and evangelical Christianity. Our conversation had ranged from telling stories about our experiences of the various factions in the industry to remembering the glory days of Christian metalcore bands like As I Lay Dying, Demon Hunter, Underoath, and Norma Jean. Having encountered some technical difficulties with Skype's recording apparatus, I was using my iPhone like an audio recorder, the handset placed near the speaker of my laptop so as to capture the conversation in as much detail as possible.

Stagg thought for a moment, and when he replied his voice was confident, yet it was obvious he was searching for the right words. "A theology of ... maybe rebellion ... [or] dissent." Dissent is not unique to Christian punk and metal, nor Christianity in general. Instead, it is evident and obvious across the whole of punk and metal. Yet there is a particular discourse of dissent that pervades Christian punk and metal, and its performance has indeed ascended to the level of a genre rule.

My conversation with Stagg illustrates this well. In response to my query about his origins in Christian heavy music, he responded almost incredulously: "The reason I got into heavy music ... just me being a boy with testosterone. Like, why is your favorite color blue ... [or] green? There's no real answer." Stagg continued by sharing how he and a friend started sneaking an older brother's Korn, Pantera, and Metallica albums in the mid-1990s because "I liked the way it sounded. I liked that it was different. I liked that it was outside of the mainstream. I liked that it was fringe. I didn't like being like all those other people that I saw in junior high and all that other stuff."

As for Christian heavy music, growing up in "a fundamentalist Christian household," heavy music in general—Christian or not—was out of bounds:

> I knew a little bit about Christian bands doing that stuff, but according to my parents or those people in youth group, that didn't exist. It wasn't a thing. So, it took a little more time to figure out who those bands were. You know, you kinda took the P.O.D. pill, or the Blindside pill, or the Stavesacre pill, or even something as light as the OC Supertones pill, and suddenly you start to learn that the kids who went to this show went to that show, or that bought this album bought that album, you know you start to dig a little bit deeper, and you start to get into a little heavier stuff.

Referencing "crossover" nu metal and ska groups from the 1990s by way of explaining his move from mainstream CCM, dominated by "middle of the road" adult contemporary and vocal pop ensembles (Howard and Streck 1999), Stagg explained how there was something about his sense of self that chaffed at what was marketed as "Christian" music.

In keeping with the spirit of our conversation, I shared how I had been a Nirvana fan, but when my parents strongly suggested that I abandon my fandom by giving me some Petra tapes, I discovered several of the bands he mentioned as an alternative to both Petra and Nirvana. His emphatic response demonstrates the sort of dissent inherent in Christian punk and metal:

> I took the same pills. I mean, that story, you would not believe—actually I'm sure you would believe—that is, there is a whole world of people who share that exact same story ... there's a line in [the comedy film] *SLC Punk!* (1998), something like, "in a city of repressive religion, rebellion spreads like wildfire." That's why [the story is so common.] When people say you can't do something, and it's something you wanna do—and one of the unfortunate things about growing up in a fundamentalist household, but also in other households when people say "you can't do that," whether it's religious or not—[is that] you're not able to find out who you are. Because they're not saying, "no, don't touch that, [because] the fire's hot," they're saying, "you can't be a certain way." And the assumption is that being that way negates some other part of who you'll be eternally! Which, to me, and even to this day, those don't add up.

While Stagg's hyperbolic use of "whole world" might exaggerate the impact of punk and metal, the importance of such experiences in shaping dissenting postures for fans of punk and metal is evident. Beyond evidencing the power of these experiences, it also illuminates the conflicts that arise when aesthetic preferences are afforded religious weight and power, and the effects these projections can have on human relationships. Several aspects of this conflict are worth describing in detail. First, the conflict arises for Stagg and others when what they desire aesthetically is prohibited without understandable reason: "the fire" was not "hot"; it was just off-limits. Furthermore, there was no fire. Second, such prohibitions did not primarily convey a proscribed set of actions so much as convey a proscribed identity: "you can't be a certain way." Finally, in the context of aesthetic preferences mapped onto soteriological prerogatives, the inverse of such a proscription of identity is the implicit imperative of eternal damnation: "who you'll be eternally." Dissent matures when these three aspects "don't add up."

Other Christian punk and metal insiders share a similar dissenting perspective to that of David Stagg. Shannon Quiggle, Head of Publicity for Facedown Records, relays a more positive spin on the origins of Facedown, which was founded in 1997 by No Innocent Victim drummer Jason Dunn as a way of distributing his band's Christian hardcore music. While Christian record companies were put off by the band's hardcore sound but attracted to their message, secular hardcore record companies were attracted to their sound but could not support their overtly Christian lyrics. From Quiggle's perspective, Dunn seized upon an opportunity to meet a need that was overlooked by "mainstream" record companies: music that featured overtly Christian lyrics and themes with punk and metal styles. Yet even the more positive spin that the Head of Publicity offers reveals the same internal frustration that characterized Stagg's reflections; there was no place within "mainstream" evangelicalism for Dunn's band to exist as a commercially viable act. In an interview with *Noisecreep*, Dunn noted that one of his goals for Facedown Records was to "break stereotypes of what people have thought of Christians to be" (Sciarretto 2010). His comments reveal one of the common refrains from within the Christian punk and metal scenes: that there is a "Christian" culture or stereotype that needs to be "broken" or rebelled against.

Mark Salomon, lead singer of pioneering 1980s Christian hardcore band the Crucified, along with numerous other post-hardcore acts including Stavesacre and Neon Horse, offered a similar rationale for presenting an alternative to popular Christian music of the period, and by extension Christianity, in his memoir *Simplicity* (Salomon 2005). He describes a scene of inauthenticity, with many pastors and industry figures disguising their true intentions, while reflexively acknowledging his own role in these events. Importantly, Salomon notes that while many of his contacts espoused a certain openness to various musical expressions, that openness was often tied to particular religious expectations. Salomon argues many within the CCM industry are more concerned with controlling others' actions than with allowing space for what he considers to be "authentic" expression. As such, he decided to leave the industry, with *Simplicity* being his farewell.

Many more Christian punk and metal musicians and fans have wished to distinguish themselves from the CCM genre and industry. Even if this distinction fails to hold up from a commercial or institutional perspective, CCM is nevertheless often considered inauthentic and artistically suspect. However, similar dissenting voices are found beyond the Christian punk and metal scenes as well, and there are myriad reasons offered for that dissent. Bob, a Christian music industry executive active in the 1990s, described such feelings during our interview:

> Christian pop music had too many gatekeepers—the bookstores, the radio stations, people at the head of the labels—to stray too far from the "message." Charlie Peacock had a song called "Kiss Me Like a Woman"—about his wife! (*Love Life*, 1991). That caused a big uproar. And of course Amy Grant's "Baby Baby" set off a firestorm in the industry that never went away (*Hart in Motion*, 1991). I was hired by [a label] to push the envelope but whenever I did, I would get my hand slapped.

As Bob, Quiggle, and Stagg suggest, a primary impetus for dissent is the CCM industry itself, with its titular connotations of Christian normatively. If "Christian" music sounds like middle-of-the-road vocal pop acts, and a given person does not like those acts, then it follows that they do not like Christian music. There are far-reaching implications for such associations. When persons of influence, such as youth pastors, teachers, or parents, deem something off-limits that has become imbricated with personal identity, as Stagg notes heavy music had for him, then questions arise about either the legitimacy of one's personal faith and subjectivity, on the one hand, or the legitimacy of an institutional religion, on the other.

These reflections point toward a much larger question about the relationship between aesthetics and subjectivity far beyond the scope of this chapter. For my purposes here I wish to point out that these associations exist and that people use them to make decisions about themselves and others in everyday life. Moreover, these decisions often reflect and involve an individual's or community's self-understanding: how they believe themselves to be situated in relation to others and their own identity. Importantly, these identities are often framed in response to some perceived expectation or norm; Stagg's reflections depict this clearly, and he offers a perceptive reason for why it was so in his experience: the need for personal discovery and identity, the "authenticity" integral to evangelical punk and other youth cultures (Abraham 2017: 37–60).

Authenticity is an important concept for punks of any persuasion, evangelicals generally, and evangelical punks especially. Authenticity is central to punk's ethos and identity, and such authenticity demands dissent from something (Lewin and Williams 2009). As Charles Taylor (1992, 2007) has documented, the concept of authenticity has become a crucial modern moral criterion. While Taylor argues that the origins of personal authenticity lie in Romanticism (if not earlier), it became much more pronounced and widespread following the sexual revolutions of the mid-twentieth century in Western societies. As in the case of the right of each individual to express and embody their own sexual preferences, the concept of being an authentic person has come to pervade contemporary life in Western society and has morphed into a meta-value for many evangelicals, especially evident in musical activity (Ingalls 2015, 2018; Myrick 2018).

Broadly understood, authenticity means living in consonance with your personal beliefs, values, convictions, and actions: being an honest person. However, being honest with yourself about yourself means coming to grips with the aspects of everyday life that do not resonate consonantly with individual values and convictions. What emerges from Taylor's observation is that authenticity is often constructed along two conflicting planes, which I call the "realist" and the "idealist." On the one hand, "realistic" authenticity means being authentic to yourself by acting in a manner that resonates consonantly with who you are: owning your personal shortcomings and foibles. Often linked to emotions, realistic authenticity reflects the assumption inherent in Taylor's (2007: 477–86) ethics of authenticity that each human being is unique and that society functions best when space is made for each to be himself or herself. On the other hand, "idealistic" authenticity recognizes the gap between who a person is and who a person wishes she or he were. From an idealistic perspective, authenticity means living into the values and conviction that a given individual holds even when those values and convictions do not resonate with who a person perceives themselves to be at a given point in time. Taylor notes this tendency has become an imperative for "self-cultivation" (2007: 477).

This conflict was brought out in a conversation I had with a student while giving a talk at Southern Methodist University. After I had described the differences between a realistic and idealistic authenticity, she noted that this distinction explained why her parents always got dressed up for church, even though they did not dress up in everyday life: they were living into their authentic ideals for religious services. She noted that their propensity to do this had bothered her for a long time, as to her this act seemed disingenuous since it appeared to project a pretense of wealth and comfort that did not resonate with her experiences. She noted that she now understood that her parents were not being pretentious but were rather authentically living into their ideals for religious worship. It just so happened that their authentic ideals aligned with certain social expectations that signified insincere conformity to her.

This anecdote sheds further light on social and institutional expectations and norms in Western society, and it is here that the tension of authenticity comes to the foreground for Christian punks: What if the gap between a social ideal and an individual ideal becomes too great to be overcome by employing either type of authentic filter? What if a social real and an individual real are in mutually exclusive conflict? What if such conflicts are intensified by the presence of religious identities and expectations? What if authentic religion, authentic aesthetics, and authentic identities collide in a given scene that must by necessity be differentiated from another such scene?

Dissent as Authenticity

I have been arguing that dissent is inherent in American evangelicalism and that part of being an authentic evangelical is dissenting from what one perceives to be the prevailing norms of society. This dissent-as-authenticity is also integral to punk ethos and values and can be construed as dissent from a perceived hegemony of Christian values (Malott 2009). Christian punks find themselves caught between these competing claims to authenticity-through-dissent and must therefore authenticate themselves by dissenting from *both* mainstream society and evangelicalism. For instance, *Alternative Press* ran a story wherein numerous prominent Christian punk and metal musicians and industry insiders responded to a series of questions about the legitimacy of Christian punk music. While the answers varied in degrees, each respondent noted that Christian punk represented a shift in evangelicalism that differentiated the "old" ideas from the "new" while simultaneously pointing out that dissent from society and evangelical norms are not mutually exclusive (Heisel 2005).

Christian punk and metal scenes include a significant number of younger evangelicals who feel disenfranchised by the evangelical cultural mainstream. Participants in these scenes have sought to construct their identity in opposition to the popular conceptions of evangelicals (Mall 2012, 2015a, 2015b; Abraham 2017). Seeking to distance themselves from the public image of scandalous televangelists and the legalistic Moral Majority, these youth found a suitable marker and discourse for identity construction in Christian punk and metal that afforded them a space to discover or construct an "authentic" identity not wholly imbricated with the dominant evangelical culture. It is therefore notable that Salomon's (2005) *Simplicity* markets itself on the back cover as "the definitive book on being authentic," and it does so by disclosing the author's involvement in, then rejection of, a music scene presented as inauthentic. More than this, it evidences how dissent can be marshalled in a multiplicity of directions—against the Christian music industry, against the evangelical churches, against one's own punk ethos, and against one's own moral failures—forming the guiding principles of an individual authenticity.

There are many ways that the value of authenticity produces conflict and dissent for Christian punk musicians and fans, but one significant site for such dissent is the confluence of gender ideals with the marketing practices of the CCM industry, the most immediate institution against which Christian punks rebel. Gender is an integral aspect of authentic identity, and there is a particular kind of gendered dissent endemic to Christian punk music, which balances the competing claims of punk and evangelical dissent as authenticity in harmonic tension.

Gendered Dissent in Christian Punk and Metal

Return to David Stagg's initial response to my question about why he liked heavy music: "just me being a boy with testosterone." Stagg's immediate justification for his preference for heavy music was linked to a core aspect of his identity: his gender. There is a long and accepted association between masculinity and, in particular, heavy metal (Walser 1993; Bayton 1997; Weinstein 2000; Moberg 2015). Specific to punk scenes, Lewin and Williams (2009: 74–5) note that for some punks, virtues are coded as inherently masculine, and women are overtly castigated for their gender. But there is more to Stagg's ascription of gender as justification for his musical tastes. CCM has had an almost mythical narrative concerning the genre's target market: a white, middle-aged housewife named Becky. There are several versions of who Becky is and what her motivations are. According to some accounts, she is 38 years old, has three kids, and volunteers at the local food bank (Acidri 2012). According to others, she is 42 and twice divorced (Gungor 2012: 196).

The revelation of Becky's existence, possibly as early as 2005 according to Acidri (2012), was by no means the origin of gendered dissent within Christian punk. Texas underground hardcore punk band Lust Control promoted a particularly hypermasculine brand of evangelical Christianity since the 1980s. Originally conceived as a satirical band, a "Christian Spinal Tap" called "Talking Ass" in reference to the biblical story of Balaam's donkey (Cummings 1990), Lust Control was active off and on from 1988 through to the present, with their most recent album being 2013's *Tiny Little Dots*. For various reasons, they kept their identities hidden until after they temporarily disbanded, wearing masks for performances and interviews and using pseudonyms when referring to each other. While their lyrical broadsides include topics such as consumerist attitudes on "Say It Like a Rock Star" (*Dancing Naked*, 1989) and secularization on "Madolyn Murray O'Hair" (*This Is a Condom Nation*, 1988), Lust Control gained notoriety among evangelical punk and metal fans for their approach to sexuality. Notable tracks include "Mad at the Girls" (*This Is a Condom Nation*, 1988), which ostensibly blames scantily clad women for the inability of the band, and by extension society, to uphold evangelical sexual mores, although the final line of the chorus admits the singer is really "mad at myself." While their satirical origins suggest their lyrics may be slightly tongue in cheek, their even more provocative *Feminazi* (1994) reveals a more straightforward endorsement of conservative evangelical sexual mores. The title track offers a shouted religious rejection of feminism: "God! God made us different / Even from the start / Role reversal never worked / You know it in your heart / Stop! Stop burning up your bra."

It may seem easy to dismiss Lust Control as an obscure act whose antics were never embraced by the majority of Christian punks. In part that may be correct, as the act never saw commercial success, yet their impact was more significant than their sales of self-recorded cassettes would suggest. Lust Control's lead singer, "Gene," whose given name was Doug van Pelt, was the owner and founding editor of *HM Magazine* who oversaw the production of Christian heavy music's flagship publication until 2013, when he sold it to present owner David Stagg. Additionally, Paul Stanley "Q-Pek" and Philip Owens, two other members of Lust Control, were simultaneously members of noteworthy 1980s Christian hardcore punk outfit One Bad Pig (Powell 2002: 652). Hailed by Mark Allan Powell as "quite possibly the most popular hard-punk act ever to arise within the Christian music scene" (2002: 652), an epitaph that seems shortsighted in hindsight, One Bad Pig enjoyed a cult following for much of their career, notably featuring Johnny Cash singing lead vocals on their cover of his song "Man in Black" (*I Scream Sunday*, 1991).

Extreme "shock-rock" acts like Lust Control and One Bad Pig are certainly outliers, and many Christian hardcore bands and fans alike did not share their propensity to saddle feminism with the blame for sexual immorality or the perceived downfall of Western civilization. Yet a common theme for nearly all Christian hardcore bands from the 1990s and 2000s was the felt need to establish an alternative Christianity to the kind represented by Becky. Such an alternative is on display in the lyrics of several Christian hardcore and metal groups whose influence is far more obvious than Lust Control and One Bad Pig. Heidi Rademacher (2015: 639) has analyzed the lyrics of Christian metal and hardcore bands, finding that "the symbolic representation of good was consistently coded as masculine." As in her analysis of non-Christian metal lyrics, women are often objectified or depicted as villains, with motherhood depicted as "the command of a punishing God rather than free choice" (Rademacher 2015: 640–3).

Yet there is more to dissent from Becky than gender alone. Steve Drees, who along with his late wife Kerri, owned and operated the Fringe, an alternative Christian radio station in northeastern Minnesota, explained this complexity in our interview:

> Utilizing cobbled together gear and a borrowed transmitter, we always ran the station on a shoestring budget. Our goal was to reach the teenagers and young adults of the Iron Range [region in northeastern Minnesota]. Most CCM stations program for a persona they call "Becky:" a 34-year-old single mom with two kids, a mini-van, who wants something safe for her to listen to while the kids are in the car. We programmed for "Todd." A 19-year-old male who liked to hunt and fish, drove a jacked-up pickup truck, and was worried his girlfriend was pregnant.

Drees's comments reveal an understanding of how gendered marketing affects both perceptions and subsequent identification for religious music. His comments also reveal the pastoral perspective shared by many of my interlocutors: that CCM's pragmatic approach to marketing had (ostensibly) unintentionally alienated many who considered themselves evangelical Christians. Drees's continued reflections also offer insight as to why pragmatic marketing decisions are often made:

> Finances were a struggle. Todd never had the expendable income that Becky did. And Todd didn't want to hear us giving him a guilt trip every six months to get our hands on his money. Lives were changed. And my bank account was emptied. The artists were chosen because the kids in the area wanted an active rock [format] station in the area. The closest one to our area had spotty coverage. So we played Project 86, Stavesacre, Underoath, Spoken, P.O.D., bands like that.

Analyzing the impact of gendered lifestyle branding in extreme sports, which is closely related to punk (Abraham 2017: 85–6), and within which cultural identities are also constructed around gender representations, Helen Parmett (2015: 205–6) notes that gender identities are not monolithic in the subcultures and that "authentic" identities are constructed to both affirm and resist such representations.

When I asked Shannon Quiggle about Facedown's marketing strategies— specifically if they have a persona such as Todd or Becky that they envision their artists resonating with—her response was almost ambivalent:

> We didn't really set out with a specific demographic in mind. The hard music
> [and] underground scene kind of comes with a built in demographic though,
> usually men ages 13–36 (something like that). We don't target our marketing to
> that demo[graphic], it just sort of happens organically. It would be great if we
> had a wider female base but that's not really how the heavy music scene works.

Asked why she thinks Christian punk and metal scenes are so male-dominant,
she was quite definite:

> It's definitely a very organic thing that metal and hardcore attract a decidedly
> male audience. There was a time in the '90s when we would make sure we
> had label and band merch[andise] printed on women's apparel, but that never
> seemed to matter, the women were just buying the unisex sizes anyway. The girls
> and women who are drawn into the underground culture of Christian punk and
> metal are unique and looking for something that fits their taste in music and in
> the way they want to worship God. I think the men feel the same way. Not just
> because they don't fit into the Becky mold, but because they like the aggressive
> truthfulness of hardcore.

There are many American evangelicals who do not identify with Becky. That the
music labeled as "Christian" was intended for "her" communicated passively to
people affiliated with scenes excluded from that demographic that they are not
welcome. Such passive (and assumedly unintentional) communication logically
results in dissent. The emergence of music for Todd, coupled with a reaction
against music for Becky, resulted in an understanding of Christian punk and
metal as a space for male Christians to gather in opposition to "inauthentic"
Christian music and institutions that, whether legitimately or not, are associated
with Becky. That Becky is a woman is both incidental and salient, as she may
be more resisted for her suburban and perceived moneyed status than for her
gender. No self-respecting punk—Christian or otherwise—wants to be a Becky.
But how much does her gender factor into that resistance?

For some punk and metal musicians, Becky's gender contributes to the felt
need to create and maintain an alternative site for Christian musical activity.
Whether this felt need is indicative of personal sensations of alienation, as Stagg's
comments suggest, or a natural result of human biological and social structures
as both Stagg and Quiggle state, or a deeper fear of male marginalization, is in
many ways unclear. For many Christian punk and metal musicians and fans,
the answers implicit in these questions are myriad forms of "yes," sometimes
converging in a single context or individual. In an interview published in *HM
Magazine*, Mattie Montgomery, the lead vocalist for now-defunct metalcore
outfit For Today, discussed at length in Chapter 3, explained to me how his

theology of gender and "male-headship" enabled his activism in opposition to human trafficking. His reflections reveal the other side of the coin represented by Lust Control mentioned above by placing the blame for sexual immorality and violence on men (Myrick 2017). When I sought clarification from him on the apparent contradiction that affirming male-headship seems to present for his desire to oppose sexual violence and abuse toward women, Montgomery doubled down. "I'm not going to throw out a truth, a biblical truth, just because some people pervert it," he insisted, revealing how Christian punks negotiate the dyadic claims of authenticity-as-dissent surrounding gender ideals in relation to both religious convictions and commercial forces.

On the other end of the spectrum, further evidencing my argument for authenticity-as-dissent in Christian punk and metal, and suggesting another iteration of dissent from prevailing perceptions of gender in evangelicalism, Brian Bowler (2016: 22–4) has argued that the lyrics of Christian metalcore band August Burns Red work against the patriarchal masculinity commonly associated with American evangelicalism. One of the most successful Christian bands in recent years, August Burns Red released two albums that reached the top ten of the Billboard 200 album chart, *Rescue and Restore* (2013) and *Found in Faraway Places* (2015). Along with the lyrics of the similarly successful Christian metalcore band The Devil Wears Prada, whose album *Dead Throne* (2011) also reached the Billboard 200 top ten, August Burns Red use their platform to confront young men with their complicity in toxic masculinity. Bowler finds the song "Treatment" (*Rescue and Restore*, 2013) particularly salient to his claim, with its passionate exhortation for Christians to "stop dwelling on what happens when we die / Start helping others while we're still alive." He relates an encounter at an August Burns Red show with Nicholas, a nonreligious audience member, who identifies that song as his reason for becoming a fan of the Christian band (Bowler 2016: 24–5). Noting that the song's lyrics challenge traditional evangelical exclusivity and closed-mindedness, especially the masculinist religious posturing of "hearts filled with hate" and "hands clenched in fists," Bowler is struck by the song's sophisticated critique of gender as a hierarchical "system of values and behaviors" (Bowler 2016: 26).

That successful Christian punk and metal bands are challenging patriarchal masculinity should not come as a surprise, given the diversity of attitudes within the broader punk and metal scenes. Focusing on the secular straight edge hardcore scene, for example, Haenfler (2006: 102–4) characterizes punk masculinities as caught between "a more progressive vision of manhood," on the one hand, and a traditional masculinity characterized by the celebration of toughness and power, on the other. Similarly, Christian metal bands have sometimes expressed strongly patriarchal values and have been simultaneously attacked for their "effeminate and gender-bending style" (Moberg 2015: 49). Punk presents us with a fascinating case study of "masculinity in contradiction" (Haenfler 2006: 102), therefore, but contradictions do not make for a sustainable set of values. If we are to theorize effectively about Christian punk, then we must have a way of making sense of its apparent contradictions. The value of dissent affords us a ready means of making sense of Christian punk's diverse perspectives on gender. To paraphrase the subjects of Heisel's (2005) article in *Alternative Press*, there is nothing more punk than being a Christian, because that is a dissenting position, from within both punk and Christian cultures.

While there are varying perspectives on gender within Christian punk and metal scenes, few of the musicians, fans, or industry insiders I have interviewed in recent years adhere to the hardline antifeminism ostensibly portrayed by Lust Control and other early Christian punk bands or even expressed agreement with the more nuanced positions of the kind advanced by Mattie Montgomery. Indeed, even Lust Control's most recent album, *Tiny Little Dots* (2013), takes a far more reflexive and even subtle approach to the issue of sexual morality, compared to their earlier efforts. Rather, it appears to be an accident of history that Becky happened to be a woman and that Todd was a necessary reaction to her. With the exception of cases such as Mars Hill Church, analyzed in Chapter 6, few evangelical punks have intentionally made an antifeminist agenda a part of their identity or program. Indeed, many contemporary Christian punks, and other evangelical musicians, prefer to avoid such controversies, as noted in Chapter 8, focusing instead on musical excellence in their chosen genre (Heisel 2005; Ingalls 2018), employing "friendship evangelism" instead of onstage apologetic argumentation (Abraham 2017: 158–9). This does not suggest that Christian punks have a unified understanding of gender or that they are apathetic on the topic. Rather, it points to the complexities and ambiguities inherent in Christian punk scenes. Furthermore, it offers compelling evidence of what I have been arguing is the value of dissent.

Conclusion

Christian punk and metal are aggressive forms of evangelical music that appeal primarily to young men. Todd represents the intended market because he is believed to be the kind of person who is drawn to this music. Shannon Quiggle laments the lack of women in Christian heavy music, but sees it as an unavoidable aspect of the genre. There is a strand of evangelicalism that I have been tracing throughout this chapter that places theological emphasis on such an idea of innate gender difference, and this strand inevitably finds a ready audience in Christian punk and metal scenes by virtue of the genre norm of dissent. When Becky has become the very thing that you oppose, it is inevitable that gendered identities and theologies take on enhanced significance.

I have argued here that the meta-value of authenticity manifests itself in a posture of dissent for many evangelical Christians, and especially for Christian punks. Bound up in the conflict over realist and idealist authenticities, Christian punks see themselves as constructing an alternative site for authentic Christian living. The primary institution that Christian punks see themselves as differentiated from, the CCM industry—especially its mainstream pop subgenres—represents shallow and inauthentic Christianity to these punks. Dissent from CCM necessarily entails dissent from CCM's intended consumer, Becky, evidenced by Todd and the gendered marketing strategies his metaphorical existence discloses. Realizing that the creation of an authentic identity often relies on engagement with commercial marketing and branding, as Parmett (2015) argues, indicates that embracing Todd in opposition to Becky provides space for a theology of gender for some influential Christian punk and metal musicians. Rather than asserting that this tendency is endemic to Christian punk music, however, I have argued that its presence is latent, and drawing attention to its presence offers an opportunity to evaluate the merits of such tendencies.

Arguing that dissent-as-authenticity for Christian punks is diffuse and dynamic means that Christian punks are likely as not to turn against gendered ideals and identities as for them. For every For Today there is an August Burns Red. If Todd becomes too established then Becky might become the godmother of new forms of Christian punk, because to be an authentic Christian punk one must dissent from the criteria that establishes that category.

8

"Lift Each Other Up": Punk, Politics, and Secularization at Christian Festivals

Andrew Mall

Introduction

Tobin Bawinkel, the lead singer and guitarist of Christian punk band Flatfoot 56, takes a few minutes near the end of his band's set at AudioFeed Festival 2017 to talk to his audience about issues important to him. The audience has been dancing, moshing, running a circle pit, singing along, and stage-diving for over an hour, and our ears are ringing. Tobin and his bandmates have gradually shed layers of clothing and are soaked with sweat. If AudioFeed had headliners, Flatfoot would be one—this is the last official timeslot of the entire festival, and it has been an energetic event. We are dirty, sweaty, and tired, but we are not yet ready to head back to our campsites. As Tobin looks out at his audience, he gestures at the quieted crowd:

> Right here, this is what real relationship looks like. Real relationship is not writing on somebody's internet feed, on their social media site. That's not what real friends do. Real friends call each other up, real friends lift each other up. Real friends dance together, real friends cry together, real friends walk together … Don't isolate yourself from people that love you. Lift each other up.

Tobin has not spoken much throughout the set. Or, rather, when he has spoken it has been to introduce a new song from the band's latest album (*Odd Boat*, 2017), direct the crowd into a circle pit, or explain the costumes and props the band has brought for the evening's theme ("classic video games"). But this moment—close to midnight on the last night of the festival, after about an hour of enthusiastic physical engagement throughout Flatfoot's set—is significant, not only because Tobin has shifted gears into discussing his values but also because his sincerity commands his audience's attention.

Through an ethnographic analysis of Christian punk performance that considers what is sung or spoken aloud and what is not, in this chapter I argue for a nuanced perspective that recognizes the importance of inclusivity along with an ambivalence toward religious politics among many Christian punks in the United States. This particular perspective is modeled by Flatfoot 56 and other Christian hardcore, metalcore, and punk rock bands, many of whom move fluidly between secular and sacred spaces.

Flatfoot 56 is a five-piece Celtic punk band from Chicago's South Side, featuring great highland bagpipes and mandolin alongside the typical distorted guitar, bass guitar, and drums. Cofounded by three brothers and currently fronted by Tobin (guitar/vocals) and Kyle Bawinkel (bass/vocals), their lyrics promoting brotherhood, community, family, scene unity, and working-class identity are as equally at home in many do-it-yourself (DIY) secular punk venues as they are in the Christian punk scene. For many years in the early 2000s, their annual sets at Cornerstone Festival—a Christian rock festival that took place in rural western Illinois—served as the de facto center of the US Christian punk scene that found a home at Cornerstone's grounds, ephemeral but repeated annually, summer after summer (Young 2012b, 2015; Mall 2015a, 2020). Cornerstone closed after its 2012 iteration, and AudioFeed emerged in 2013 in its wake. AudioFeed is run by a different group of organizers at a different location, but they intend to support the same musical community, cater to the same festival audience, and are clearly indebted to Cornerstone's inclusive and inquisitive spirit. Luke Welchel, a cofounder of AudioFeed who directs the festival's programming, acknowledged in an interview with me: "We've never hid that we did it [AudioFeed] because of Cornerstone. We've been vocal about it. We've been sad that Cornerstone is gone."

Flatfoot 56 has been playing, touring, and recording consistently since 2001, self-releasing several of their albums and EPs. At Cornerstone, the brothers' father Dan Bawinkel ran the Fat Calf Stage, one of the unofficial generator stages also discussed in Chapter 3. Flatfoot often played one set at Fat Calf and another at an official festival stage, such as the Underground Stage or one of the Encore Stages. They have continued releasing albums and touring widely since Cornerstone ended in 2012, and they have only become more central to the Christian punk scene that gathers at the Champaign County Fairgrounds in Urbana, Illinois, every summer for AudioFeed. Dan is not involved with AudioFeed officially, but the Bawinkel brothers have become elder statesmen of Christian punk there. As active and ethical members of the Christian punk scene for over fifteen years, Tobin and his bandmates have earned the respect of other bands, concert and festival promoters, and fans.

On Sunday, July 2, 2017, he and Kyle hang out all afternoon at their merchandise tent. I have a tenuous personal connection to the Bawinkels, and Tobin and I gamely toss out names until we discover the affiliation (one of my cousins was acquainted with his sister over a decade earlier). Throughout our conversation, there is a steady stream of fans and admirers—some younger than the band—who want to speak with Tobin and Kyle, shake their hands, and buy a T-shirt, CD, or vinyl LP. Tobin is gracious and cheerful, friendly and supportive, giving his attention to each person who approaches. Most punk scenes, Christian or not, expect an egalitarian relationship between artists and fans. Tobin's reputation in the Christian punk scene thus depends, in part, on this humility and accessibility. So he sets that reputation aside to live his ethics, and he makes everyone feel valued.

Politics, Punk, and US Evangelicalism

Later that night, Flatfoot 56 plays the most anticipated and last official set at AudioFeed. Like many other punk shows, Flatfoot shows are fun and physical, but they are also serious and serve a greater purpose than merely enjoying a good band perform live. Punk shows provide both a conceptual space and a physical place where band members and showgoers can articulate, embody, and enact their values. Bernard Gendron (2002: 233–4) summarized celebrated rock journalist Lester Bangs's (1988) three elements of early punk aesthetics as aggressiveness, minimalism, and "defiant rank amateurism." There may not be a universal politics of punk, but the genre's relative simplicity and aggression make it particularly well suited for scenes that foreground participants' ethics over musical complexity or virtuosity.

There is a long history of punk bands around the world using their platform, however modest, to discuss a wide range of issues important to them. Christian punks are therefore not the only punks who "preach" from the stage or the pit. Ethical discourse is common at punk shows, where participants debate their communities' ethical values and boundaries alongside their aesthetic ones. Bands who fail to live up to their scene's ethical expectations might be ostracized and excommunicated, no matter how closely their sound fits—diverge too far outside of the accepted boundaries and you may find yourself shut out of the scene entirely. In short, in punk, as in many other music genres, scenes, and communities, ethics and aesthetics are interrelated and provide barometers of appropriateness against which artists, bands, and other participants are measured for inclusion. These debates are discursive processes of authentication that, crucially, involve all participants: musicians, listeners, and cultural intermediaries (Moore 2002).

In punk—particularly DIY punk—ethical expectations are often made explicit, sometimes aggressively so. Lewin and Williams (2009) argue that belongingness in punk depends more on one's adherence to ideological commitments (they specifically address rejection, reflexivity, and self-actualization) than to the stylistic elements and material culture that Hebdige (1979) and other early observers noted. Foregrounding ethics may actually be punk's unifying politics. We might expect Christian punk bands at Christian music festivals in the United States to foreground causes popularly associated with white US evangelicalism, such as antiabortion, gender normativity, premarital sexual abstinence, "traditional" marriage, and others. Christian punks are mostly white and evangelical, after all. And indeed, these discourses are never far from the surface at US Christian music festivals, at both the largest (such as Creation Festivals) and the smallest (including the comparatively marginal AudioFeed and Cornerstone). For example, journalists Andrew Beaujon (2006: chap. 9) and Daniel Radosh (2008: 181–9) described encounters with antigay seminar speakers and antiabortion activists at Cornerstone. In 2009, when I first attended Cornerstone for fieldwork, antiabortion groups with booths in the merchandise tents included Cupcakes for Life (which organizes National Pro-Life Cupcake Day every year on October 9), Rock for Life, Save the Storks, and Stand True selling T-shirts with slogans such as "Jesus is pro-life," "Pray to end abortion," "She's a child, not a choice," and "Social justice begins in the womb," among others.

But although organizations, speakers, and vendors promote these values at festivals, and although attendees discuss them around the campfire and proclaim them on T-shirts, they are noticeably absent from Christian rock festivals' most highly anticipated acts on their largest stages. Christian bands performing hardcore, heavy metal, metalcore, and punk rock—especially those who regularly transgress boundaries between the Christian and secular (or "general") markets—typically avoid discussing divisive issues in songs, interviews, and performances. Some even make explicit their distaste for divisive issues. For example, when joining Flatfoot 56's official fanclub, the "Ollie Mob," new members agree to rules of conduct including "the Mob is a community of positive music fans and will not be a platform for negativity or for exclusionary conduct," and "Ollie Mob is not in any way a politically motivated group, and will not be used as a platform for political division" (Ollie Mob, n.d.).

It would be easy to attribute such bands' avoiding these potentially controversial or divisive topics to a commercial strategy intended to make them less alienating and thus more accessible to a wider swath of potential listeners, including non-Christians. Outsiders might otherwise assume that these bands harbor antiabortion and antigay beliefs similar to those that Beaujon (2006) and Radosh (2008) encountered at Cornerstone. But in doing so we would be attributing a common set of values to a large community whose diverse participants hold a heterogeneous collection of values in favor of an essentializing homogeneity that happens to harmonize with the political perspectives of the loudest and most conservative voices within white US evangelicalism.

As early as Hebdige's (1979) analysis of punk, observers have identified acts of questioning and resisting the values that dominant cultures proclaim the loudest and with the most certainty as key elements of punk. Surely we participants and observers—outsiders or not—should interrogate our assumptions if we find ourselves presuming that Christian punks follow dominant conservative evangelical politics unquestioningly and unambiguously. Otherwise we might also neglect the likelihood that some bands harbor more progressive ideals that, if publicized, would alienate them within the larger Christian rock and evangelical communities. And we would miss the spirit of relatively peripheral Christian festivals like Cornerstone and AudioFeed, both of which have reflected what Young (2012a: 335) describes as an "ongoing dalliance with pluralism": a broader, more ambiguous, more open-minded, and more diverse set of theological, ideological, and political beliefs among fans of Christian rock.

Christian Rock Festivals

Christian rock festivals such as Cornerstone and AudioFeed exist on the peripheries of the mainstream markets for Christian popular music. This is true both in terms of the festivals' size and in terms of their content. The biggest Christian festivals in the United States include Creation Festivals, which draw over one hundred thousand attendees annually to two locations, one in central Pennsylvania in June and another in southeastern Washington state in July. Creation started in 1979 and is one of the longest-running, best-known, and largest Christian events in the country. Creation Festivals articulate the theologies, ethics, and aesthetics of mainstream Christian rock, contemporary Christian music, and white US evangelicalism. By contrast, at its peak Cornerstone drew over twenty-five thousand attendees; in its final year (2012), there were only around three thousand paying festivalgoers. AudioFeed's attendance is roughly the same size, although at times its crowds can feel deceptively larger than those during Cornerstone's later years because the attendees are concentrated on a smaller fairgrounds with fewer available concerts.

A former organizer at Cornerstone Festival, Jeremy, described his goal for the event in an interview as a communal space for believers who feel marginalized within their churches or other communities:

> It's an annual gathering of people that are either Christians or have some connection to the Christian faith who are more interested in discussion, the arts, I think creative music, fellowship. It's an annual renewal. A lot of these folks live all over the country, and ... they live lives and interact everyday with people that are not like-minded. This is a chance to come together.

The parallels between Jeremy's description of Cornerstone and punk subcultures are clear: both provide safe spaces and places where participants can meet others who share similar values and express themselves without fear of being (further) alienated from mainstream or dominant culture. Jeremy further clarified that Cornerstone emerged, in part, because no other festivals at the time booked artists who were on the margins of the mainstream Christian pop music market. When Cornerstone launched in 1984, according to Jeremy, its organizers intended it as a way to feature

> more and more independent, really creative artists that were Christians. Maybe they were a little too evangelical in who they were and what they stood for to make it in the general market, but a little too wild to really play a part of the fairly conservative Christian music scene at the time. We decided that there was probably room for another festival, and went for it. It was a little more alternative.

Cornerstone was always a haven for underground Christian rock, and it helped sustain a geographically disbursed niche market: fans from around North America gathered at Cornerstone to see alternative Christian bands like the Choir, Daniel Amos, the Lost Dogs, Charlie Peacock, the 77's, and many others throughout the 1980s and 1990s (Thompson 2000). Cornerstone's organizers, members of the Chicago-based intentional community Jesus People USA (JPUSA), promoted and validated Christian punk, and other marginal genres, from the beginning. Early ads intentionally referenced the design of punk show flyers, using cut-and-paste lettering, clip art, and hand-drawn illustrations; a drawing of a spike-haired punk in a leather jacket appears in an ad for Cornerstone 1987 and again in 1990, for example, and an ad for Cornerstone 1989 features a drawing of a skinhead (see Figures 8.1 and 8.2). The punk DIY ethic was alive and well at the festival itself, where bands promoted their Cornerstone shows by papering the grounds with flyers, and organizers sanctioned attendee-operated generator stages as unofficial performance spaces.

From the mid-1980s through the 1990s, foundational Christian punk bands like Altar Boys, the Crucified, One Bad Pig, and Undercover played Cornerstone regularly, as did Christian punk bands that included JPUSA members, such as Crashdog, Ballydowse, and the Blamed, among others. In the mid-1990s, Tooth & Nail Records emerged as the most prominent label to sign Christian punk bands, and performing at Cornerstone every summer was an annual

Figure 8.1 Early Cornerstone ad © 1987 Jesus People USA. Reproduced with the permission of Jesus People USA.

Figures 8.2 Early Cornerstone ad © 1989 Jesus People USA. Reproduced with the permission of Jesus People USA.

highlight for the label's artists and their fans. Notably, this included MxPx, the most successful Christian punk band to emerge from Tooth & Nail during this period. For several years, the label sponsored an entire day of performances the day before the festival's official programming began. Brad, a former manager at Tooth & Nail, recalled Cornerstone as a locus of community during this time: "Playing at Cornerstone was huge … It was fun, the sense of community back in those days. That was the only time we'd see each other, we'd go play Cornerstone. It was so much more tight-knit. We'd go to everybody else's shows, we were all friends, we'd run into each other." Gerrard, another former Tooth & Nail employee, told me that even as aggressive rock subgenres were increasingly prominent at general market rock festivals like Lollapalooza, Ozzfest, Warped Tour, and the 1990s iterations of Woodstock, large Christian festivals did not follow suit and Cornerstone remained more accepting of Tooth & Nail's artists: "Cornerstone's always been like, 'Come one, come all,' and I think [it] has a similar mentality about the music as probably Tooth & Nail does as a whole … We love it. They have always been really good supporters of us."

In the early 2000s, Jeremy began to book fewer rock and pop artists and more hardcore, metalcore, and punk rock bands at Cornerstone. He described this shift in programming to me as replicating the festival's original emphasis on "independent, really creative artists": JPUSA had originally hoped to support underappreciated Christian rock artists at the outset. Booking relatively unknown Christian hardcore and punk bands simply updated that ethic for a changed market. Another way to explain this is that as rock itself had become more accepted within the mainstream Christian market, Cornerstone turned to more peripheral styles as much out of financial necessity (rock artists were increasingly expensive to book) as out of ideology. Many of these bands had small audiences and benefitted from the exposure; AudioFeed's Luke Welchel explained that although not all of these bands were very popular, many were very good and worth supporting. While Creation and other large (and deep-pocketed) Christian music festivals' programming gradually included more hard Christian rock bands during this time (Skillet and Red are two festival favorites)—which had been Cornerstone's domain in prior years—Jeremy and his staff trended further into subgenres like emo, hardcore, and metalcore: all scenes in which Christian bands were becoming increasingly prominent. When I first attended Cornerstone in 2009, the festival itself was well past its peak at the turn of the century, but its Main Stage lineup included bands near the peak of their critical and commercial success: Underoath and Haste the Day (both metalcore bands), mewithoutYou (an eclectic indie-punk band), Emery, Project 86 (both post-hardcore bands), and Living Sacrifice (a hardcore band), among others.

There were multiple results of this shift in programming. The most obvious, and probably the most predictable, result was that as Cornerstone became the festival home for the most aggressive Christian rock genres, it also became noticeably louder and less inviting to attendees who were not fans of these genres and bands. The festival grounds, a private farm outside Bushnell, Illinois, owned by its organizers and colloquially known as Cornerstone Farm, included several official stages and many more unofficial generator stages, such as Dan Bawinkel's Fat Calf Stage, operating with little oversight from festival staff. The generator stages, of which there were two dozen in 2009, primarily booked hardcore, metalcore, and punk rock; walking the grounds was often a disorienting experience because of the auditory cacophony that these bands generated. Anecdotally, many longtime Cornerstone attendees who post in several different Facebook groups devoted to the event tell of gradually losing interest during this time. McDowell (2018: 63) describes watching a panel of middle-aged adults debate the value, utility, and overwhelming noisiness of Christian hardcore ("screaming music") at Cornerstone 2010 (see Chapter 3).

As Jeremy admitted to me:

> There are people that feel like we put way too much emphasis on the kids at Cornerstone. "What about us—we've been there for twenty, twenty-five years and we want more old-timer bands?" I'm really pretty determined to keep Cornerstone as a youth event. My target audience is that 16- to 25-year-olds … I'm sure we alienated some folks.

Yet if old-timers felt alienated during Cornerstone's waning years, younger Christian rock fans increasingly felt welcomed at the festival. Every year there were more young artists and bands that suited their tastes, true to Jeremy's intention to keep Cornerstone as a youth event. Although organizers scheduled a "Jesus Rally" in 2011 featuring to feature Christian artists from the 1970s and 1980s—Daniel Amos, E Band, Phil Keaggy, Barry McGuire, Petra, Resurrection Band, Servant, and Randy Stonehill—reflecting the roots of Christian rock and JPUSA in the Jesus Movement, as noted in the Introduction, Christian hardcore, metalcore, and punk rock dominated the festival's schedules in its last several years.

The Underground Stage was home to the Christian punk scene at the event itself, hosting Flatfoot 56 and many other bands every year. In addition to concerts all afternoon and evening, punks slept and ate at the stage, never straying too far. One of Cornerstone's final two T-shirt designs memorialized the Underground as a site of "only the finest circle pits" (see Figure 8.3). But the concentration of subcultural styles was not the only reason for Cornerstone's popularity among Christian punks. Even as the festival itself faltered financially, its organizers

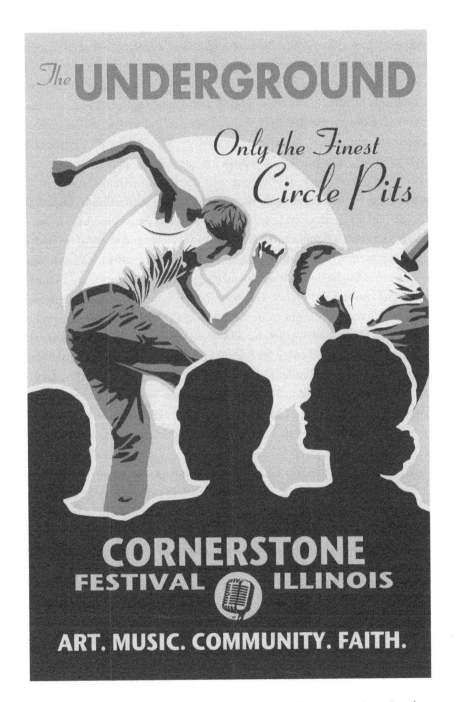

Figure 8.3 Memorializing Cornerstone's Underground Stage © 2012 Jesus People, USA. Reproduced with the permission of Jesus People, USA.

retained its inclusive spirit. The "Cornerstone experience," as many attendees described it to me, was valued because it remained a space free from judgment, where one could sidestep divisive issues (walking away from the antiabortion organizations in the merchandise tents, for example) and instead build real relationships by finding common ground with fellow fans, attendees, and even musicians. Cornerstone certainly was not secular, but neither did it promote mainstream evangelical positions exclusively. The politics of participation outweighed any collective need to affirm a single political cause.

AudioFeed grew out of a desire not to let Cornerstone's politics of participation perish along with the festival itself. Cornerstone's organizers refocused their resources on new initiatives closer to their communal home in Chicago's Uptown neighborhood. But for Luke Welchel and many of his friends (including members of bands that had played the festival), Cornerstone's absence proved to be both a tragedy and an opportunity. "The common thread of all of us [AudioFeed organizers] was that we were Cornerstone people ... We all didn't want there not to be Cornerstone," Welchel explained to me in an interview. For several years, he and some other friends had organized a pre-festival cookout and party for friends and bands traveling to Cornerstone, "and after Cornerstone [ended]," Welchel said, "people were like, 'Hey, are you guys gonna book something?'" Working together with his partners, several of whom had been involved in organizing and operating generator stages at Cornerstone, Welchel used that network and experience as the core of the first AudioFeed in 2013.

When I asked Welchel why he and his partners organize AudioFeed and what this festival's objectives are, he was quick to explain that there is no evangelical intent. They are officially registered as a 501(c)(3) nonprofit ministry, but "that ministry pretty much only exists to do AudioFeed ... We're not trying to evangelize everybody through some ministry of that sort." Instead, their emphasis is on supporting a music community:

> We want people to come together, love each other, and listen to music ... We love this community. We love music. I think our objective is to keep a strong place that bands can come and play, people can listen to the music, discover new bands, find the support of other people who are trying to do the same thing.

Importantly, Welchel and his partners intend for AudioFeed to be accessible to non-Christians and Christians alike.

Unlike most genres of Christian music, Christian punk rock, hardcore, and metalcore have been successful in attracting non-Christian audiences. Welchel reflected:

There was smaller bands coming up that non-Christians would be like, "this band is sick, I don't care what they think. I don't even know what they're talking about." … Trying to support that was a big goal, so those indie bands have a place to go … We want you to come and listen to bands you've never heard.

Festival promoters commonly rely on their headlining acts to draw paying attendees and use lower-profile timeslots (often scheduled during the afternoon) to showcase artists at earlier stages in their careers or who attract a smaller, niche audience. As an artist's profile and audience grows over time, they may be booked for successively higher-profile slots and festivals. By contrast, Cornerstone's organizers often scattered high-profile artists throughout the program, depending on their audience. Punk and metal bands that appealed to younger listeners would play late-night sets at the Encore Stages, for example, while singer-songwriters and rock artists with older fans frequently performed late afternoon sets at the Gallery Stage. For a Christian festival, appealing to potential attendees who do not share evangelical beliefs and politics can be fraught. AudioFeed's organizers have navigated this issue by minimizing the religious content during the festival and "not trying to evangelize everybody." There are a few seminar speakers, and partner organizations (such as Nashville's Anchor Fellowship church and Christian apologetics publishers Athanatos) offer worship services and more speakers, but by and large the festival's official programming emphasizes music, consistent with Welchel's stated goals.

Flatfoot 56 and Secularization

In her writings on Christian hardcore, Amy McDowell (2018: 74) examines a scene and community invested in "collectively reimagining church against mainstream Christian congregations and in spaces and forms that are also secular." Doing so is a kind of outreach that would be recognizable to members of the Jesus Movement, in Chapter 1, that reframed Christianity in contexts familiar to participants in the hippie counterculture, inasmuch as "they build Christian space in subcultural environments where rejected youth feel most comfortable" (McDowell 2014: 266). The bands, ministers, and fans she describes find religious meaning in the contexts, rituals, places, and activities of the punk and hardcore subcultures. They perform and attend Christian punk shows to reaffirm and strengthen their faith, sacralizing what non-Christian punks would view as secular places. Ibrahim Abraham (2015) describes a blurring of sacred and secular expression in punk's postsecular "overlapping consensus," in which secular and Christian punks find common values that enable them to share space, both on the stage and in the scene. While this might appear to be less evangelistic than the scenes that McDowell describes, Abraham notes that many Christian punks are committed to the vitality of punk scenes in general, because doing so would ensure the availability of "creative self-expression reflecting and celebrating Christian beliefs and creative self-expression presenting Christian belief to non-believers," particularly in the form of Christian punk music (2015: 98).

But Flatfoot 56 and many other punk and hardcore bands that have performed at Cornerstone and AudioFeed do not easily fit into these theoretical frameworks. For one, they do not obviously use their musicking to praise or worship God or otherwise express their religious beliefs. And although they are indeed interested in performing for diverse audiences that include nonbelievers, they do not use those performances to present, reflect, or celebrate Christian beliefs. Instead, Flatfoot promotes ideals that would fit punk's "overlapping consensus" without necessarily transitioning into Christian affirmation at their secular shows: brotherhood, community, family, scene unity, and working-class identity. At their Christian festival sets, they reiterate these and then explain how these values intersect with their faith to sustain the hard work of being a DIY punk band. Like McDowell's interlocutors, Flatfoot's members are simultaneously punk and Christian—those components of their identity are inseparable—and yet, unlike the Christian subculturalists McDowell encountered, Tobin, Kyle, and their bandmates are sensitive to the divisive potential of foregrounding their faith. This ambivalent religious politics is present at their Cornerstone and AudioFeed sets as well, where they avoid divisive issues in favor of appealing to punks' consensus ideals to create a safe, inclusive, and fun space for all fans, no matter their faith identity. As Abraham (2017: 78) recognizes, within punk scenes where Christian and non-Christian bands coexist, this reflects "a culture of mutual respect" for the bands' diverse audiences, "one that acknowledges the legitimacy—and probably inevitability—of individual religious and spiritual journeys." If a politics of cultural conservatism has become the public face of white US evangelicalism, then instead of sacralizing secular places Flatfoot 56 secularizes the otherwise sacred places of Christian festivals by decentering evangelicalism's most controversial public positions in favor of inclusivity.

When I first see Flatfoot play at Cornerstone in 2009, I only realize while standing there at the Underground Stage that this is the same South Side Chicago punk band to which I had taken a class of twenty-two students in 2007. They did not strike me as particularly Christian at the time, but I recall the show itself being particularly fun and attuned to DIY punk values, if a bit incoherent to my music major students, to most of whom punk music and its rituals were foreign. The Cornerstone crowd truly love this band and the mayhem they inspire. The show's theme is "Mexican Fiesta," and the Underground Tent gets hot, smelly, and dusty soon after they start playing as sweaty bodies run, jump, and crash into each other in time with the music. They play another Cornerstone set the following afternoon at the Fat Calf Stage. At this afternoon set, I am struck by the band's energy as well as that of the crowd. The band plays blistering punk songs with a tight precision; Tobin directs the circle pit (with hoarse shouts of "Circle up!" and making circular motions with his index finger), and the kids have not stopped moving since the music started.

There is little in Flatfoot's music about their religious beliefs, but they do talk about building subcultural unity through sharing a common faith. They describe the encouragement that they get from attending Cornerstone each year and the fellowship they experience with like-minded bands and fans at the festival as sustaining their work touring and recording the rest of the year. Tobin describes similar sentiments the following summer, when Flatfoot plays the Legacy Stage. They take a lot of time explaining how this festival is so important and meaningful in the lives of bands and performers who need the encouragement and brotherhood found here to take back home with them and on tour.

When I have seen Flatfoot 56 perform at secular venues—such as at the Beat Kitchen in Chicago in 2007 or Reggies, also in Chicago, in 2010—Tobin does not talk about his faith at all. Instead, he promotes the value of brotherhood and relationships, as I illustrated at the beginning of this chapter, and which he reiterates on record. In the song "Brotherhood" (*Knuckles Up*, 2004), for example, he sings of friends sticking together in the face of violence: "I remember the boys who took a stand / Who stood there strong when things got tough / ... / Never look back never give up / There's someone behind who will pick you up." When Tobin speaks of brotherhood at a Christian festival, he might be referencing to congregational cohesion; at a secular punk venue, however, scene unity is just as likely an interpretation; but in both cases he is suggesting that a fractured collective cannot sustain individual members through difficult periods.

For many years, Flatfoot has announced a theme in advance of its July festival show (first at Cornerstone and now at AudioFeed) and brought stage props, costumes, and audience activities related to that theme. The themes are a way to make punk more fun than serious, and they also enable the band to engage their fans in creating community: many audience members also dress up and bring props, while many more are involved in the games the band plays with them during the set.

The 2017 theme is "classic video games," and the band members have dressed up as video game characters: Link from the *Legend of Zelda* franchise, Donkey Kong, and Mario, Bowser, and Toad from the *Mario* franchise. They have devised crowd activities that include a crowd-surfing Pac-Man avoiding crowd-surfing ghosts and a game of *Pong* that involves bouncing someone in an inflatable sphere from one half of the crowd to the other, which quickly devolves into slam-dancing.

This audience is the most engaged I have seen at AudioFeed 2017 so far: moshing, playing along with the band's silly antics, running a circle pit (including a young father with his toddler on his shoulders), singing along, and stage diving and crowd-surfing. Tobin notices the enthusiasm and thanks the crowd in between songs: "Every year, we stand out there getting ready for the show. It kinda looks sparse around the campground, a lot of people are going home. And then, all of a sudden, before the show starts this room just like crams out. And we're like, 'Where did all these people go? Where did they come from?'" Kyle chimes in to single out the younger audience members:

> I grew up going to punk rock shows, the young kids were just stomped on. We were never appreciated, never said thank you to, and I don't think that's cool. Thank you for coming to shows, keep on going to shows, go to local shows, support your local scene. Don't let the old people beat you down for nothing.

Two songs later, Kyle asks if this is anyone's first Flatfoot theme show, and several dozen hands go up: "We got some new people? That's awesome. I appreciate—thank you for coming out and participating." "Welcome to the family, welcome to the family," Tobin repeats, before launching into the band's rendition of Southern gospel song "I'll Fly Away" (*Toil*, 2012).

At this show, Flatfoot 56 affirms difference—honoring both video game nerd culture and punk subcultures—and inspires physical engagement (circle pit, moshing, stage diving) that sets its performance apart from other concerts at the festival. They accomplish this by avoiding divisive issues and by encouraging an inquisitive approach to spirituality. Tobin tells the audience:

> I've heard a lot of people this weekend talking about how they're searching for something more, how they're searching for something that's real to them ... It's good that you're searching. Never stop looking. Never stop pursuing God. Never stop asking him the tough question, never stop asking him the things that your heart cries, wants to answer. It's through relationship with him that you get your answers, guys. It's through asking him, and saying, "Lord, show yourself to me."

It is during this moment, late in the set, that Tobin foregrounds his faith as an important component of his identity. Importantly, however, he frames the notion of faith as the result of continued questioning and searching, and not necessarily as the starting point for religious belief. For Tobin, asking questions about and pursuing answers to your spiritual life are important parts of a sustainable faith. "Never stop asking him the tough questions," he says. "There's nowhere in scripture that tells you not to ask, where it tells you not to question." Tobin's own searching has brought him closer to God, and when he talks about questioning one's faith he does so with the conviction that such a pursuit will strengthen it:

> Just keep talking to him [God], keep pursuing him, and he'll show himself faithful. There's times where you're going to pound on his chest, and you're going to say, "I want answers now, I'm hurting, I'm in pain." And he's going to stand there and he's going to hold you. He may not say anything at that particular point, but as he stands and holds you ... you're going to remember that for the rest of your life. Because I've been at that very place, where my life fell apart, where I didn't know what to do, and he just held me.

In "Same Ol' Story" (*Jungle of the Midwest Sea*, 2007), Tobin sings of the spiritual salvation that Christians experience as a result of Jesus Christ's crucifixion: "On that hill upon a tree / Hung a man who died for me / ... / He said, 'My son, your sins are vast / But they are gone now, thrown to the past.'" This song is unique among Flatfoot 56 songs in that its accompaniment is primarily acoustic guitars, accordion, mandolin, instead of distorted electric guitars. As a result, it is much easier to comprehend the lyrics of "Same Ol' Story" than in other Flatfoot songs. The song "I Believe It" (*Toil*, 2012) starts with Tobin singing over a single mandolin, but quickly breaks into a full-band performance (with drums accenting the two and four, distorted guitar, and bass guitar joining the mandolin). The lyrics are more opaque, but from a faith-based perspective Tobin appears to refer to salvation and the responsibilities that entails: "I believe in a hope that is true / And I believe in a purpose we did not deserve / Who gave them right before wrong? / Who gave us joy for this song? / I believe in second chances." In live performance the song is joyful, with the audience responding with the refrain "I believe it" to the verses and singing along with a wordless melody ("whoa") between the first and second verses and as the song's outro.

Conclusion

At AudioFeed 2017, close to midnight, Flatfoot 56 pauses, and an expectant silence envelopes the crowd. Fifteen songs into a two-hour-long set that draws from five of their seven albums, Tobin takes some time to speak about values important to him. As he speaks to the audience gathered under the tent at the Black Sheep Stage and says, "Right here, this is what real relationship looks like," I cannot help but think back to the model he set earlier that afternoon: approachable and available to anyone who wanted some of his time. Flatfoot operates in both the Christian and general markets simultaneously, although it largely sticks to the punk subcultures and niche markets. It is possible that, for Tobin, there is no real boundary between the two, and that discussing brotherhood in the secular punk scene is equivalent to musing about the nature of friendships in the context of spiritual communities, that inclusion is paramount, and that the personal is the political. This means you have to be careful about alienating and excluding others if you value them more for their ability to contribute to your community than as potential voters to be won to your side (or souls to be converted). But even when these two markets overlap, they remain conceptually distinct spaces. In one, it is safe to discuss faith and teach your audience members about God's love. In the other, it is not. For the Christian punks who gleefully run into each other at Flatfoot sets at Cornerstone and AudioFeed, however, what they hear is a band who is one of them, in both subcultural identity and faith identity. This is what real relationship looks like.

All this is to say that when Tobin Bawinkel speaks—which is not often—his fans listen. At AudioFeed, Tobin uses his stage for a teaching moment to promote community and faith during this final breather in their set. Importantly, for his last lesson of the evening, Tobin is clear about which is more important: faith can sustain you when your community fails.

> I'm serious you guys, listen up. I don't preach very often, but I feel like there's something that needs to be heard this weekend … I'm sorry you've been hurt by the church, I'm sorry you've been hurt by people that you looked up to. People are flawed. Be in any scene, be in any place, and you're going to run into hypocrisy. Whether it be in the punk scene, the hardcore scene, the metal scene—hypocrisy is what people do. [But] where are you going with it, what are you pursuing? Are you pursuing the one that can help make it better, or are you going to sink back into your anger and frustration and hate? I want to lift you up, I want to build you up as the children of God that you are.

Tobin does not preach often, as he tells us, although I have witnessed moments like this one at almost every Christian festival set that Flatfoot has played. He does not ask his audience to segregate themselves from a worldly society that believes and acts differently, nor does he advocate for political positions that would be divisive (no matter which side of the divide one falls).

But during tonight's set, he does encourage us to pay attention to each other and also to rely upon God for support because all humans are ultimately fallible. Plenty of Cornerstone and AudioFeed attendees have, at best, an ambivalent relationship with organized Christianity, and Tobin pleads with them not to let human flaws impact their relationship with God. Religious politics are erased in favor of faith, and this is perhaps the biggest distinction between Flatfoot 56 and their counterparts in non-Christian punk bands: that the ethics of inclusion are not an end in themselves but ultimately serve a greater purpose of connecting individuals to transcendent experiences.

After Tobin finishes speaking, the peal of bagpipes signifies the final song of the evening (and of every set that Flatfoot has played at a Christian festival). We lift our voices with those of the band and sing the first verse of "Amazing Grace" (*Knuckles Up*, 2004) in an expression of brotherhood and faith, swaying side to side, accompanied only by the pipes. The full band kicks back in after the first verse and the audience erupts into motion: one last circle pit, one last stage dive, fists raised in the air.

9

Christian Punk in (Post)secular Perspectives

Ibrahim Abraham

Introduction

A curious feature of Christian punk is its emergence as a vibrant cultural movement at the very time and place in which conventional Christian belief and practice appears to be in decline, especially among the young men to whom the music primarily appeals. To understand this apparent paradox, this chapter explores diverse sociological theories of secularization to examine Christian punk from three perspectives, drawing on published studies of Christian punk and data from my interviews and ethnographic observations with Christian punk musicians. My desire in this chapter is not to argue which approach to secularization is absolutely correct; Rob Warner (2010) and Steve Bruce (2011) offer complimentary overviews of the debate, and there is much that can be dredged from Charles Taylor's (2007) tome, *A Secular Age*. Rather, my desire is to show how these different paradigms can shed light on different aspects of Christian punk. Accordingly, Christian punk can be understood as a typical example of the compartmentalization of religion in secularizing societies in general and American Christianity's self-secularization in particular. Or, as an example of the vibrancy of Christianity in America's free market for salvation. Or, as an example of the resilience, but limited relevance, of religion in fragmented postsecular public spheres.

From the perspective of the established secularization paradigm, in the first section of this chapter, Christian punk can be seen as engaged in a rather predictable compromise with secular modernity. I will draw on the work of Bryan R. Wilson and Steve Bruce to argue that the internal secularization of American evangelicalism has allowed Christian punk to take its place in the "ideologically uncommitted" entertainment industry (Wilson 1966: 40). From the perspective of the religious market theory, in the second section, Christian punk will conversely be understood as an example of the efficiency of open markets in religion. Following Rodney Stark and Roger Finke, who could doubt the perpetual demand for religious products, and the adaptability of religious providers, when even punks are starting their own churches? Finally, Christian punk will be analyzed as a postsecular phenomenon, making particular use of the work of Jürgen Habermas. From this perspective, Christian punk is an illustration of the ongoing importance of religion to a significant minority of individuals in seemingly secularized cultures, still capable of impact upon secular spaces.

Christian Punk and the Secularization Paradigm

A basic sociological definition of secularization is "the process whereby religious thinking, practice and institutions lose social significance" (Wilson 1966: xiv). The secularization paradigm sees secularization as a cumulative historical process, which has happened unevenly and principally in Western Europe and its settler colonies. Focusing on the individual implications of what often appears in sociological literature as an abstract assembly of interrelated social processes, secularization is presented by Taylor (2007: 3) as "a move from a society where belief in God is unchallenged and indeed unproblematic to one in which it is understood to be one option among others, and frequently not the easiest to embrace."

The simplified argument, glossed from Wilson (1966, 1985) and Bruce (2002, 2011), runs something like this. The reformation of Christianity (in Protestant *and* Catholic forms, I hasten to add) leads to the rationalization of religion, as well as its individualization, replacing the "diverse mysteries" of a primal religious society with internalized doctrine (Wilson 1966: 23). Denominations emerge as revivalist carriers of variations of this doctrine to different social groups, although they typically moderate their positions over time. This process is ongoing, in Pentecostal rivals in the Global South, for example, but over time this denominational diversity undermines religious influence, as rival religious values become strongly contested. It is difficult to insist upon a privileged truth in societies that are diverse and egalitarian; toleration is a practical necessity, but if toleration leads to the view that "all roads lead to god … it becomes harder to persuade people that there is special merit in any particular road" (Bruce 2011: 3). In such cases, no single church is capable of sustaining the entire society, and so "religious values cease now to be community values" (Wilson 1966: 30). Concern with individual morality becomes concern with public order, a matter for the state, just as the punishment of "sin" gives way to the punishment of "crime" (Wilson 1966: 63).

The rationalization and internalization of religious belief, notably in the middle class, lead to pragmatic and empirical outlooks, as in Weber's (1992) famous Protestant ethic thesis, but hardly limited to that context, which in turn leads to the growth of technology and wealth through specialization across social spheres. "At work we are supposed to be rational, instrumental, and pragmatic," Bruce (2011: 40) notes. "We are also supposed to be universalistic: to treat customers alike." As another of these social spheres, science, has proven better able than religion to provide the "tangible fruits" such pragmatic worldviews respect, so it gained much of the social status that religion once had (Wilson 1966: 47).

The consequence of all this, in short, is that life has been compartmentalized in such a way that religion has lost the "general presidency" it once had (Wilson 1966: 57). Religion becomes differentiated; it becomes an identifiably separate institution that loses authority over other separate institutions, such as education and the "ideologically uncommitted" entertainment industry (Wilson 1966: 40). Socializing children into religion becomes more difficult as a result. Parents can choose religious education and entertainment, often paying a premium to do so, but such religiously regulated alternatives exist alongside or within the margins of secular institutions. The entertainment industry is particularly significant in that it consumes leisure time that might be spent on religious activities, and it is so influential in the socialization of young people that Christian youth ministry essentially comes into existence to challenge or co-opt it. Some scholars have argued for the analogous religious nature of popular culture, a tendency neatly summarized and critiqued by Marcus Moberg (2012) in the case of heavy metal, but as Bruce (2011: 81) argues, the fact that "young people are more likely to find ecstasy in a dance hall than in a church or invest more of their energy and wealth in following a football team than worshipping God seems pretty compelling evidence for, rather than refutation of, the secularization paradigm." As religion has been compartmentalized, it has also been privatized; if churches want to engage in public debates, or offer public services, they have to follow "secular rules of engagement" (Bruce 2011: 39).

Critics of the secularization paradigm, such as proponents of the market theory of religion, below, have insisted that this process does not apply to the United States. However, various surveys, neatly extracted in Kevin McCaffree's

(2017) study, show clear generational differentiations, suggesting that American secularization is "slow and gradual and, thus, somewhat difficult to perceive within any one person's lifespan" (2017: 101). One thing that accounts for this gradualness is successive waves of immigration, another is the comparative insecurity and inequity of life in the United States. When I've shared the modern sociological classic *Soul Searching* (Smith and Denton 2005) with students in Europe and Australia, they've been struck by the brutality of the lives of many young people in the world's wealthiest nation.

Wilson's (1966: 89) early formulation of the secularization paradigm addressed some aspects of the sociological conundrum that is American religion, noting that while the United States "manifests a high degree of religious activity ... no one is prepared to suggest that America is other than a secularized country," in which rationalism and self-interest are pervasive. Wilson picks up on the classic thesis on American religion, Will Herberg's (1955) *Protestant—Catholic—Jew*, to argue that secularization in the United States has been internal more than external, a process happening primarily within religious institutions themselves. Rather than religion being the source of moral order and identity, as in the European past, Herberg's thesis argues persuasively that American society itself is the source of moral order and identity. All but the most sectarian religions reflect these values, embodying them in ready-made communities for alienated individuals and waves of immigrants. Today, even those sectarian religions seem to be secularized, insofar as Rowan Williams (2012: 15–6) recognizes the hallmarks of secularization in the functionalism and managerialism of identity-based, prosperity-based, and well-being-based religions. Even Pentecostals, sometimes seen as "defeating" secularization (Jennings 2015), are now, generally speaking, pleasure-seeking and world-affirming. "When they could afford the work of the Devil, they relaxed their disapproval" (Bruce 2011: 42). What Bruce (2002: 140–50) describes as secularizing religion's "regression to the mean," and Williams (2012: 16) describes as fundamentalism's inability to conceive that "God's seeing of the world and the self is very strictly incommensurable with any strictly human perspective," is summed up in David Gushee's (2019: 14) lamentation over whether the term "evangelical" means anything in the United States other than "aggrieved white conservative." Is there any "theological-ethical substance" left in evangelicalism in the era of Donald Trump, he wonders (Gushee 2019).

From the perspective of the secularization paradigm, Christian punk appears as unexceptionally marginalized, then secularized. It was confined to religious spaces until it came to terms with its own partiality and started to follow punk's

"secular rules of engagement" (Bruce 2011: 39). Early Christian punk, of the 1980s
and 1990s, as discussed in Chapter 2 in particular, was restricted to evangelical
youth subcultures. It emerged as an explicit alternative and antagonist to the
secular music industry that caused such concern to conservative Christians, as
discussed in Chapter 7. But this began to change in the 1990s, part of religion's
"regression to the mean" (Bruce 2002: 140–50) wherein even conservative
American evangelicals became critical consumers of secular popular culture,
rather than conspicuous for their rejection of it. William Romanowski's (2001)
Eyes Wide Open: Looking for God in Popular Culture is a good example of this,
a text intended to offer some scholarly direction (and theological challenges)
to conservative Protestants consuming film, television, and music of the kind
that would have been boycotted not much earlier. Religion's regression to the
mean involves not just abandoning certain distinctives but taking up elements
of dominant secular culture. This has been much the case with contemporary
Christian music (CCM) in general, but also evangelical worship music that has
become heavily influenced by the norms of secular pop and rock. Combined,
this renewed appreciation of secular popular culture, and musical virtuosity
within evangelical culture, sets the stage for the emergence of Christian punk in
the secular scene.

This emergence of Christian punk in the secular punk scene also relied
upon a broader change in religious outlook, evincing a perhaps surprising level
of toleration. On the whole, lyrics of Christian punk bands active in secular
scenes in the late 1990s and 2000s were far less millenarian and sectarian,
prescriptively doctrinal, or condemnatory, than in the 1980s. Lyrics that still
were so were largely expressed in the incomprehensible orcish growls and goblin
shrieks of metalcore or restricted to the straight edge sub-subculture where
judgmentalism can be a virtue. In general, lyrics became personal and poetic
with a few standard evangelical touchstones, demonstrating the individualization
of religion, including Christianity, discussed in Chapter 4. The introspective
nature of the lyrics mimicked the general introspective turn in punk at the time
(Azerrad 2007), as well as Bruce's (2011: 13) acerbically accurate description of
contemporary popular theology: "Evil and sin have been turned into alienation
and unhappiness. The vengeful God has been replaced by Christ the inspiring
big brother or Christ the therapist."

This process of internal secularization has allowed Christian punk to take
its place in the "ideologically uncommitted" entertainment industry (Wilson
1966: 40). The experience of Christian punk, to all but the most committed of its
fans willing and able to decipher the personal reflection and scriptural allusion

underlying its incoherent vocals, reflects the values of contemporary American crossover punk. Absent political radicalism (of the left or the right) it focuses on the frustrations of adolescence and early adulthood. Live performances are purely affective, a precognitive experience of exhilaration and aggression, and just like the more spectacular forms of contemporary worship music—minus the megachurch smoke machines and laser shows—there is nothing axiomatically Christian about punk effervescence (Jennings 2008; Abraham 2018). Moreover, whatever the exclusivity of the onstage messages, usually delivered formulaically between songs toward the end of the set, and necessary to nominally contain the experience in a Christian framework, the behavior of the bands is inclusive. This is a combination of punk's egalitarianism and the general imperative in business life to act pragmatically and universally (Bruce 2011: 40). In a very real way, the professed values of these bands—brotherly love, subcultural solidarity, and expressive individualism—are placed at the service of the broader punk scene, just as Wilson (1966: 98) notes America's churches underlabor American civil religion, not least through the effective nationalization of the evangelical hymnal, especially with such "secular spirituals" as "Amazing Grace" and "We Shall Overcome" (Stowe 2004: 249). Exclusivist messages of salvation and damnation do circulate, of course, rhetorically undermining egalitarianism. However, when viewed from the pit, rather than the stage, the propositional truth values of these statements are often morally or literally incomprehensible in a culture in which non-doctrinal "moral therapeutic deism" is the default belief system (Smith and Denton 2005: 162–70; Smith 2010).

Christian Punk and Religious Market Theory

The most direct repudiation of the secularization paradigm has come from the United States, called the religious market theory or the religious market model, it seeks to reverse some of its foundational findings. One foundational approach building upon insights from this "new paradigm" comes from R. Stephen Warner (1993: 1050), arguing for the incompatibility of the Eurocentric secularization paradigm with the "disestablishment of the churches and the rise of an open market for religion" in American history. Another pertinent approach drawing on the logic of the market model is Christian Smith's (1998) subcultural theory of evangelical identity and resilience, which argues that the conflict arising from living amid such pluralism strengthens, rather than weakens, conservative denominations. By and large, however, the market thesis has been dominated by the personalities of other, strongly ideological scholars. Rodney Stark and Roger Finke, whose work I focus on in this section, have fully embraced and applied the classical liberal economic doctrines of rational action (or rational choice) theory to explain religious life.

Although Stark and Finke (2000: 41) reject the rational action or rational choice label, for fear of being confused with "initiates of some theoretical 'sect' of crypto economists unable to deal with the subtleties of religious realities," they probably protest too much. Rational action theory clearly underpins the market thesis, insofar as it is the application of classical liberal economics to all spheres of social life; people seek to maximize their utility within their budgetary constraints in the supermarket, so why not in church? The thesis is as follows:

> Religious economies consist of a market of current and potential followers (demand), a set of organizations (suppliers) seeking to serve that market, and the religious doctrines and practices (products) offered by the various organizations ... [T]he most significant single feature of a religious economy is the degree to which it is unregulated and therefore market-driven ... the founders of the social sciences were entirely wrong about the harmful effects of pluralism and religious competition. Rather than eroding the plausibility of all faiths, competition results in eager and efficient suppliers of religion, just as it does among suppliers of secular commodities, and with the same results: far higher levels of overall "consumption". (Stark and Finke 2000: 36)

To this general thesis, the market theory adds some specifics, such as liberal churches' rejection of exclusive claims to salvation or supernatural rewards placing them at a competitive disadvantage, as they lose their unique selling point, and that Europe's comparative secularization, compared to the United States, is explained by "a lack of energetic and attractive religious 'firms' rather than a lack of religious 'demand'" (Stark and Finke 2000: 22).

One review of an early formulation of the theory described it—satirically, perhaps—as "gloriously American" in that it assumes an image of the human being as "a unit constantly on the prowl for rewards and never seized with the notion that there are, in principle, insurmountable social obstacles to achieving rewards" (Simpson 1990: 371). Bruce (1999), on the other hand, offers an explicit critique of the market theory, arguing against the evidence offered by its proponents—noting, for example, that American evangelicals can avoid pluralism by retreating into a subculture almost as Christian as medieval Europe—but also the underlying logic of applying economic decision-making to spirituality. One does not have to be particularly reverential toward religion to see "cynicism" or even "crassness" in the market theory (Bruce 1999: 122). Take, for example, the idea that the only significant difference between commercial transactions with people and transactions with God is that the latter "can involve far more valuable payoffs" (Stark and Finke 2000: 113). Or the idea that ministers in Scandinavian churches—"civil servants as well as union members"—are happier with empty churches because they receive the same salary for less effort (Bruce 1999: 122; Stark and Finke 2000: 230). The disestablishment of the Church of Sweden and the increasing diversity of the religious landscape in the Nordic countries generally—including a smorgasbord of American and African Pentecostal churches in my former home, Finland, and even a Mormon temple on the outskirts of Helsinki—have accompanied ongoing declines in churchgoing this century.

In spite of this criticism, Christian punk seems like an ideal example of the religious market theory in action, the vitality of contemporary religion, through response to niche market interests. When even the punks have their own missionaries, who could doubt that "the American religious economy continues to generate new methods for appealing to the people" (Finke and Stark 2005: 252)? In Amy McDowell's (2018: 74) research on "institutional entrepreneurs" in evangelical hardcore punk parachurch projects, she observes that these missions grow by differentiating themselves from "mainstream" evangelicalism, as discussed also in Chapter 3. She gives the example of Andrew, who felt "burned" by his church that did not accept his punk identity, which was embraced by the punk parachurch mission. "As a punk, the group reasoned, Andrew was charged with the task of being church in secular spaces for those who feel alienated from the mainstream" (McDowell 2018: 68). In the language of the market theory, these alienated punks have very little "religious capital" invested in their regular churches (Stark and Finke 2000: 120–1). The cultural conduct of the services, and the general habitus of the congregation, may well render them outsiders with little in common with the congregation other than a basic creedal commitment. In my research I found that evangelical churches are more tolerant of individual idiosyncrasies than we might assume, but stories of churches' rejection of punks reverberated. Their lack of emotional investment in their congregational communities makes them willing to affiliate elsewhere.

The emergence of these parachurch missions may also say something about the "efficiency and variety of existing religious firms" (Stark and Finke 2000: 203). McDowell's punks seem to innovate within or against churches, such as Calvary Chapel that pioneered youth subcultural ministry, that were themselves once radically innovative, "with an infusion of fresh music, new strategies for founding new churches, [and] new methods for recruiting members" (Finke and Stark

2005: 252). Ethan, a British punk musician and youth pastor who spent a lot of time in South Africa, expressed a common frustration with the standardization of evangelicalism, especially its worship music. "I just can't understand why mainstream Christianity accepts one particular style of music as 'worship,'" he said. "It really pushes people into a box; we all look the same, we all listen to the same thing." As I have noticed variations on these punk parachurches around the world, as well as more formal examples such as regular services for various alternative youth at Coventry's Anglican Cathedral, and heavy metal masses in Finnish Lutheran churches, meeting these "demand niches" might be seen to maintain competition and market diversity in youth-focused Christianity (Stark and Finke 2000: 219).

Another virtue of these punk parachurch projects, from the perspective of the market theory, is their low start-up cost. Rory, a Scottish Christian punk, was given a modest payment to function as a part-time pastor in his local punk scene, but most missions are even less formal than that, being organic outgrowths of youthful religious enthusiasm and institutional alienation. Insisting that "church is not a place to *go*; church is a state of being that Christians can express and mobilize in a range of social settings" (McDowell 2018: 74), there is no need for formal meeting spaces or clergy. The start-up costs for new religious "firms" are U-shaped, high in contexts of religious monopolies and saturated free markets alike (Stark and Finke 2000: 203), and the punk parachurches seem to have found a sweet spot in the middle, given the punk scene's relative openness and the evidently niche market they are serving.

Christian Punk and Postsecular Theory

The emergence of Christian punk in secular scenes, as analyzed from the perspective of the secularization paradigm, and the accompanying emergence of missionary organizations in the secular punk scene, as analyzed from the perspective of the market theory of religion, sets the stage for the final key theoretical approach in this chapter, postsecular theory. In contemporary social science and social theory, "postsecular" typically refers to a new recognition of the internal vitality and public resilience of religion within Western societies, which had been considered so thoroughly secularized that religion ceased to be important in public life. As Gregor McLennan (2007: 859) observes, the "post" in postsecular theory rarely means "after-secular" or "anti-secular," but something more conceptual: "The key postsecular move is simply to question and probe the concept of the secular, and to re-interrogate the whole 'faith versus reason' problematic that has so consistently punctuated modern thought." A postsecular perspective seeks to move beyond the view of religion in modern society as simply a "subtraction story" (Taylor 2007: 22) and the view of secularity as natural, inevitable, or morally neutral. A society doesn't need to experience any overall increase in religiosity to be considered "postsecular," therefore, just as a society doesn't need to be a theocracy for political debates to be pushed by religious communities and concerns (Williams 2012: 11).

The idea of the postsecular emerged in a significant way after the 9/11 attacks. For Habermas (2008a: 61–2), who is particularly associated with postsecular theory, three emergent elements provoked the postsecular turn: increasing religiosity in the developing world, increasing visibility of fundamentalist forms of religion, and high-profile acts of religious violence. Globalization underpins this, glimpsed in the immigration of evangelicals from the Global South to the Global North, for example. Habermas (2008b) also recognizes that the increasing fragmentation of public spheres and cultural spaces in Western societies gives greater prominence to religious voices. This is not to say that postsecular culture gives religion any real power, evangelicals may be one mutually incomprehensible subculture among many others, but the decentering of dominant discourses other than the liberal individualism discussed throughout this book creates a kind of equality in marginality.

Punk's own postsecular turn occurred rather differently than the violence and global migrations that ushered in the broader postsecular turn. The subcultural realization that religion retains enough vitality such that it is likely to claim and maintain a presence in punk spaces has three sources locatable within the almost inexhaustible plurality of contemporary punk forms. Firstly and primarily, from the commercial and critical success enjoyed by evangelical punk bands in the early twenty-first century, notably in the hardcore and metalcore subgenres. Secondly, from the subcultural controversy surrounding a small number of North American Muslim punks around the same time (Abraham and Stewart 2017: 247–8), as the boundary between legitimate criticism of religion and illegitimate racism and xenophobia was not always clear to non-Muslim punks. And thirdly, in a rather residual manner, from the Krishnacore subgenre. A handful of relatively prominent American hardcore bands, largely active between the mid-1980s and the mid-1990s—the Cro-Mags, 108, Shelter—embraced the Hare Krishna movement, a missionary branch of Hinduism (Abraham and Stewart 2017: 245–6). Despite noting the visibility of Krishna Consciousness in American hardcore scenes in the 1990s, twenty years later Colin Helb (2014) cannot quite believe what he lived through in his youth, treating the subgenre as an historical improbability in search of a rational explanation.

Perceptive punk and metal fans would have had an inkling about religion's resilience at some point in the noughties, perhaps upon seeing Christian bands feted in glossy secular magazines such as *Alternative Press* in the United States or *Kerrang* in Britain. In his journalistic study of contemporary Christian rock, Beaujon (2006: 72) recounts the surprise of a schoolteacher being informed that Underoath is a Christian band—"I see their shirts every day!" While the commercial success of some of these bands has been significant, even punk's anti-consumerist consumers, mimicking the most paranoid religious fundamentalists by boycotting anything with a barcode on it, will probably have encountered Christian bands in secular venues.

In contrast to earlier attempts by Christian punk and metal bands to evangelize through occasional disruptive spectacles in secular scenes (Luhr 2009: 111–43), punk's crisis of subcultural secularism was not produced by Christianity's mere presence, or confrontational activities, but by the exceptional technical abilities and creative innovations of Christian punk musicians. Christian punk became a talking point in the global punk and metal scenes in the twenty-first century because a number of bands—especially in the metalcore subgenre—were critically lauded in the secular music press and online forums and established a significant non-Christian fan base. This secular success was of an order of magnitude far exceeding Krishnacore, but also very different from earlier waves of CCM in the 1970s and 1980s. At that point, CCM could be characterized as derivative with a reasonable amount of critical objectivity, as in Thompson's (2000) history of the genre, given the focus on the message in the lyrics rather than the quality or originality of the music. Even in the early 1990s this was arguably the case. As the Australian ska and punk guitarist Mitch explained, "Christian music, in general, at the time, was probably a couple of years behind the mainstream; it would follow a phase but come out later." Jeff, who played in a grunge band, argued that among secular musicians "in the nineties it was really looked down upon to be Christians in a band" partly because of the perception of derivative music.

Evangelicalism's "regression to the mean" (Bruce 2002: 140–50), combining with now ubiquitous rock and pop-styled worship music in church services, created a new evangelical appreciation for musical excellence. Into this mix remerged the secular culture industry, with a renewed sense of the commercial possibilities of the Christian market. Will, an Australian metalcore and contemporary worship musician, explained that the success of Christian hardcore and metalcore in the mid-2000s radically changed the perception of Christian music:

> All my friends started getting into bands like Beloved, and mewithoutYou, and Emery, Project 86, and Underoath. With bands like Underoath, all of a sudden in the hardcore and metal genres, Christian bands started leading the way. Guys like Norma Jean, As I Lay Dying, August Burns Red. With all these bands it wasn't quite cool to be a Christian, but we didn't have dudes out there making us look bad. Guys like Underoath were just owning everything.

Punk's postsecular turn, then, came about when musicians and fans were obliged to (re)consider the position of religion within the scene because talented and original Christian artists started appearing on their musical radar.

What this sudden recognition of religion's presence has required in punk scenes, as in punk's parent societies, is a postsecular "adjustment" by nonreligious social actors. As Habermas (2008a: 63) argues, since religious individuals and institutions have been adjusting to increasingly secular societies for quite some time, a certain reflexivity and flexibility is not unreasonable. So rather than the "condescending benevolence" of the nonreligious toward the religious, which rests on the assumption that religion will eventually evaporate, something more inclusive is required for the sake of social justice (Habermas 2006: 4). This adjustment requires moving beyond a certain limit Habermas (2008b: 115–16) identifies in progressive thought that cannot regard religion as anything other than the remnants of tradition and struggles especially with comprehending the "vitality" of conservative religion.

Three broad approaches toward Christianity—as the most and often only prominent expression of religion within punk—can be identified within punk scenes in the West, all of which reflect this postsecular turn, but do not necessarily embrace the ethical message that Habermas wants to take from it. The first approach is hostile and reactive, if not reactionary, viewing Christianity's presence as threatening or weakening punk culture. Such an approach is in direct contrast to the second observable approach, that of liberal toleration. The third approach is the one most amenable to Habermas's postsecular ethic, acceptance of the legitimacy of a Christian presence in punk through a specifically punk perspective.

In a purely hostile mode, Christianity is viewed by a section of the punk subculture through a subcultural lens of Jacobin neurosis, a periodic theme throughout Charles Taylor's (1989, 2007) writings on religion and modernity. It is as if suburban Christianity is a rival center of power that must be constrained for punk's new order to flourish. In Malott's (2009) view, the circulation of anti-

Christian attitudes within even commercial pop punk is evidence that punk's rebel heart keeps beating. Such an approach was also evident in the "God-free youth" movement periodically active within some hardcore scenes, which saw itself as a form of subcultural self-defense against the growing prominence of Christian bands. As Williams (2012: 292) notes, social harmony is defined by whoever is in power at the time, so it was not surprising for young punks to feel apprehensive about the emergence in their midst of a sub-subcultural current that might disrupt the prevailing stable values of the scene. According to Connor, a musician and Christian hardcore collector in Ohio, the movement was especially active in the American Midwest, but British and Australian hardcore musicians also encountered the movement. What was problematic about the God-free youth was that in spite of its justifiable anxiety, it was the movement itself that sought to create conflict in local scenes; ironically, by trying to provoke a violent response from Christian punks to constant aggravation, the idea was to prove the inherently intolerant nature of religion. The movement now seems to be largely restricted to online archives, but it has been around in one form or another since at least the mid-1990s, coterminous with the emergence of the Spirit-filled hardcore bands, and was visible through its T-shirts and other merchandise. As Ciminio and Smith (2007) argue, contemporary atheism mimicked American evangelicalism's development of particular subcultural expressions, making it a more claimable and performative identity, and both mimicked the band merchandise many people wear to punk shows.

Although partly predating it, the God-free youth movement could be folded into the broader "New Atheist" current, a small part of the rise in anti-religious rhetoric in often youth-focused popular culture, especially notable in the years following the 9/11 attacks (McCaffree 2017: 100–4). It was this cultural context that was really "new" about the New Atheism. With the intellectual arguments supposedly settled decades ago, postmodern relativization and multicultural accommodation of conspicuous religiosity became as much the target as religion itself. Punks are less commonly the atheistic militants one might suspect, however, and I have found apatheism—a portmanteau of "apathy" and "atheism"—far more common in punk scenes than explicit anti-religiosity or conventional religiosity. Illustratively, Ty and Rory, Christian punk musicians in Scotland, discussed a particular performance in which they were heckled by the audience. "During our set people started chanting 'Dawkins! Dawkins! Dawkins!'" Rory said, referring the author of *The God Delusion* (Dawkins 2006). "When the song finished [Ty] was like, 'right, who here has read *The God Delusion*?' And only him and our bass player had."

This reactive stance toward religion in the postsecular context of renewed recognition of its public presence is apparent in Bestley's (2015: 120) irritated critique of contemporary punk and punk studies, even though religion is almost an afterthought. He laments academia's political correctness, its "paranoid, self-defeating arguments relating to *equality* in every aspect of race, gender, sexuality or, more recently, belief," and that these norms have found their way into the study of punk. Bestley also takes aim at the "new age of punk identity politics," and the new generation of moral gatekeepers, "with the increasingly thin-skinned hypersensitivity that seems to define much social activity in the modern world" (2015: 121). Reading Bestley's analysis, I was reminded of comments I encountered in the United States, that for some punks, the presence of Christians in the scene was analogous to the presence of women; both signify how far contemporary punk has fallen from its ideal form as a carnivalesque subculture repulsive to all but the most dysfunctional young men.

What is explicitly at stake here is the right to offend in a genre that has thrived on offensiveness, including through the blasphemy discussed in Chapter 10. But what is implicitly at stake, as is the case for the New Atheists and the God-free youth, is the right to police the public sphere and determine the extent to which religious expression is to be accepted, respected, or even protected in public. Strange as it may seem, we can make an analogy with postsecular politics in Turkey, in which the electoral defeat of an explicitly secularist ruling class, at the hands of a post-Islamist party, resulted in religion's greater conspicuousness in the public sphere, from personal style to political language (Abraham and Parmaksiz 2015). Similarly, if punk spaces are no longer policed by a relatively homogenous group of anti-religious heterosexual white males, with a concomitant lack of sensitivity around race, gender, sexuality, or belief, the policing of punk's public space will change.

Here we move to the second approach to religion in general, and Christianity in particular, evident in punk's postsecular turn, not to the public religiosity of the Turkish analogy, but to a general commitment to diversity and toleration in the punk scene. Since the vast majority of Christian punk musicians, since at least the turn of the millennium, have grown up as participants within secular punk scenes, or at least as fans of secular punk music, one finds a general commitment to the flourishing of punk as a genre of music indistinguishable from that held by non-Christian punks. Similarly, as explored notably in Chapter 3, one finds far more toleration of Christianity in punk scenes than one might anticipate. This is the case for "not just Christians but *scary* Christians," in the form of evangelicals, in the words of Rory, who was warmly embraced by the broader secular scene in Glasgow. Representatively, his band was able to freely borrow recording equipment, to record poetically cryptic but nevertheless religious songs, and nonreligious musicians responded with a surprising degree of seriousness when invited to perform at a punk Christmas carols show.

It is nevertheless the case that, in keeping with Habermas's general argument about the postsecular adjustment required of nonreligious social actors, in accommodating religious diversity most of the heavy lifting has been done by Christians, as by far the most—and often only—notable religious presence in punk scenes, at least in the West. Christian punks accept the "contestability" of their beliefs in the punk scene, to use the language of William Connolly (1999: 9), understanding that Christianity will inevitably be challenged and cannot dominate punk spaces. There is a recognition that just as Christianity can be given a voice by punk's constitutive commitment to explore different ways of living and thinking, contra what Leblanc (1999: 62–3) refers to as "mainstream political, vocational, and moral imperatives," punk also gives voice to many other contradictory beliefs. This gives rise to a necessarily self-reflexive approach to evangelical culture and belief. As noted in Chapter 8, in which the idea of the punk scene as a "safe space" is also discussed, there has been a general consensus on keeping the most conservative or controversial evangelical attitudes out of public utterances in secular or mixed religious spaces.

Related to this acceptance of punk as a secular subculture is the individual and collective acknowledgment that Christianity is just one of many truths circulating within punk. In fact, it is not argumentative atheism that especially troubles Christians in the punk subculture, as much as the sense that, as noted above, so many punks are simply apatheistic. These young people, to paraphrase Bruce (2002: 42), couldn't care enough about religion to bother being atheists. This introduces a different parenthetical understanding of the postsecular; Ingolf Dalferth's (2010) conceptualization of societies in which religion has retreated so far from public consciousness that even secularity makes little sense. Such subcultural norms make the third approach to punk's postsecular turn, the acceptance of the legitimacy of a Christian presence in punk through a specifically punk framework, difficult to realize in anything other than a shoulder-shrugging manner.

As McLennan (2007: 867) glosses Habermas's argument, hinting at the overly ambitious reasonableness and intellectualism of it all, within "Habermasian postsecularism, non-believers, just like believers, are required to undergo an equivalent, and intertwined, learning process … by accepting the continuing value of the religious consciousness and by genuinely appreciating not only the human *motivation* for, but also the possible *truth-content* of, religious worldviews." Subcultural dialogue is necessary to develop these kinds of relationships between religious and nonreligious actors within punk, mirroring the process of dialogue that Habermas undertook with then Cardinal Joseph Ratzinger—the future Pope Benedict XVI—which he hopes can take place on a larger scale (Habermas and Ratzinger 2007). Within punk, such dialogue is made possible by the foundational desires of punk to exploring alternative subjectivities and passionate self-expression. Punk provides what the theologian Jürgen Moltmann (2001) calls a "third language" external to the parties in dialogue and capable of mediating between religious and thoroughly atheistic viewpoints so long as each party can accept both the legitimacy of religious and nonreligious viewpoints within the logic of punk culture. As a mediator of dialogue, the third language of punk can allow atheist punks to accept the presence of religious beliefs they may otherwise find unacceptable, and vice versa.

Dialogue of this kind in the punk context is primarily informal, taking place at punk shows where musicians and fans naturally gather, but dialogue can also be more formal when it is carried out online. Christian punks are often the exceptional sub-subculture, but punk's diversity throws up a number of other sub-subcultures, too, and Christians I have spoken with have been disabused of their misconceptions about straight edge intolerance, discussed in Chapter 4, while simultaneously disabusing nonreligious straight edge punks about Christianity. As many live performances by Christian punk bands are in secular spaces or feature non-Christian bands on the bill, bands tend to be judged for the quality of the music rather than the religious specificities of their lyrics at these shows, which are almost always incomprehensible in live performances, and often also in recordings. Dialogue then occurs as those who want to engage with a band's spiritual message are typically invited to speak with them after their performance or contact them online. In this way, the shared musical experience does not rely upon a shared spirituality, but the shared musical experience can nevertheless form the basis for dialogue and mutual understanding.

Conclusion

Emerging in times and places in which Christian belief and practice is, quantitatively speaking at least, at rather a low point, Christian punk is an interesting case study for thinking through the status of religion in Western society. This chapter has made use of three separate sociological theories, or perhaps paradigms, for understanding the decline, or perhaps the rise, of the social influence of religion over time, or perhaps over the North Atlantic. As that sentence demonstrates, the secularization paradigm, the market theory of religion, and postsecular theory offer some contradictory understandings of the contemporary status of religion in Western society. These three approaches nevertheless draw out some of the salient and perhaps contradictory features of Christian punk.

Examining Christian punk from the perspective of the secularization paradigm emphasizes, above all, the contrast between the early Christian punk of the 1980s and early 1990s, restricted almost entirely to the evangelical youth subculture, and latter iterations of Christian punk, which gained acclaim from secular audiences by embodying a radically different attitude. There was not only an embrace of musical excellence, something earlier generations of evangelical musicians hardly concerned themselves with given that they were producing popular music for people boycotting popular music, but there was also an embrace of pluralism, with doctrine buried beneath feedback and within personal, poetic abstraction. Conversely, viewed from the perspective of the religious market theory, Christian punk shows that religion is still able to mobilize activist youth. Even if they are not recruiting the unchurched, the dynamism of evangelicalism is predicated on its missionary impulses to reach market niches. Mainline and progressive churches are far less likely to shun punks, but their toleration may belie the reality that music-based identities are "thicker" cultures than we may assume, and if religion is not going to be compartmentalized, then it must find subculture-specific expressions. Finally, viewed from the perspective of postsecular theory, Christian punk demonstrates the resilience of religion as a minority concern in public spheres, as well as a range of reactions to that presence. Some punks have reacted with hostility to religion in punk, perhaps as part of a deeper discomfort with punk's ongoing pluralization; some punks have shown benign indifference to religious truth claims that are barely comprehensible to them; and some punks have embraced the ethical imperative of our postsecular age and engaged in dialogue toward mutual understanding between religious and secular worldviews.

10

Blasphemy, Conversion, and Liberation:
"Christian" "Punk" in Theological Perspective

Michael J. Iafrate

Introduction

This chapter asks, what makes Christian punk "Christian" and what makes Christian punk "punk"? This critical theological engagement with Christian punk will interrogate the adequacy of both terms as they are typically used to describe this genre, as neither "Christianity" nor "punk" is monolithic, and each contains very different and even opposing ideas and practices. As a liberation theologian, I am compelled to interpret both Christianity and punk relative to their ability to generate liberating communities, movements, and ways of life, which are congruent with the original liberationist impulses of both movements. Bringing a liberationist theological perspective to bear on the genre of Christian punk, I argue that it tends to reproduce a settled, conservative Christian identity and practice, while many expressions of secular punk carry a liberating impulse that is indeed more punk, more Christian, and more theologically satisfying than most of what is identified as Christian punk. Such a view seems counterintuitive for a genre with a propensity toward irreverence and blasphemy, yet Christians claim to worship a divine person who was executed, in part, for the crime of religious and political blasphemy. This chapter shall also argue, therefore, that punk may have something to teach the church about the role of blasphemy in Christian life.

These arguments draw on my study and practice of liberation theology, including previous work on the theological significance of secular punk, but it is also rooted in my own experiences as a musician and activist in punk and other independent music circles for nearly thirty years. Indeed, my first reflections on the relationship between Christian faith and punk rock took place not long after my full immersion baptism into the world of hardcore in a small town in

West Virginia in the early 1990s. My initiation into punk took place when a fellow altar server from my Catholic parish handed me two cassettes: a copy of Fugazi's *13 Songs* (1989) and a mixtape of various straight edge hardcore bands. As I have described elsewhere (Iafrate 2017), receiving those tapes was like being handed a copy of scripture, and before long, my friend and I were writing songs together and acquiring the equipment to start our own straight edge hardcore band with the theologically weighty name of Anamnesis. Only a few months later, Anamnesis made our debut at a local community hall alongside a Krishnacore band, joining a small but diverse scene that included hardcore, metal, grunge, and noise bands. For its size, our town had a surprisingly active scene, especially in those days before the internet, connecting with scenes throughout the region and across the country, and well-known touring bands started to come through town.

Out of my hometown scene came a Christian metalcore band that grew to be quite famous. Although they grew out of a local Pentecostal youth group, they played mostly for a nonreligious audience, and I was always impressed with the boldness with which the singer preached and prayed with sincere devotion during their shows. Although their approach to Christianity was different from my own Catholic faith, I remain very good friends with some of its members to this day. Through them I became exposed to the emerging Christian punk scene, although I was always drawn more toward secular punk, even including those bands with anti-religious views reflected in provocative artwork or band names, or whose lyrics explicitly criticized religion. I often found the latter type of band to be much more authentic, much more interesting, and much more inspiring of conversation and deeper understanding. Perhaps I secretly reveled in these sentiments, sensing a kind of liberatory dynamic taking place.

My involvement in the punk scene in later high school and college accompanied—and, I would argue, helped to facilitate—a sort of gradual political awakening and a conversion from a fairly passive type of religious faith to a more "activist" faith, as well as a desire to study theology. During my master's degree, I played in a band that toured occasionally, and while on the road I recall studying for a Hebrew exam while selling CDs and shirts, fielding questions from fans about the "God books" lying open in front of me. During these formative years, music and religion continually interacted with and informed one another, each one deeply involved with my evolving intuitions about life. Theologian Clive Marsh (2007: 540) describes this process well: "Bible-reading, participation in worship, prayer, social and political action all happen alongside the consumption and use of art, media and popular culture, and the multiple influences of one activity on another is not always easy to grasp." My interests increasingly gravitated toward liberation theologies and other forms of radical Christianity, and after a few years of pastoral work, I decided to pursue doctoral studies. Throughout my doctoral work I have discovered resonance between my early punk rock "catechesis" and my chosen approach to doing theology, as well as with the intuitions of a wider community of "punkademics" across disciplines (Furness 2012; Iafrate 2013). I take the relationship of punk and religion seriously, not only as a curious topic of interest but as part of my self-reflection on my formation as a theologian and as a potential resource for theology and church practice (Iafrate 2011, 2013, 2017).

As theology and religious studies increasingly come to recognize the spiritual relevance of culture outside of traditional religions and churches (Cady 2001), liberation theologians will find that the process of reflection on praxis must turn toward those new expressions of church and of spirituality outside of the church. The liberationist theological critique of Christian punk that follows provides an intervention into the existing body of scholarship on religion and punk music, which tends to focus on explicit references to religious language, images, and traditions while largely ignoring signs of spirituality or religiosity that are less explicit but, from my theological perspective, arguably deeper, and perhaps even more Christian, than music that carries the Christian label. The critical engagement with Christian punk that follows does not debate the issue of whether or not Christianity belongs in punk or punk in Christianity. My concern is rather what kinds of Christianity seem to be embodied, mobilized, and promoted in the specific genre called Christian punk when viewed from a perspective informed by liberation theology.

Christian Punk in Liberationist Perspective

Gustavo Gutiérrez's (1988) classic description of liberation theology as the critical reflection on praxis in light of the Christian gospel remains most helpful. But liberation theology is not primarily the product of religious authorities or academic theologians; it is first and foremost the reflection of marginalized peoples on the meaning of their struggles for liberation from oppression that, as analyzed in Chapter 2, can be seen as the concrete expression of sin and contrary to God's will for the world. Liberation theology arises in specific contexts from the people themselves, and it often takes the form of popular writing and artistic expression rather than encyclicals, academic essays, or books (Oliveros 1993: 13).

Liberation theologies are less concerned with orthodoxy (right belief), which tends to be of utmost concern to official theologies, and instead prioritize orthopraxis (right action). The priority of orthopraxis is seen in the agency people of faith exert with regard to inherited faith traditions, using aspects of these traditions in ways that best serve movements for liberation and rejecting aspects that contribute to oppression (Boff 1988: 17). Liberation theologies tend to share the assumption that authentic Christian life requires participation in movements for liberation as a participation in the Reign of God (Boff and Boff 1987). Or, as James Cone (1990) put it in the starkest of terms, theology and practice that do not place the liberation of the oppressed at the center of their concerns are simply not Christian. For liberation theologians, then, the norm of liberation enables critical reflection on ecclesial praxis, but it can also be "mobilized as the norm through which culture is explored" (Beckford 2006: 9).

Bringing a liberation ethic to bear on Christian punk will mean examining the genre's origins, the general features of the theology as seen through its "texts" (i.e., its music), and any communal action in the world that the music appears to generate. In addition to my own impressions garnered from decades of involvement in independent music, I also rely on existing sociological studies of Christian punk. These studies provide a consistent narrative of Christian punk's origins as well as several of its features, most of which resonates with my own experience.

Despite the universal-sounding moniker "Christian punk," as previous chapters have illustrated, the genre originates in a specific expression of Christianity, North American evangelicalism, and has largely remained an evangelical project. The first expressions of Christian punk emerged on the fringes of the contemporary Christian music (CCM) scene in the 1980s, blending punk with conservative evangelical theology, as noted in the Introduction and Chapter 2. The later Spirit-filled hardcore subgenre of 1990s emerged during a time when hardcore bands and fans had become more open in their explicit engagement of religious traditions of all kinds (Abraham and Stewart 2017: 242–3). This wave of Christian punk partly parted ways from the CCM scene, especially in the way these new bands did not isolate themselves from secular music scenes (Abraham and Stewart 2017). Nevertheless, the conclusion remains that "self-identified Christian punk bands are almost exclusively evangelical in origin and outlook" (Abraham and Stewart 2017: 244).

This becomes apparent in any survey of Christian punk lyrics. Combining Abraham's study (2012) with my own survey of popular bands from this period, several consistent themes emerge:

- Iterations of familiar Protestant conversion narratives; once lost, now found
- Iterations of familiar Protestant critiques of inauthentic institutional Christianity
- Fear of divine judgment, for one's self and others, underlining the importance of evangelism
- Expression of devotion to Jesus/God as evidence of salvation
- Emphasis on personal sins rather than social sins, with the exception of critiques of the secularization and sexualization of society
- Existential focus on personal suffering

Certainly there have been exceptions to these generalizations. As analyzed in Chapter 2, some bands such as Crashdog, Ballydowse, and Psalters have emphasized social justice in a way similar to liberation theology. These exceptions notwithstanding, what is particularly relevant for a liberationist critique is Christian punk's focus on personal spiritual change, rather than social and political change (Abraham 2017: 34; McDowell 2018). Although Christian punk lyrics reveal a variety of social positions, Abraham (2017) argues that it can broadly be framed within the notion of "populist traditionalism," which he takes from Tex Sample's (1996) sociological and theological study of class, Christianity, and country music. Socially conservative, but economically egalitarian, and distrustful of both the state and the free market, populist traditionalism is a somewhat contradictory position.

McDowell's (2018) analysis moves beyond lyrical content to Christian punk's communal practices, namely the tendency of bands to understand their work as a redefinition of "church" beyond the institutional walls of mainstream Christianity. In McDowell's view, these bands demonstrate a certain "tolerance" of non-Christians by performing in secular spaces, but they retain a fundamentalist attitude, focusing on a fear of damnation and encouraging association with like-minded Christians. Christian punk's "openness" to secular culture does not eliminate its basic conservatism. As theologian Tom Beaudoin (2011) has argued, the willingness to "engage culture" is often a condescending and conservative move: "'Meeting people where they are' ... always borders on patronizing: people can't 'get' to where 'we' are, so 'we' must 'go out' and meet 'them.'"

Christian punk is often interrogated by non-Christian punks based on whether it adheres to the substance of punk, rather than merely its style. But Christian punk could also be interrogated based on whether it adheres to the substance of Christianity, which, from the perspective of liberation theology, concerns adherence to the original prophetic impulses of Judaism and Christianity in their resistance to Roman imperialism (Taylor 2004: 41). Indeed this question is at the very heart of any attempt to evaluate Christian punk from a liberationist theological perspective. Viewed from this perspective, Christian punk—like most forms of US Christianity—departs from the liberationist impulse that was central to early Christianity and various radical Christian movements throughout history. As much as the Christian punk genre has sought to set itself apart from previous forms of CCM, as analyzed in Chapter 7, it still tends to reproduce a quite conservative brand of Christianity. Moberg's (2015: 151) point about Christian metal stands for Christian punk also; what differs is the "*way* and *style*" in which conventional theological ideas are expressed through the music, not the ideas themselves.

As we will see in the next section, studies of secular punk from a variety of disciplines look beyond musical output to individual and communal lifestyle and political practices. Observers of Christian punk have shown how this music generates community (Abraham and Stewart 2017: 242), but what kind of communities are they? What "ways of life" and what kinds of praxis has Christian punk inspired? Sociological studies suggest bonds have weakened between members of music-based subcultures, if they ever seriously existed in the first place (Abraham 2017: 15–35), but from a liberationist theological perspective, the test of whether Christian punk embodies the substance of Christianity is the extent to which it generates communities of liberationist praxis. On the other hand, recognition of the liberationist impulse shared by many forms of secular punk and liberationist Christianity recasts the question of Christian punk into a different kind of focus, enabling us to see secular punk as quite "Christian," even at its most blasphemous.

DIY Punk as Liberating Movement

We have seen how liberation theology provides a norm for critiquing the particular substance of Christianity expressed and promoted in much of Christian punk, but a theological criticism of Christian punk will need to think through the substance of punk as well. Sociological studies of Christian punk tend to define punk in a diverse and descriptive manner, rejecting approaches, such as that of Greil Marcus (1989), which place punk in the tradition of religious and artistic rebellion. Deferring to the various views of participants who self-identify as punk, these approaches favor "studies of specific punk scenes which reveal more banal and contested everyday realities" and "emphasize the diverse and contested nature of punk" (Abraham and Stewart 2017: 242). But definitions that are too broad can end up reducing punk to a style of music that merely decorates any number of beliefs and ideologies, or to a vague set of punk attitudes such as "thinking for yourself" or "going against the mainstream," which rarely seem satisfying from a theological perspective. Coming up with a usable theological understanding of the substance of punk requires moving past these vague definitions, following Michael Azzerad (2001: 390) who points out that there are "different interpretations of punk, just like various Christian denominations come up with different interpretations of the Bible," and these interpretations often conflict with one another. Just as various expressions of Christian belief and practice can be analyzed according to the liberationist theological norm identified earlier, some forms of punk rock have maintained a liberationist norm as well, what we might call a "liberatory *a priori*": the "pervasive tendency to assume, desire, and imagine" political, economic, social, cultural, and personal freedoms (Taylor 2003b: 27). In their strong criticism of punk deemed to be apolitical, various expressions of political DIY (do-it-yourself) punk provide a liberationist approach within the diverse punk genre.

It is precisely this liberationist focus that allows us to see secular punk's deeper theological significance, which is overlooked in most discussions of religion and punk because they tend to limit their consideration to those expressions that are explicitly religious. This narrow view ends up normalizing orthodox expressions of religious punk and neglects the spirituality of punk that is not obviously religious, including punk that is irreverent or blasphemous (Hopps 2017: 84). My theological reading of secular punk attempts to look beyond the obvious use of religious language and imagery to the deeper issues and struggles contained in cultural expression (Heartney 2018: 50). Following Taylor (1996: 127), I believe that "neither beliefs in general, nor specific beliefs (in Allah, a divine plan, Christ, et al.) are in themselves key marks of the spiritual." Rather, from a liberationist theological perspective, it is precisely the impulse toward liberation that is the most important indicator of the presence of spirituality (Taylor 1996; Taylor 2003a).

From within this approach, it is therefore reasonable to question the extent to which punk is a liberating movement at all. Since its first expressions among British and North American youth in the late 1970s, punk has included a wide range of political and ideological commitments. Early punk, at least, "was riven through with sexism, homophobia and racism" (Sabin 1999: 4). But it is important not to overlook the fact that internal critique seems to have always been integral to punk rock (Thompson 2004) and that punk has always been "haunted" (Taylor 2003b: 29) by the liberatory norm prioritized by specific expressions of political DIY punk. As a result of this always present liberationist tendency, I believe it is reasonable to describe punk as a liberation movement, albeit complex and contradictory, like most others.

Most accounts of punk rightly place the DIY ethic at the center of the narrative, but they tend to focus primarily on the production of alternative music commodities parallel to those of the commercial culture industry (Thompson 2004; O'Connor 2008). Relatively few emphasize the deeper political significance of DIY music-making practices or the influence of these practices on the rest of the lives of punks, including political practices (Holtzman et al. 2007; Dale 2008; Furness 2012). Specifically, what tends to be overlooked or downplayed is the use of DIY ethics as a liberating political tactic. "It is precisely this ambition—to 'fuck the system', to use one of the punk movement's favourite crudities—which seems to so often get forgotten in scholarly accounts of the indie movement" (Dale 2008: 177).

The inherent political significance of DIY punk is not understood because the severity of the political context from which punk emerged is often forgotten. British punk's DIY music and culture was a politically inspired response to the poverty and despair brought about by the economic crisis in Britain in the 1970s (Holtzman et al. 2007: 46; Johnson 2014). After punk's first wave self-destructed, DIY punk remerged with even stronger political ferocity in the British anarcho-punk movement, particularly the band Crass, which influenced punk's reemergence as hardcore in the United States in the 1980s. Both anarcho-punk and US hardcore advocated an alternative, radical politics and underground info-sharing through zines and other alternative media (Holtzman et al. 2007: 46–8; Dale 2008: 177; Berger 2009).

The DIY ethic, in short, is "the idea that you can do for yourself the activities normally reserved for the realm of capitalist production" (Holtzman et al. 2007: 44). Because it is "part of the process of undermining capitalism by forming relationships not intended by capitalism" (Holtzman et al. 2007: 45), the DIY ethic is not merely anti-consumerist. Such an ethic is also certainly not limited to music, and many interpretations of punk agree that what begins as a cultural expression of personal agency and the rejection of consumer culture comes to overflow into the rest of one's life (Davis 2006; Iafrate 2013: 45–7; Stewart 2017). Punks introduced to the DIY ethic through music scenes come to believe that "staying punk" has everything to do with the way we choose to live within a consumer society, influencing what we buy, what we eat, what careers we choose, and so on, following the invitation of the Minutemen lyric "Our band could be your life" (*Double Nickels on the Dime*, 1984; Azerrad 2001).

Even this assertion that punk is about more than music can neglect the depth of DIY's political significance in favor of the liberal individualism of DIY moralities and spiritualities analyzed in Chapter 4. More than this, radical DIY punk includes a preference for the "politics of the act" over the "politics of demand," creating change rather than petitioning politicians for it (Day 2005: 14–15), not only as an "alternative" but precisely because it is a powerful tactic for the marginalized (Holtzman et al. 2007: 44). Likewise, DIY punk involves what a liberation theologian might call a preferential option for the oppressed, for "while many punks come from privileged sectors of dominant society, to identify as a punk is a maneuver to intentionally position one's self in solidarity with oppressed and colonized people, both locally and globally" (Miner and Torrez 2012: 31). According to this logic, punk identity must be "intimately intertwined" with a great many radical causes, "not even mentioning the most fundamental desire to produce new and liberated societies 'within the shell of the old'" (Miner and Torrez 2012: 29).

One of the clearest examples of this type of liberationist DIY punk is the "Revolution Summer" that took place in the Washington DC scene in 1985. Bands associated with Dischord Records, such as Rites of Spring, Beefeater, and Nation of Ulysses, challenged the scene's growing macho, violent, depoliticized, and even racist tendencies by creating a new scene (Azerrad 2001: 378–82; Andersen and Jenkins 2003; *Salad Days* 2014). Launched with an anti-apartheid protest outside the South African embassy, Revolution Summer reconnected music and politics, leading to the founding of Positive Force DC, a youth-based punk activist group. Positive Force continues to embody the particular kind of DIY punk politics I am describing through serving the needs of local marginalized people while taking on the larger systems that cause oppression (Andersen and Jenkins 2003). To DC musician and writer Ian Svenonius (2007), "the idea of Revolution Summer was to demolish the fetid body of punk while retaining its constructive aspects," a rebirth that Svenonius christens with religious comparison as "an auditing of belief systems and orthodoxies." Indeed, this sort of self-critical movement within a tradition bears resemblance to religious reformers like the Hebrew prophets and Jesus.

Following on the heels of Revolution Summer, the newly formed band Fugazi advanced this approach to punk politics by challenging almost every assumption of what it means to be a band (Azerrad 2001: 376–410; Iafrate 2013: 42–5). "Hardcore and punk had been marked by a victim complex," says Svenonius

(2007), "the expression of a caste who felt perpetually under-represented. The Fugazi ethos countered this with the idea that the group—and by extension the audience (since the punk announcement was that they were one and the same)—could be at the reins if they so desired." Through word and action, Fugazi's entire existence as a band was a reminder that music did not have to be a mere product for individual consumption but could be linked to a potentially liberating set of communal practices.

For many of its participants, DIY punk has included reclaiming spiritual agency and experiencing spiritual liberation alongside other types of liberation. Some punks have experienced this through the total rejection of religion, while others have experienced a sense of liberation through commitment to particular religious traditions (Peterson 2009; Abraham and Stewart 2017). For still other punks, spiritual liberation has led them to a more "DIY" approach to faith, rejecting inherited (and perhaps oppressive) forms of religion to explore new approaches to faith and religious practice, analyzed in Chapter 4. Punk scenes have therefore become spaces for punks to rethink religion, de-linking it from the perceived status quo and re-linking it to liberationist political and cultural movements. Consequently, punks have often developed tools through local scenes that make them well adapted for a world in which interfaith encounter is increasingly the norm (Bidwell 2018).

The Washington DC scene provides rich examples of the specifically liberationist impulse within DIY spiritualities, such as the DC "clown/prophet" Tomas Squip, who drew freely from multiple traditions for his lyrics in Beefeater and Fidelity Jones, bands at the center of DC's DIY scene. Squip described punk as a context for "open-ended growth," which did not automatically rule out religious traditions as sources for living life and for participating in movements for justice (Squip 1990; Andersen and Jenkins 2003: 256–7, 274, 297; Iafrate 2017: 29). Squip's approach to DIY spirituality cannot be boxed into any single religious tradition, nor does it seem to be influenced by the individualistic or consumerist spirituality critically analyzed in Chapter 4. It is, rather, a hybrid or "postcolonial" approach (Kwok 2005: 186–208), resembling the approach of Jesus who did not say "yes" or "no" to Judaism in its totality but carefully sifted that tradition, believing that Judaism's core transcended the boundaries of that faith. It likewise resembles the early church, which was not exclusively "Christian" or "Jewish," but at the crossroads of traditions (Taylor 2004: 52). Often practicing in fluid ways that do not map onto rigid sociological frameworks, punks formed in this kind of DIY spiritual culture exhibit an impulse that is arguably more "Christian," from a liberationist theological perspective, than what is often seen in Christian punk.

Blasphemy as a Sacrament of Spiritual Liberation

I am convinced that, at its best, punk has been a movement for spiritual liberation. But how can this claim hold up, given the anti-religious and blasphemous nature of much punk rock? Although it seems counterintuitive, I argue that punk is spiritually liberating in a very positive and constructive sense not in spite of its tendency to be blasphemous but precisely because of it. Blasphemy can indeed be a sacrament of spiritual liberation.

The word "blasphemy" is used in a number of different ways for different purposes and is therefore difficult to define, but in general, by blasphemy I mean "profane speech" perceived to be an "offense against the sacred" that transgresses the border between the sacred and the profane as deemed by some kind of public criteria (Plate 2006: 36–40). Words and images perceived to be "blasphemous" can function as "culturally symbolic markers" publicly used by authorities to define the boundaries of acceptability (Plate 2006: 27). Given the largely underground nature of punk, blasphemous expression within its cultures has rarely risen to the level of public scrutiny, but it can nevertheless function as a kind of cultural marker within those scenes.

At least since the Sex Pistols sang "I am an Antichrist" (*Never Mind the Bollocks, Here's the Sex Pistols*, 1977), punk has demonstrated a propensity toward blasphemy in a variety of ways: in the names of bands themselves, in the imagery used by bands in their album art or clothing, in song lyrics, and in actions that bands might engage either during or outside of music performances. The first type of expression, the naming a band using religious imagery in a subversive way, is a very common punk tradition. Bands might select a religious name for a variety of reasons, such as pure shock value as in names like The Damned, Econochrist, Jesus Crust, Bad Religion, or Burn the Priest. But even the choice of a religious name without any obvious attempt at shock value (e.g., Golgotha, Eucharist, Jesuit, Three Studies for a Crucifixion, Iconoclast, or Judas Iscariot) can be a subtle but provocative reclaiming of language from religious authorities who police the sacred by policing the use of sacred language and images (Plate 2006: 126). In whatever form they take, punk expressions of blasphemy can be silly or irreverent types of parody, or for shock value, or they can be more serious and analytical criticism of religion. I suggest that individual expressions of punk blasphemy sit somewhere along a spectrum of at least three types, but whether an expression is perceived as serious or silly depends very much on the audience and the context.

Firstly, expressions of punk blasphemy can be pure shock value without much depth, usually in blasphemous band names or imagery. Once religion is addressed in song lyrics, there tends to be an automatic movement toward more substance, although songs like "Fuck the Pope" by Anti-Flag (*Rock'n with Father Mike*, 1993) demonstrate the existence of relatively non-substantive lyrical content. Secondly, expressions of punk blasphemy can offer blanket criticism of religion itself, often contrasting religious dogmatism to punk's value of autonomous thought and expression. Combined with hardcore punk's focus on personal relationships, criticism of religion can focus on religion's impact on friends or family, as in "Filler" by Minor Threat: "Your brain is clay / What's going on? / You picked up a Bible / And now you're gone" (*Minor Threat*, 1984). Another common theme is religious hypocrisy, as in "Body and Blood" by Eucharist: "Your corrupt institution has such precious possessions / Your brethren suffer spiritual famine" (*Eucharist*, 1996).

Finally, and most significantly, expressions of punk blasphemy can offer deep critical engagement with specific theological issues or provocative ideas about spirituality. Beyond mere shock value or the blanket rejection of religion, this type of criticism can be sustained across the entire career of a band, such as Crass or Bad Religion. Rather than simply rejecting religion, such criticism looks more deeply at specific themes, perhaps by questioning certain Christian practices such as the combination of religion and nationalism in Bad Religion's "American Jesus" (*Recipe for Hate*, 1993). Some expressions in this category affirm religion or spirituality in general but reject forms that the musicians believe are not life giving, such as "No Spiritual Surrender" by Inside Out (*Inside Out*, 1990), or they can be mystically suggestive as in Dan Higgs's simultaneously devotional and blasphemous punk hymns to "Holy Holy Christ Beast" as vocalist for Lungfish (*Love Is Love*, 2003).

A good example of articulate but often severely blasphemous punk is the British anarcho-punk band Crass (1977–1984). The band's career includes an ongoing criticism of religion as seen in the band's logo, which provocatively combines religious and political symbols, as well as in album titles that parodied Christianity (*Feeding of the 5000*, 1978/1980; *Stations of the Crass*, 1979; *Christ — The Album*, 1982). Some of their anti-religious output seemed to be for the sake of shock value, while some merits serious theological attention, particularly the contributions of drummer Penny Rimbaud. Before the founding of Crass, Rimbaud was moved to deep anger at the death of his friend Wally Hope. Rimbaud came to believe that Hope was murdered by the British government for his provocative activism and that Hope, inspired by the death of Jesus, welcomed his own death as a kind of martyr: "In Wally's behavior I recognised the same stupidity that I interpreted in the Christ story" (Berger 2009: 69–70). In response, Rimbaud wrote and self-published the lengthy poem *Christ's Reality Asylum*, a dialogue with Jesus in which Rimbaud rejects Christ and the martyrological aspects of the Christ myth.

After the founding of Crass, portions of the poem were used as lyrics for the song "Asylum," which was slated to appear on their first record, *Feeding of the 5000* (1978/1980). The song, however, was censored on the initiative of the workers at the pressing plant, and Crass released it as a 7″ single on their own label instead (Gordon 2015: 18). While taking the form of a "remarkably aggressive comment on the idea of Christ" (Berger 2009: 136), band members and others interpret the poem and the song as critical not of Christ himself but of the way institutional Christianity uses Christ to uphold misogyny and imperialism. Crass's Eve Libertine would later reflect, "I do see it as an attack on religion, even though it's seemingly attacking Christ. It's attacking what religion took from this man" (Berger 2009: 135).

Rimbaud's nuanced and articulate critique of imperial Christianity would be sustained through Crass's career, including their poetic art-noise album *Yes Sir, I Will* (1983). Written as an attack on UK Prime Minister Margaret Thatcher after the Falklands War and tracked as an album-length song divided into seven parts, *Yes Sir, I Will*'s blasphemous lyrics reject and subvert imperial Christianity with an alternative "Crasstology" drawn in part from the words of the Gospels as well as the Hebrew prophets. Part five, "Rock 'n' Roll Swindler," describes imperial Christianity as a violent "robbery of life" that encourages "servility as a bargain for dignity" and "death as a bargain for living," deriving its power from a warped interpretation of Christ's martyrdom. Part six, "Burying the Hatchet," continues the critique: "Still we lay prostrate before a stylized figure on a crucifix / As if the stone fool might be resurrected / ... Military acts are bathed in those gory tales." Crass bluntly condemns this version of Christianity: "Fuck his loaded deity" (*Yes Sir, I Will*, 1983).

Like Rimbaud's *Christ's Reality Asylum* poem, *Yes Sir, I Will* seems like a brutal rejection of Christ, yet central to Crass's critique are Christianity's victims who are identified with Christ himself in part seven, "Taking Sides": "We regret to inform you / That today another Christ was shot in the back of the head ... / That another Christ, not yet ten years old, was shot today / By agents of Her Majesty's Government with a plastic bullet" (*Yes Sir, I Will*, 1983). This identification, at the heart of an otherwise blasphemous piece of art, is an unexpected but sensitive christological awareness shared with liberationist christologies such as Sobrino's (2001) "view from the victims." Finally, the album's echo of the prophets' lament, "For Christ's sake how long? How long, O Lord, how long?" is answered with a call to responsibility and action that draws on Christ's healing words to the paralytic, "Get up, take up your bed, and walk" (Jn 5:8): "Take up your mind and think! / Take up your life and act!" (*Yes Sir, I Will*, 1983).

Indeed, Rimbaud and Crass would not be able to make such subtle christological observations without an "invisible but eminently apparent vein of spirituality running through their output and attitudes" (Berger 2009: 137). It is a spirituality that Christian fans of Crass would apparently recognize. "After Asylum," says Eve Libertine, "we did have some letters from Christians saying they sort of understood it ... I can't remember getting any letters that said 'How could you do this?'" (Berger 2009: 136). Likewise, Pete Wright, founder of Current 93 and a longtime friend of the band who is Roman Catholic, has said that "Penny's take on Christianity and culture was very articulate" and indeed a vision of "clarity and beauty" (Berger 2009: 121).

The kind of "articulate" criticism demonstrated in the work of Crass demonstrates the liberationist impulse discussed throughout this essay at work in both punk and Christianity. But even punk artists who seem less precise about what they are trying to communicate seem to be concerned to varying degrees with engaging in a critical interrogation of received orthodoxies of any kind. So even at its most blasphemous, punk music can express a kind of backhanded affirmation of the sacred. As Beaudoin (1998: 123) argues in his work on the spirituality of Generation X in popular culture, rather than indicating irreligiosity, blasphemy "may indeed reveal a deep—if unorthodox—religiosity." One cannot express doubt or blaspheme without an already present sense of belief. "To be 'heretical', then, [one] must have strong spiritual intuitions" (Beaudoin 1998: 125). Eleanor Heartney (2018: 41) takes a similar approach in her work on the religious sensibility of blasphemous postmodern Catholic visual art. Beaudoin and Heartney invite us to ask what is really being said in punk music that seems "blasphemous" rather than automatically dismissing it as theologically irrelevant.

Aside from whatever is going on in particular expressions of punk blasphemy, I would argue that the tendency toward blasphemy in punk culture is very much a part of the gradual process of conversion and spiritual liberation present in punk, perhaps moving through three identifiable moments. First, blasphemy in punk culture can give the listener permission to question, reject, and even repudiate certain expressions of religious belief, including entire traditions. As Berger (2009: 121) says of Crass, "The attacks on Christianity and the person of Christ were extraordinary and must have made most listeners feel that they'd led lives more sheltered than they'd ever imagined." Second, once the initial permission is granted, engagement of blasphemous punk can be part of a deeper working through of spiritual-religious beliefs. Listeners need not reproduce punk's often dramatic rejections of religion, but the music may simply help to continue a process of affirmation and negation of specific religious ideas and doctrines. Third, blasphemous speech can move the personal sifting of religious ideas toward more public expression, becoming sacramentalized as individuals, bands, and communities find their voices in resistance to structures of religious and political power. As Plate (2006: 125) puts it, "Until someone stands up and cracks the joke, exclaims the treason, paints the blasphemous image, the discussion will not open." The blasphemies of punk, in other words, can provide an entry into wider public discourse.

The blasphemous tendencies of punk are also an example of the reality of "deconversion" in and from religious traditions, a process only beginning to be taken seriously by theologians (Beaudoin 2008; Hornbeck 2011). Theological attention to this kind of religious speech, rather than limiting theological attention to religious speech expressive of Christian belonging, is important because it can complicate religious identities, "make room for ways of religious belonging that move beyond the traditional binary of affiliation and disaffiliation, and [enable us] to appreciate deconversion as a theological act, one among many possible ways that a person might live out the values that she has learned" in Christian community (Hornbeck 2011: 21).

Toward a "More Punk" Christianity

Blasphemy seems to be an important ingredient in the liberative process of conversion provoked by punk, perhaps even a sacrament of religious and ethical liberation itself. Indeed, blasphemy is so central to punk that it seems fair to me to say that Christian punk, if it is to be true to both Christianity and punk, must be willing to be a little more blasphemous. I pose this challenge not simply because blasphemy is intrinsic to punk but rather because blasphemy is intrinsic to liberation and therefore intrinsic not only to punk but to Christianity when viewed from a liberationist perspective. Indeed, perhaps one reliable indicator of how Christian and how punk something is, is how blasphemous it is.

Just as practitioners of Christian punk can learn about the blasphemous dimension of the liberative impulse of their own religious tradition from punk, so too can Christian churches learn something from blasphemous punk that might influence their own practices of faith. In short, both Christian punk and Christianity itself need to be made more punk by being more disruptive of the political and religious status quo of which blasphemy is an important part. Christians in fact already believe that blasphemy is a necessary ingredient to their religious tradition, for although Christian communities have not always adequately grappled with it, the fact remains that Christians worship a person who was executed, in part, for the crime of religious and political blasphemy. As Mark Johnson (2014) has argued, Jesus's practice of sedition vis-à-vis Judaism and the Roman Empire bears a family resemblance to the seditious nature of punk. This is an attitude and a practice that Christianity needs to recover, as it is rooted in the life of Jesus himself (Johnson 2014). By becoming more blasphemous, churches can indeed become more Christian.

We can already identify Christian communities that have been influenced in one way or another by punk, quite apart from the conservative Mars Hill and Acts 29 network analyzed in Chapter 6, including radical expressions of contemporary Christianity such as the New Monasticism movement, various expressions of Christian anarchism, and newer waves of the Catholic Worker movement. There is much to learn from these, but perhaps becoming more blasphemous in Christian practice will involve something along the lines of what Mark Van Steenwyk (2017) suggests about "taking protest to church": "If we want to confound and disrupt the narratives of oppression, we need to raise our angry voices in the pews as well as the streets ... I don't mean that figuratively ... I literally mean we should disrupt our churches." Likewise, punkademic theologians will need to discern ways that the practice of theology might be informed by radical DIY punk (Iafrate 2013), including the recognition of blasphemy as a basic Christian spiritual attitude and as a theologically relevant category, and will need to put blasphemy into practice in theology itself.

Perhaps a solid guide for Christian punk, churches, and theologians is the Russian performance art punks Pussy Riot whose unsanctioned performance in the sanctuary of Moscow's Cathedral of Christ the Savior resulted in charges of blasphemy. Pussy Riot's (2013) musical intercessory prayer, begging the Virgin Mary to "become a feminist" and "drive away Putin," made headlines but also inspired quite a bit of analysis from theologians and religious studies scholars for the way the band justified not only their opposition to the repressive church and state relationship ("the Lord's shit") but also their blasphemous actions with rich theological reasoning based on the prophetic impulse of Christianity of speaking truth to power (Korte 2014: 47–8). Christian communities have much to learn from this kind of liberative "spirit" at the heart of punk. As "a community that has persisted, imperfectly but powerfully, to raise a vision of a better world that might still be" (Andersen and Jenkins 2003: 397), punk has much to teach churches that aim to be the same kind of community in the world. One of the most important lessons punk can teach the church and the Christian punk genre is the art and power of blasphemy that is integral to the liberative impulse it shares with Christianity. For punks know that building a better world involves tearing this shit down—all of it, including "the Lord's shit."

Conclusion: Performing Christian Punk Identity

Ibrahim Abraham

Performing Evangelical Identity

The ten chapters in this book have highlighted three key aspects of Christian punk performance integral to the subgenre's music: the performance of evangelical identity, of masculine identity, and of punk identity. Each is inseparable from the other, in the contexts in which they are presented, such that Christian punk is as much a product of the secular punk genre as it is a product of evangelical youth culture or contemporary Christian music (CCM). In fact, the aspects of Christian punk that offend bourgeois decency—its narrow demographics, its moral absolutism, its masculinist posturing—owe as much to punk as they do to evangelicalism.

Recalling David Bebbington's (1989: 1–17) four pillars of evangelicalism from the Introduction—activism, Bible-centrism, conversion, and a focus on Christ's crucifixion—draws out specific aspects of evangelical identity in Christian punk. Chapters 1 and 2, by Eileen Luhr and Eric Strother, examine Christian punk in its earlier years, while still embedded exclusively within evangelical churches, on the margins of the CCM industry. Christian punks at this time took a strongly activist approach to music, aimed at solidifying the identity of evangelical youth against the secular world. This approach has been significantly modified by bands embedded within secular scenes, as in Andrew Mall's analysis of Flatfoot 56 in Chapter 8, which shows a band as committed to upholding the values of the punk scene as early Christian punk bands were committed to upholding their ideas of the values of the church.

Christian punk lyrics frequently feature biblical references, but these are not always utilized in a straightforward evangelistic manner, and even when they are, they are not always understood or interpreted in the same way, given the diversity of audiences that many more contemporary bands appeal to. An example is Underoath's use of the Psalms, analyzed in Chapter 5. Religious references can quite often be "opaque," as Andrew Mall notes in relation to Flatfoot 56, but songs will often still feature variations upon the evangelical pillars of conversion and crucifixion. The extent to which these themes, and their underlying soteriological imperative, are comprehensible to audiences is taken up in Chapter 9, noting not only the decline of conventional religious knowledge, but the musical genre norms of punk subgenres that can render lyrics literally incomprehensible and changing value systems that can make such evangelical truth claims morally incomprehensible within the cultures of therapeutic individualism and spiritual egalitarianism, analyzed also in Chapter 4 in the context of punk's straight edge movement.

The evangelical subject presented in this book is therefore one who struggles to make his beliefs consistent and comprehensible—and it almost always is a "him" in punk. Christian Smith's (2000: 194) general reflections on American evangelicals are accurate in this specific context, too; they are "ordinary Americans of a particular religious bent who are beset by the same kinds of incongruities, made interesting by the same kinds of complexities, and tempered by the same kinds of ambivalences that characterize other Americans." They are consequently not the angels they would like to think of themselves as, which is an essential observation given the kinds of pressures placed upon often very young men to live up to idealized public personas, noted in Chapter 5. But with the possible exception of Mark Driscoll from Chapter 6, evangelicals are rarely the reactionary devils their critics are wont to think of them as (Smith 2000: 193–4). Approached in this way, Christian punk seems to me to be one more way of making evangelicalism inhabitable and explicable within everyday life. The disagreements over evangelism noted in Chapter 3, the individualism noted in Chapter 4, and the disavowals noted in Chapter 5 are a vital part of this, as evangelicals are awkward and reluctant evangelists more often than we might assume, and tolerance is less a virtue than a necessity.

Performing Masculine Identity

The chapters in this book suggest that Christian punk continues the foundational punk desire of creating homosocial spaces within which to explore its various identities (Thompson 2004). Nathan Myrick's analysis of the deliberate differentiation of Christian punk and metal's "Todd" from mainstream CCM's "Becky" in Chapter 7 is revealing in this regard, but Christian punk in its entirety is coded male; women are primarily present as absent problems, also addressed in the lyrics analyzed in Chapter 2. Deena Weinstein's (2000: 105) study of heavy metal suggests that the presence of women presents two key problems for men in that subculture, and the chapters in this book suggest that this carries over into punk, too. Firstly, they become disruptive objects of desire, most evident in the lyrics about adolescent sexuality analyzed in Chapters 2, 5, and 7. But in Weinstein's analysis, femininity is also representative of repressive authority, not just of one's own mother but of late modern society in general. In Chapter 5, Joshua Kalin Busman notes the suspension of adulthood in the metalcore scene, in which these scene "kids" remain kids in part because they seem unwilling or unable to engage with women in more than the most cursory of ways. Maren Haynes Marchesini's analysis of Mark Driscoll's Mars Hill megachurch in Chapter 6 offers the most fully realized example of this. "It all began with Adam, the first of the pussified nation," Driscoll (2000a) hammered into an internet forum, "when he shut his mouth and listened to his wife who thought Satan was a good theologian." Self-help guru Jordan Peterson would earn a fortune mythologizing such status anxieties and neuroses among adolescent males.

In my own research, I never noticed male Christian punks to be less gender inclusive than their secular subcultural peers, but like Christian Smith (2000: 194) calming nerves about American evangelicals by reminding readers they are only "ordinary Americans" after all, this may not be saying very much. Some were highly critical of the gendering of music in churches, carried over into secular projects and spaces, in which young women are directed toward keyboards, classical instruments, and decorative vocal styles. As is the case in Chapter 7, I also encountered those who simply shrugged at what they viewed as innate gender differences in musical taste. The differences I observed in Christian sub-scenes were marginal, but the presence or absence of a single female musician or a small group of female audience members could be consequently quite significant. Christian bands that enlist the support of their local church—not automatic—can sometimes coax young women from their church to shows, but this can produce a backlash from some male punks, scandalized by the idea that their punk scene is a place to invite girls from Sunday school.

Performing Punk Identity

In the earliest days of Christian punk, analyzed in Chapters 1 and 2, it was a rather politicized sense of religious otherness that formed the link between evangelicalism and punk. Punk's energy and attitude were enlisted to enliven pop culture–friendly evangelical churches in danger of repeating the routinization common throughout church history, making compromises with "the world." Reminiscent of John Lydon—once Johnny Rotten of the Sex Pistols, once a latter-day John of Leyden to Greil Marcus (1989)—appearing in commercials for Country Life butter, J. Milton Yinger (1982: 301) calls this "the John Wesley syndrome." In Chapter 1, Eileen Luhr links this to earlier American Protestant revivals, while in Chapter 2 Eric Strother links this to the biblical prophetic tradition, a tradition with more than passing relevance to the liberationist punks—Christian, non-Christian, and anti-Christian—introduced by Michael J. Iafrate in Chapter 10. But the figure of the punk as preacher or prophet, calling for the world to repent, or to be turned upside down, or to be shunned, seems to become problematic when Christian punk begins to embed itself in secular scenes, beginning with the Spirit-filled hardcore movement in the mid-1990s. At this point, punk has turned inward, as the success of grunge and emo demonstrates (Azerrad 2007), so Christian punks share stories of individual salvation from despair, in the example of For Today in Chapter 3, hope amid institutional dysfunction and distrust, in the example of Flatfoot 56 in Chapter 8, and nominally universal truth claims are at once disavowed, in the example of Underoath in Chapter 5.

These ideological changes continue to resonate; Christian punk coexists with punk pornography in an ever-expanding metagenre that has come to terms with its likely permanent partial presence in the mainstream culture industry. Something else noticeable about Christian punk, and contemporary punk tout court, is the declining concern with class distinction and performance in all but the crustiest corners of the subculture. For Mars Hill, in Chapter 6, punk was part of its strategy of identifying as an explicitly working-class church, or at the very least as an anti-bourgeois church, and implicitly also as white and patriarchal. Working-class identity is also a part of the identity of Flatfoot 56, closely analyzed in Chapter 8, but this is a reified convention of the Celtic folk-punk genre, which has little interest in the Celtic world after about *Ulysses*. It once was considered foundational—and not just in the UK—for punks to at the very least demonstrate their divestment from middle-class status, as Daniel Traber (2001, 2008) has shown, as part of punk's broader progressive political project, which has implied a variety of solidarities noted in Chapter 10.

Progressive politics, or a preferential option for the oppressed as noted in Chapter 10, hardly seems to require working-class solidarity and identity in punk today. To borrow a phrase from Gáspár Miklós Tamás's (2013: 13) work on class and knowledge, it is as if a "terrific moral switch" has been flicked, and the privileged status of the working class has been revoked. The "inversion of the moral hierarchy" that established the epistemological privilege of the working class on the left, expressed in a variation on the language of the Sermon on the Mount (Tamás 2006: 245–6), has itself been inverted. In this regard, John Lydon is unusual in still insisting upon the historical and moral agency of his own traditional working class. Analyzing comments Lydon made both for and against Trump and Brexit—in the latter case arguing that the working class have made their judgment, so history has spoken—music journalist Tim Sommer (2017) observed that if "Lydon hears that the working class is making some kind of noise, he will immediately respond to that with some instinctual empathy; later, he'll take a breath and use his rather enormous intellect to parse the issue with some greater depth." Sometimes he may do this in reverse.

This neglect of class is understandable in Christian punk, as from an evangelical perspective personal faith eclipses any material measurement, and as Eric Strother notes, in comparing approaches to sin in Chapter 2, feminist and liberation theologians have criticized conservative Christianity for emphasizing the universality of sinful human nature over categories of material inequality. From a punk perspective it is more significant. On the one hand, perhaps capitalism has taken its prophesized course and erased meaningful distinctions between the working and middle classes, hence the subjects of economic justice becoming the "99%" and indebted university graduates, as hinted at again in Chapter 2, noting the work of Susan Willis (1993) a generation ago. On the other hand, the privileging of questions of gender, racial, and sexual inequality is observed in Russ Bestley's (2015) state-of-the-field essay on punk studies and evidenced in subtle ways by the authors in this collection. Punk's bad conscious has turned to focus on other things, as noted in Chapter 9, revealing the declining influence of punk's early generations, with their lack of sensitivity around such questions. Willis (1993: 373) may have been right about American hardcore representing—consciously or not—"a white male separatist response" to popular culture, and Christian punk may be viewed as a similarly separational expression of contemporary muscular Christianity, a place where young white men can avoid the obligatory egalitarian relationships required *out there* (McCaffree 2017: 91–2). British punk occasionally overlapped with reggae and ska, but it was only the South African Christian punks I met who seriously wrestled with the social and religious implications of punk's narrow demographics, some turning to hip hop as the only music now living up to rock's mythology as the sound of liberated youth. There is also a deeper, final political logic at work, I believe, reminiscent of C. Wright Mills's (1960) famous critique of the British New Left for their "Victorian" devotion to the working class. "Who is it that is thinking and acting in radical ways?" he asked, "it is the young intelligentsia" (1960: 22).

Christian punk, in short, replicates the same tensions and contradictions as its parent cultures: secular punk, CCM, and evangelical youth culture. But as this concluding chapter has suggested, these are often performed simultaneously. This complexity of Christian punk performance is a consequence of the rather remarkable and unexpected achievement of many Christian punk bands to have successfully embedded themselves within secular music scenes, gained the respect of non-evangelical peers, gained the acclaim of non-evangelical critics, and gained a significant number of non-evangelical fans. In surpassing the limitations of CCM and evangelical youth culture more broadly, Christian punk in turn highlights a new set of tensions and contradictions, also analyzed in this book, around the ability of Christianity to make itself comprehensible to young people in increasingly secularizing societies.

References

Bibliography

Abraham, Ibrahim (2012). "A Sociology of Christian Punk," PhD diss., University of Bristol.

Abraham, Ibrahim (2015). "Postsecular Punk: Evangelical Christianity and the Overlapping Consensus of the Underground," *Punk & Post-Punk*, 4 (1): 91–105.

Abraham, Ibrahim (2017). *Evangelical Youth Culture: Alternative Music and Extreme Sports Subcultures*, London: Bloomsbury Academic.

Abraham, Ibrahim (2018). "Sincere Performance in Pentecostal Megachurch Music," *Religions*, 9 (6): article 192.

Abraham, Ibrahim and Umut Parmaksiz (2015). "Australia and Turkey in Postsecular Perspectives," in Michalis Michael (ed.), *Reconciling Cultural and Political Identities in a Globalized World: Perspectives on Australia-Turkey Relations*, 91–111, Basingstoke: Palgrave Macmillan.

Abraham, Ibrahim and Francis Stewart (2014). "Desacralizing Salvation in Straight Edge Christianity and Holistic Spirituality," *International Journal for the Study of New Religions*, 5 (1): 77–102.

Abraham, Ibrahim and Francis Stewart (2017). "Punk and Hardcore," in Christopher Partridge and Marcus Moberg (eds.), *The Bloomsbury Handbook of Religion and Popular Music*, 241–50, London: Bloomsbury Academic.

Acidri, Michael (2012). "Becky the Golden Calf of Christian Radio," *A Twisted Crown of Thorns*, February 19. Available online: https://atwistedcrownofthorns.com/2012/02/19/becky-the-golden-calf-of-christian-radio/ (accessed December 1, 2018).

Adams, Deanna R. (2002). *Rock 'n' Roll and the Cleveland Connection*, Kent, OH: Kent State University Press.

Alfonso, Barry (2002). *The Billboard Guide to Contemporary Christian Music*, New York: Billboard Books.

Ammerman, Nancy (1998). "North American Protestantism Fundamentalism," in Linda Kintz and Julia Lesage (eds.), *Media, Culture, and the Religious Right*, 55–113, Minneapolis: University of Minnesota Press.

Andersen, Mark and Mark Jenkins (2003). *Dance of Days: Two Decades of Punk in the Nation's Capital*, New York: Akashic Books.

Appadurai, Arjun (1996). *Modernity at Large: Cultural Dimensions of Globalization*, Minneapolis: University of Minnesota Press.

Aranza, Jacob (1983). *Backward Masking Unmasked*, Lafayette, LA: Vital Issues Press.

Arrupe, Pedro (1978). "On Inculturation, to the Whole Society," *Jesuit Studies Portal*. Available online: https://jesuitportal.bc.edu/research/documents/1978_arrupeinculturationsociety/ (accessed December 1, 2018).

Astley, Tom (2017). "'Ours Is a Strange Pornography': Reflections on Performing Punk in Academia," *Punk & Post-Punk*, 6 (1): 41–61.

Azerrad, Michael (2001). *Our Band Could Be Your Life: Scenes from the American Indie Underground 1981–1991*, Boston: Little Brown.

Azerrad, Michael (2007 [2004]). "Punk's Earnest New Mission," in Theo Cateforus (ed.), *The Rock History Reader*, 331–5, New York: Routledge.

Babylon Bee (2018). "MxPx Appeals to Early Fans with Special Christian Edition of New Album," *Babylon Bee*, July 25. Available online: https://babylonbee.com/news/mxpx-appeals-to-early-fans-with-special-christian-edition-of-new-album (accessed December 1, 2018).

Baker, Paul (1979). *Why Should the Devil Have All the Good Music? Jesus Music: Where It Began, Where It Is, and Where It Is Going*, Waco: Word Books.

Baker, Paul (2004). *Fantabulosa: A Dictionary of Polari and Gay Slang*, London: Bloomsbury Academic.

Balmer, Randall (2004). *Encyclopedia of Evangelicalism*, rev. edn, Waco: Baylor University Press.

Bangs, Lester (1988). *Psychotic Reactions and Carburetor Dung*, New York: Vintage Books.

Barr, Brian (2005). "A Decade of DIY: 'No Depression' Celebrates American Music," *The Stranger*, September 22. Available online: https://www.thestranger.com/seattle/Content?oid=23188 (accessed December 1, 2018).

Barr, James (1977). *Fundamentalism*, London: SCM Press.

Bayton, Mavis (1997). "Women and the Electric Guitar," in Sheila Whiteley (ed.), *Sexing the Groove: Popular Music and Gender*, 37–49, London: Routledge.

Beaudoin, Tom (1998). *Virtual Faith: The Irreverent Spiritual Quest of Generation X*, San Francisco: Jossey-Bass.

Beaudoin, Tom (2008). *Witness to Dispossession: The Vocation of a Postmodern Theologian*, Maryknoll, NY: Orbis Books.

Beaudoin, Tom (2011). "Twenty-Somethings and Catholicism: Reflections on the Fordham Conference," *America Magazine*, January 31. Available online: https://www.americamagazine.org/content/all-things/twenty-somethings-and-catholicism-reflections-fordham-conference-updated (accessed December 1, 2018).

Beaudoin, Tom (ed.) (2013). *Secular Music and Sacred Theology*, Collegeville, MN: Liturgical Press.

Beaujon, Andrew (2006). *Body Piercing Saved My Life: Inside the Phenomenon of Christian Rock*, Cambridge, MA: Da Capo Press.

Bebbington, David W. (1989). *Evangelicalism in Modern Britain: A History from the 1730s to the 1980s*, London: Unwin Hyman.

Beckford, Robert (2006). *Jesus Dub: Theology, Music and Social Change*, London: Routledge.

Beer, Dave (2014). *Punk Sociology*, Basingstoke: Palgrave Macmillan.

Bellah, Robert N., Richard Madsen, William Sullivan, Ann Swidler, and Steven Tipton (1985). *Habits of the Heart: Individualism and Commitment in American Life*, Berkeley: University of California Press.

Bennett, Andy (1999). "Sub-Cultures or Neo-Tribes? Rethinking the Relationship between Youth Style and Musical Taste," *Sociology*, 33 (3): 599–617.

Bennett, Andy (2000). *Popular Music and Youth Culture: Music, Identity, and Place*, Basingstoke: Palgrave Macmillan.

Bennett, Andy (2011). "The Post-Subcultural Turn: Some Reflections 10 Years On," *Journal of Youth Studies*, 14 (5): 493–506.

Berger, George (2009). *The Story of Crass*, Oakland: PM Press.

Bergler, Thomas E. (2012). *The Juvenilization of American Christianity*, Grand Rapids: Eerdmans.

Bestley, Russ (2015). "(I Want Some) Demystification: Deconstructing Punk," *Punk & Post-Punk*, 4 (2&3): 117–27.

Bidwell, Duane R. (2018). *When One Religion Isn't Enough: The Lives of Spiritually Fluid People*, Boston: Beacon Press.

Blessitt, Arthur (1972). *Tell the World: A Jesus People Manual*, Old Tappan, NJ: Fleming H. Revell Company.

Blush, Steven (2001). *American Hardcore: A Tribal History*, Los Angeles: Feral House.

Boff, Leonardo (1988). *When Theology Listens to the Poor*, San Francisco: Harper & Row.

Boff, Leonardo and Clodovis Boff (1987). *Introduction to Liberation Theology*, Maryknoll, NY: Orbis Books.

Bonomi, Patricia (1986). *Under the Cope of Heaven: Religion, Society, and Politics in Colonial America*, New York: Oxford University Press.

Borthwick, Stewart and Ron Moy (2004). *Popular Music Genres*, Edinburgh: Edinburgh University Press.

Bosch, David J. (1991). *Transforming Mission: Paradigm Shifts in Theology of Mission*, Maryknoll, NY: Orbis Books.

Bouma, Gary (2006). *Australian Soul: Religion and Spirituality in the Twenty-First Century*, Melbourne: Cambridge University Press.

Bowler, Brian W. (2016). "Masculinities and Christian Metal: A Critical Analysis of August Burns Red Lyrics," MSc diss., Utah State University.

Boyer, Paul (1978). *Urban Masses and Moral Order in America, 1820–1920*, Cambridge, MA: Harvard University Press.

Bramadat, Paul (2000). *The Church on the World's Turf: An Evangelical Christian Group at a Secular University*, New York: Oxford University Press.

Bromley, David G. (2012). "The Sociology of New Religious Movements," in Olav Hammer and Mikael Rothstein (eds.), *The Cambridge Companion to New Religious Movements*, 13–28. Cambridge: Cambridge University Press.

Bruce, Steve (1999). *Choice and Religion: A Critique of Rational Choice Theory*, Oxford: Oxford University Press.

Bruce, Steve (2002). *God Is Dead: Secularization in the West*, Oxford: Blackwell.

Bruce, Steve (2011). *Secularization: In Defence of an Unfashionable Theory*, Oxford: Oxford University Press.

Brunner, Jim (2002). "Rules Loosened for All-Ages Dances," *The Seattle Times*, August 13. Available online: http://community.seattletimes.nwsource.com/archive/?date=20 020813&slug=teendance13 (accessed December 1, 2018).

Burgess, Aaron (2006). "Underoath – Define the Great Line," *Alternative Press*, June 7. Available online: http://www.altpress.com/reviews/entry/definethegreatline/ (accessed December 1, 2018).

Cady, Linell E. (2001). "Loosening the Category That Binds: Modern 'Religion' and the Promise of Cultural Studies," in Delwin Brown, Sheila Greeve Davaney, and Kathryn Tanner (eds.), *Converging on Culture: Theologians in Dialogue with Cultural Analysis and Criticism*, 17–40, Oxford: Oxford University Press.

Canedo, Ken (2009). *Keep the Fire Burning: The Folk Mass Revolution*, Portland, OR: Pastoral Press.

Carpenter, Joel A. (1997). *Revive Us Again: The Reawakening of American Fundamentalism*, New York: Oxford University Press.

Carrette, Jeremy and Richard King (2005). *Selling Spirituality: The Silent Takeover of Religion*, London: Routledge.

CCM (1991). "Feedback: You Say You Want a Revolution?" *CCM*, March: 6.

Chastagner, Claude (1999). "The Parents' Music Resource Center: From Information to Censorship," *Popular Music*, 18 (2): 179–92.

Ching, Barbara and Pamela Fox (2008). "Introduction: The Importance of Being Ironic—Toward a Theory and Critique of Alt.Country Music," in Pamela Fox and Barbara Ching (eds.), *Old Roots, New Routes: The Cultural Politics of Alt.Country Music*, 1–27, Ann Arbor: University of Michigan Press.

Christopher, Allison, John Bartkowski, and Timothy Haverda (2018). "Portraits of Veganism: A Comparative Discourse Analysis of a Second-Order Subculture," *Societies*, 8 (3), article 55.

Ciminio, Richard and Christopher Smith (2007). "Secular Humanism and Atheism beyond Progressive Secularism," *Sociology of Religion*, 68 (4): 407–24.

Clarke, John, Stuart Hall, Tony Jefferson and Brian Roberts (1976). "Subcultures, Cultures and Class: A Theoretical Overview," in Stuart Hall and Tony Jefferson (eds.), *Resistance through Rituals: Youth Subcultures in Post-War Britain*, 9–74, London: Hutchinson.

Clifford, James (1983). "On Ethnographic Authority," *Representations*, 2: 118–46.

Cohn, Norman (1957). *The Pursuit of the Millennium: Revolutionary Millenarians and Mystical Anarchists of the Middle Ages*, New York: Oxford University Press.

Cone, James H. (1990). *A Black Theology of Liberation*, 20th an. edn, Maryknoll, NY: Orbis Books.

Congdon, David (2015). *The Mission of Demythologizing: Rudolf Bultmann's Dialectical Theology*, Minneapolis: Augsburg Fortress Press.

Connolly, William (1999). *Why I Am Not a Secularist*, Minneapolis: University of Minnesota Press.

Cross, Terry L. (2007). "The Holy Spirit," in Timothy Larsen and Daniel J. Treler (eds.), *The Cambridge Companion to Evangelical Theology*, 93–108, Cambridge: Cambridge University Press.

Cummings, Tony (1990). "Lust Control: Investigating the Mysterious and Controversial Band from Austin, Texas," *Cross Rhythms*, May 1. Available online: http://www.crossrhythms.co.uk/articles/music/Lust_Control_Investigating_the_mysterious_and_controversial_band_from_Austin_Texas/36239/p1/ (accessed December 1, 2018).

Dale, Pete (2008). "It Was Easy, It Was Cheap, So What? Reconsidering the DIY Principle of Punk and Indie Music," *Popular Music History*, 3 (2): 171–93.

Dalferth, Ingolf U. (2010). "Post-Secular Society: Christianity and the Dialectics of the Secular," *Journal of the American Academy of Religion*, 78 (2): 317–45.

Dancis, Bruce (1978). "Safety Pins and Class Struggle: Punk Rock and the Left," *Socialist Review*, 8 (3): 58–83.

Davis, Joanna R. (2006). "The Scene Is Dead, Long Live the Scene: Music, Identity, and the Transition to Adulthood," PhD diss., University of California, Santa Barbara.

Dawkins, Richard (2006). *The God Delusion*, London: Bantam.

Day, Keith (1987). "Good News!," *Gospel Metal*, Fall: 32–4.

Day, Richard J. F. (2005). *Gramsci Is Dead: Anarchist Currents in the Newest Social Movements*, Toronto: Between the Lines.

DiDonna, John A. and Alexis Levy Neptune (1993). "Who Done It?" *Thieves and Prostitutes*, 8: 7.

Diehl, Matt (2007). *My So-Called Punk*, New York: St Martin's Griffin.

Dixon, Robert (2014). "The Science of Listening: Context and Challenges Facing the Catholic Community in Australia," *Australasian Catholic Record*, 91 (3): 264–80.

Donadio, Rachel (2004). "Faith-Based Publishing," *The New York Times*, November 28. Available online: https://www.nytimes.com/2004/11/28/books/review/faithbased-publishing.html (accessed December 1, 2018).

Doyle, J. D. (2007). "Bear Music: A Look at the Music of the Bear Community," *Queer Music Heritage*, February 1. Available online: http://queermusicheritage.com/feb2007s.html (accessed December 1, 2018).

Driscoll, Mark (2000a). "Pussified Nation," *Mars Hill: Midrash Blog*, May 12. Available online: http://web.archive.org/web/20020921060555/http://www.marshill.fm:80/ubb/Forum1/HTML/000048.html (accessed December 1, 2018).

Driscoll, Mark (2000b). "Seasons of Grace: The Story of Mars Hill," *Mars Hill Fellowship*, December 10. Available online: http://web.archive.org/web/20001210191200/http://www.marshill.fm:80/who/our_history.htm (accessed December 1, 2018).

Driscoll, Mark (2001). "Men and Masculinity," sermon, Mars Hill Church, Seattle, October 28.

Driscoll, Mark (2005). "Isaac Marries Rebekah," sermon, Mars Hill Church, Seattle, March 13.

Driscoll, Mark (2006). *Confessions of a Reformission Rev.: Hard Lessons from an Emerging Missional Church*, Grand Rapids: Zondervan.

Driscoll, Mark (2013). "Mars Hill Music Is Partnering with Tooth & Nail," *Mars Hill Church*, January 15. Available online: http://web.archive.org/web/20140328093500/http://marshill.com/2013/01/15/mars-hill-music-is-partnering-with-tooth-nail (accessed December 1, 2018).

Driscoll, Mark and Jon Dunn (2012). "'We're Starting a Record Label': Pastor Mark Interviews Jon Dunn," *YouTube*, May 2. Available online: https://www.youtube.com/watch?v=fDr0B59_jZA&t=29s (accessed December 1, 2018).

Duncombe, Stephen (1997). *Notes from Underground: Zines and the Politics of Alternative Culture*, New York: Verso.

Edmondson, Jr., Frank M. (1972). "Deviation: Explo '72 Afterthoughts," *Rock in Jesus*, September/October: 22–7.

Eldredge, John (2001). *Wild at Heart: Discovering the Secret of a Man's Soul*, Nashville: Thomas Nelson.

Erricker, Clive (2001). "Living in a Post-Punk Papacy: Religion and Education in a Modernist World," *Journal of Beliefs and Values*, 22 (1): 73–85.

Eskridge, Larry (2013). *God's Forever Family: The Jesus People Movement in America*, New York: Oxford University Press.

Finke, Roger and Rodney Stark (2005). *The Churching of America, 1776–2005: Winners and Losers in Our Religious Economy*, New Brunswick, NJ: Rutgers University Press.

Flory, Richard and Donald E. Miller (2008). *Finding Faith: The Spiritual Quest of the Post-Boomer Generation*, New Brunswick, NJ: Rutgers University Press.

Force, William Ryan (2011). "Consumption Styles and the Fluid Complexity of Punk Authenticity," *Symbolic Interaction*, 32 (4): 289–309.

Fuist, Todd Nicholas and Amy D. McDowell (2019). "Jesus Would Turn the Tables Over: Five Dimensions of Authenticity Applied to Countercultural Christianity," *Symbolic Interaction*, 42 (3): 374–94.

Furness, Zach (ed.) (2012). *Punkademics: The Basement Show in the Ivory Tower*, Wivenhoe, UK: Minor Compositions.

Gardner, Christine J. (2011). *Making Chastity Sexy: The Rhetoric of Evangelical Abstinence Campaigns*, Berkley: University of California Press.

Garnett, Robert (1999). "Too Low to Be Low: Art Pop and the Sex Pistols," in Roger Sabin (ed.), *Punk Rock: So What? The Cultural Legacy of Punk*, 17–30, London: Routledge.

Gendron, Bernard (2002). *Between Montmartre and the Mudd Club: Popular Music and the Avant-Garde*, Chicago: University of Chicago Press.

Goffman, Erving (1963). *Stigma: Notes on the Management of Spoiled Identity*, New York: Simon and Schuster.

Gordon, Alastair (2015). "Pay No More Than 45 Copies: The Collection Legacy of the Crass Record, *Reality Asylum* (1979)," *Punk & Post-Punk*, 4 (1): 7–27.

Gordon, Kenneth D. (2012). "Newbigin as Preacher and Exegete," in Mark T. B. Laing and Paul Weston (eds.), *Theology in Missionary Perspective: Lesslie Newbigin's Legacy*, 88–101, Eugene, OR: Pickwick Publications.

Gormly, Eric (2003). "Evangelizing through Appropriation: Toward a Cultural Theory on the Growth of Contemporary Christian Music," *Journal of Media and Religion*, 2 (4): 251–65.

Gorski, Philip (2017). *American Covenant: A History of Civil Religion from the Puritans to the Present*, Princeton, NJ: Princeton University Press.

Graham, Ruth (2014). "How a Megachurch Melts Down: What the Dissolution of One of America's Fastest-Growing Churches Means for Evangelicalism," *The Atlantic*, November 7. Available online: https://www.theatlantic.com/national/archive/2014/11/houston-mark-driscoll-megachurch-meltdown/382487/ (accessed December 1, 2018).

Greeley, Andrew (2004). *The Catholic Revolution: New Wine, Old Wineskins, and the Second Vatican Council*, Berkley: University of California Press.

Greeley, Anthony and Michael Hout (2006). *The Truth about Conservative Christians: What They Think and What They Believe*, Chicago: University of Chicago Press.

Greve, Justine (2014). "Jesus Didn't Tap: Masculinity, Theology, and Ideology in Christian Mixed Martial Arts," *Religion and American Culture: A Journal of Interpretation*, 24 (2): 141–85.

Grossberg, Lawrence (1990 [1986]). "Is There Rock after Punk?" in Simon Frith and Andrew Goodwin (eds.), *On Record: Rock, Pop and the Written Word*, 111–26, London: Routledge.

Gungor, Michael (2012). *The Crowd, the Critic, and the Muse: A Book for Creators*, Colorado Springs: Woodsley Press.

Gurrentz, Benjamin T. (2013). "'A Brotherhood of Believers': Religious Identity and Boundary-Work in a Christian Fraternity," *Sociology of Religion*, 75 (1): 113–35.

Gushee, David P. (2008). *The Future of Faith in American Politics: The Public Witness of the Evangelical Center*, Waco: Baylor University Press.

Gushee, David P. (2019). "2018 AAR Presidential Address: In the Ruins of White Evangelicalism: Interpreting a Compromised Christian Tradition through the Witness of African American Literature," *Journal of the American Academy of Religion*, 87 (1): 1–17.

Gutiérrez, Gustavo (1988). *A Theology of Liberation: History, Politics, and Salvation*, rev. ed., Maryknoll, NY: Orbis Books.

Habermas, Jürgen (2006). "Religion in the Public Sphere," *European Journal of Philosophy*, 14 (1): 1–25.

Habermas, Jürgen (2008a). *Europe: The Faltering Project*, Cambridge: Polity.

Habermas, Jürgen (2008b). *Between Naturalism and Religion*, Cambridge: Polity.

Habermas, Jürgen and Joseph Ratzinger (2007). *The Dialectics of Secularization: On Reason and Religion*, San Francisco: Ignatius Press.

Haenfler, Ross (2006). *Straight Edge: Hardcore Punk, Clean Living Youth, and Social Change*, New Brunswick, NJ: Rutgers University Press.

Haenfler, Ross (2013). "'More Than the Xs on My Hands': Older Straight Edgers and the Meaning of Style," in Andy Bennett and Paul Hodkinson (eds.), *Aging and Youth Cultures: Music, Style and Identity*, 9–23, London: Bloomsbury Academic.

Hall, Stuart and Tony Jefferson (eds.) (1976). *Resistance through Rituals: Youth Subcultures in Post-War Britain*, London: Hutchinson.

Hammer, Olav (2010). "I Did It My Way? Individual Choice and Social Conformity in New Age Religion," in Stef Aupers and Dick Houtman (eds.), *Religions of Modernity: Relocating the Sacred to the Self and the Digital*, 49–67, Leiden: Brill.

Hansen, Collin (2008). *Young, Restless, Reformed: A Journalist's Journey with the New Calvinists*, Wheaton, IL: Crossway Books.

Harding, Susan (1991). "Representing Fundamentalism: The Problem of the Repugnant Cultural Other," *Social Research*, 58 (2): 373–93.

Harding, Susan (2000). *The Book of Jerry Falwell: Fundamentalist Language and Politics*, Princeton: Princeton University Press.

Harper, Judd (1988a). "Eternal Life," *Rizzen Roxx*, 20: 2.

Harper, Judd (1988b). "Denomination Dance," *Rizzen Roxx*, 20: 4–5.

Heartney, Eleanor (2018). *Postmodern Heretics: The Catholic Imagination in Contemporary Art*, 2nd edn, New York: Silver Hollow Press.

Heaven's Metal (1986). "Abortion Is Murder!" *Heaven's Metal*, 2 (6): 15.

Hebdige, Dick (1979). *Subculture: The Meaning of Style*, London: Methuen.

Heelas, Paul (1996). *The New Age Movement: The Celebration of the Self and the Sacralization of Modernity*, Oxford: Blackwell.

Heelas, Paul (2008). *Spiritualities of Life: Romantic Themes and Consumptive Capitalism*, Oxford: Blackwell.

Heelas, Paul and Linda Woodhead (2005). *The Spiritual Revolution: Why Religion Is Giving Way to Spirituality*, Oxford: Blackwell.

Heisel, Scott (2005). "Building the Church on the Punk Rock," *Alternative Press*, 208: 87–102.

Helb, Colin (2014). "'The Time Is Right to Set Our Sight on Salvation:' The Strange Tale of How the Hare Krishnas Came to Play Hardcore Punk," in Eric James Abbey and Colin Helb (eds.), *Hardcore, Punk, and Other Junk: Aggressive Sounds in Contemporary Music*, 139–67, Lanham, MD: Lexington Books.

Hendershot, Heather (2004). *Shaking the World for Jesus: Media and Conservative Evangelical Culture*, Chicago: University of Chicago Press.

Henry, Tricia (1989). *Break All Rules!: Punk Rock and the Making of a Style*, Ann Arbor, MI: UMI Research Press.

Herberg, Will (1955). *Protestant—Catholic—Jew: An Essay in American Religious Sociology*, New York: Doubleday.

Heylin, Clinton (2005). *From the Velvets to the Voidoids: The Birth of American Punk Rock*, 2nd edn, London: Helter Skelter.

Heyrman, Christine Leigh (1997). *Southern Cross: The Beginnings of the Bible Belt*, Chapel Hill: University of North Carolina Press.

Hollywood Free Paper (1969). "Wanted: Jesus Christ," *Hollywood Free Paper*, 1 (1): 7.

Hollywood Free Paper (1970a). "Christian You're Next," *Hollywood Free Paper*, 2 (3): 1.

Hollywood Free Paper (1970b). "All Power through Jesus," *Hollywood Free Paper*, 2 (18): 8.

Hollywood Free Paper (1971a). "Jesus Is the Liberator," *Hollywood Free Paper*, 3 (1): 14.

Hollywood Free Paper (1971b). "All Power to the People thru Jesus," *Hollywood Free Paper*, 3 (3): 2.

Holmes, Peter R. (2007). "Spirituality: Some Disciplinary Perspectives," in Kieran Flanagan and Peter C. Jupp (eds.), *A Sociology of Spirituality*, 23–42, Aldershot: Ashgate.

Holtzman, Ben, Craig Hughes, and Kevin Van Meter (2007). "Do It Yourself, and the Movement beyond Capitalism," in Stevphen Shukaitis, David Graeber, and Erika Biddle (eds.), *Constituent Imagination: Militant Investigations/Collective Theorization*, 44–61, Oakland: AK Press.

Home, Stewart (1995). *Cranked Up Really High: Genre Theory and Punk Rock*, Hove: Codex.

Hookway, Nicholas (2015). "Moral Decline Sociology: Critiquing the Legacy of Durkheim," *Journal of Sociology*, 51 (2): 271–84.

Hookway, Nicholas (2018). "The Moral Self: Class, Narcissism and the Problem of Do-It-Yourself Moralities," *The Sociological Review*, 66 (1): 107–21.

Hopps, Gavin (2017). "Theology, Imagination and Popular Music," in Christopher Partridge and Marcus Moberg (eds.), *The Bloomsbury Handbook of Religion and Popular Music*, 77–89, London: Bloomsbury Academic.

Hornbeck, J. Patrick, II (2011). "Deconversion from Roman Catholicism: Mapping a Fertile Field," *American Catholic Studies*, 122 (2): 1–29.

Horne, Stephen A. (1992). "Concert Review," *CCM*, May: 35.

Houtman, Dick and Stef Aupers (2010). "Religions of Modernity: Relocating the Sacred to the Self and the Digital," in Stef Aupers and Dick Houtman (eds.), *Religions of Modernity: Relocating the Sacred to the Self and the Digital*, 1–29, Leiden: Brill.

Howard, Jay R. (1992). "Contemporary Christian Music: Where Rock Meets Religion," *Journal of Popular Culture*, 26 (1): 123–30.

Howard, Jay R. and John M. Streck (1999). *Apostles of Rock: The Splintered World of Contemporary Christian Music*, Lexington: University Press of Kentucky.

Hunter, James Davison (1991). *Culture Wars: The Struggle to Define America*, New York: Basic Books.

Iafrate, Michael J. (2011). "'I'm a Human, Not a *Statue*': Saints and Saintliness in the Church of Punk Rock," paper presented at the Catholic Theological Society of America Annual Convention, San Jose, CA, June 10.

Iafrate, Michael J. (2013). "More Than Music: Notes on 'Staying Punk' in the Church and in Theology," in Tom Beaudoin (ed.), *Secular Music and Sacred Theology*, 35–58, Collegeville, MN: Liturgical Press.

Iafrate, Michael J. (2017). "Punk Rock and/as Liberation Theology," in Michael O'Connor, Hyun-ah Kim, and Christina Labriola (eds.), *Music, Theology, and Justice*, 21–42, Lanham, MD: Lexington Books.

Ingalls, Monique M. (2015). "Transnational Connections, Musical Meaning, and the 1990s 'British Invasion' of North American Evangelical Worship Music," in Jonathan Dueck and Suzel Ana Reily (eds.), *The Oxford Handbook of Music and World Christianities*, 425–45, New York: Oxford University Press.

Ingalls, Monique M. (2018). *Singing the Congregation: How Contemporary Worship Music Forms Evangelical Community*, New York: Oxford University Press.

Isaac, Rhys (1982). *The Transformation of Virginia, 1740–1790*, Chapel Hill: University of North Carolina Press.

Jennings, Mark (2008). "'Won't You Break Free?' An Ethnography of Music and the Divine-Human Encounter at an Australian Pentecostal Church," *Culture and Religion*, 9 (2): 161–74.

Jennings, Mark (2015). "An Extraordinary Degree of Exaltation: Durkheim, Effervescence and Pentecostalism's Defeat of Secularisation," *Social Compass*, 62 (1): 61–75.

Johnson, Mark (2014). *Seditious Theology: Punk and the Ministry of Jesus*, London: Routledge.

Judson Press (1971). *The Street People: Selections from "Right On!" Berkeley's Christian Underground Student Newspaper*, Valley Forge: Judson Press.

Julian, J. J. (1990). "K.C. News," *The Burning Bush*, 13: 18–19.

Kahn-Harris, Keith (2007). *Extreme Metal: Music Culture on the Edge*, New York: Berg.

Kennedy, Dan (1984). "Review of Under a Blood Red Sky by U2," *Cutting Edge*, 1 (2): 1.

Kennedy, Dan (1992). "That's 100 Issues Not 100 Years! An Interview with Dan Kennedy by David Clay," *Cutting Edge*, 9 (3–4): 7.

Kennedy, David (1990). "Frankenchrist versus the State: The New Right, Rock Music, and the Case of Jello Biafra," *Journal of Popular Culture*, 24 (1): 131–48.

Kent, Stephen A. (2001). *From Slogans to Mantras: Social Protest and Religious Conversion in the Late Vietnam War Era*, Syracuse: Syracuse University Press.

Kern County Kid (2006). "Underoath – Define the Great Line," *HM Magazine*, July. Available online: https://web.archive.org/web/20120910130329/http://www.hmmagazine.com/reviews/album/u/underoath0606.php (accessed December 1, 2018).

Korte, Anne-Marie (2014). "Pussy Riot's Punk Prayer as a Case of/for Feminist Public Theology," *Journal of the European Society of Women in Theological Research*, 22: 31–53.

Kwok, Pui-Ian (2005). *Postcolonial Imagination and Feminist Theology*, Louisville: WJK Press.

Lahickey, Beth (1997). *All Ages: Reflections on Straight Edge*, Huntington Beach: Revelation Records Books.

Lahr, Angela M. (2007). *Millennial Dreams and Apocalyptic Nightmares: The Cold War Origins of Political Evangelicalism*, New York: Oxford University Press.

Laing, Dave (2015). *One Chord Wonders: Power and Meaning in Punk Rock*, 2nd edn, Oakland, CA: PM Press.

Lamb, Hillary (2017). "'Shot by Both Sides': What It's Like to Be a Punk in Academia," *Times Higher Education*, February 9. Available online: https://www.timeshighereducation.com/news/shot-by-both-sides-what-its-like-to-be-a-punk-in-academia (accessed December 1, 2018).

Larsen, Alan Edward (2008). "Selling (Out) the Local Scene: Grunge and Globalization," PhD diss., State University of New York at Buffalo.

Lausanne Movement (1974). "The Lausanne Covenant: The Urgency of the Evangelistic Task," *Lausanne Movement*. Available online: https://www.lausanne.org/content/covenant/lausanne-covenant (accessed December 1, 2018).

Lausanne Committee for World Evangelization (1978). "Lausanne Occasional Paper 2—The Willowbank Report: Consultation on Gospel and Culture," Lausanne Committee for World Evangelization. Available online: https://www.lausanne.org/content/lop/lop-2 (accessed December 1, 2018).

Lawhead, Steve (1981). *Rock Reconsidered: A Christian Looks at Contemporary Music*, Downers Grove, IL: InterVarsity Press.

Leblanc, Lauraine (1999). *Pretty in Punk: Girl's Gender Resistance in a Boy's Subculture*, New Brunswick, NJ: Rutgers University Press.

Lentini, Pete (2003). "Punk's Origins: Anglo-American Syncretism," *Journal of Intercultural Studies*, 24 (2): 153–74.

Lewin, Philip and J. Patrick Williams (2009). "The Ideology and Practice of Authenticity in Punk Subculture," in Philip Lewin and J. Patrick Williams (eds.), *Authenticity in Culture, Self and Society*, 65–83, Farnham, UK: Ashgate.

Lindsay, Hal (1970). *The Late Great Planet Earth*, Grand Rapids: Zondervan.

Living Bible: Paraphrased, The (1971). Carol Springs, IL: Tyndale House.

Lopez, Steve (1999). "The Mutant Brady Bunch," *Time*, August 30. Available online: http://content.time.com/time/magazine/article/0,9171,991840,00.html (accessed December 1, 2018).

Ludy, Eric (2003). *God's Gift to Women: Discovering the Lost Greatness of Masculinity*, Colorado Springs: Multnomah Books.

Luhr, Eileen (2009). *Witnessing Suburbia: Conservatives and Christian Youth Culture*, Berkeley: University of California Press.

Luhr, Eileen (2010). "Punk, Metal and American Religions," *Religion Compass*, 4 (7): 443–51.

Luhr, Eileen (2013). "'A Revolutionary Mission': Young Evangelicals and the Language of the Sixties," in Axel R. Schäfer (ed.), *American Evangelicals and the 1960s*, 61–80, Madison: University of Wisconsin Press.

MacDougall, Joy Ann (2011). "Sin," in Ian A. McFarland (ed.), *The Cambridge Dictionary of Christian Theology*, 472–5, Cambridge: Cambridge University Press.

Maffesoli, Michel (1996). *The Time of the Tribes: The Decline of Individualism in Mass Society*, London: Sage.

Magolda, Peter and Kelsey Ebben Gross (2009). *It's All about Jesus! Faith as an Oppositional Collegiate Subculture*, Sterling, VA: Stylus.

Mall, Andrew (2012). "'The Stars Are Underground': Undergrounds, Mainstreams, and Christian Popular Music," PhD diss., University of Chicago.

Mall, Andrew (2015a). "'This Is a Chance to Come Together': Subcultural Resistance and Community at Cornerstone Festival," in Anna Nekola and Tom Wagner (eds.), *Congregational Music-Making and Community in a Mediated Age*, 101–21, Farnham, UK: Ashgate.

Mall, Andrew (2015b). "'We Can Be Renewed': Resistance, Renewal, and Worship at the Anchor Fellowship," in Monique Ingalls and Amos Yong (eds.), *The Spirit of Praise: Music and Worship in Pentecostal-Charismatic Christianity*, 163–78, University Park, PA: Pennsylvania State University Press.

Mall, Andrew (2020). "Music Festivals, Ephemeral Places, and Scenes: Attending and Producing Cornerstone Festival," *Journal of the Society for American Music*, 14 (1).

Malott, Curry (2009). "Christotainment in Punk Rock: Complexities and Contradictions," in Shirley Steinberg and Joe Kinchlove (eds.), *Christotainment: Selling Jesus through Popular Culture*, 247–68, Boulder: Westview Press.

Marcus, Greil (1989). *Lipstick Traces: A Secret History of the Twentieth Century*, London: Secker & Warburg.

Marsh, Clive (2007). "Theology as 'Soundtrack': Popular Culture and Narratives of the Self," *Expository Times*, 118 (11): 536–41.

McCaffree, Kevin (2017). *The Secular Landscape: The Decline of Religion in America*, Basingstoke: Palgrave Macmillan.

McDannell, Colleen (1995). *Material Christianity: Religion and Popular Culture*, New Haven: Yale University Press.

McDowell, Amy D. (2014). "Warriors and Terrorists: Antagonism as Strategy in Christian Hardcore and Muslim 'Taqwacore' Punk Rock," *Qualitative Sociology*, 37 (3): 255–76.

McDowell, Amy D. (2017). "Aggressive and Loving Men: Gender Hegemony in Christian Hardcore Punk," *Gender & Society*, 31 (2): 223–44.

McDowell, Amy D. (2018). "'Christian but Not Religious': Being Church as Christian Hardcore Punk," *Sociology of Religion*, 79 (1): 58–77.

McLennan, Gregor (2007). "Towards a Postsecular Sociology?" *Sociology*, 41 (5): 857–70.

Miller, Kiri (2008). *Traveling Home: Sacred Harp Singing and American Pluralism*, Urbana: University of Illinois Press.

Mills, C. Wright (1960). "Letter to the New Left," *New Left Review (1st Series)*, 5: 18–23.

Miner, Dylan and Estrella Torrez (2012). "Turning Point: Claiming the University as a Punk Space," in Zach Furness (ed.), *Punkademics: The Basement Show in the Ivory Tower*, 27–35, Wivenhoe, UK: Minor Compositions.

Moberg, Marcus (2012). "Religion in Popular Music or Popular Music as Religion? A Critical Review of Scholarly Writing on the Place of Religion in Metal Music and Culture," *Popular Music & Society*, 35 (1): 113–30.

Moberg, Marcus (2015). *Christian Metal: History, Ideology, Scene*, London: Bloomsbury Academic.

Moltmann, Jürgen (2001). "Dialogue or Mission? Christianity and the Religions in an Endangered World," in John Hick and Brian Hebblethwaite (eds), *Christianity and Other Religions*, 172–87, Oxford: Oneworld.

Monger, James Christopher (2006). "Define the Great Line," *AllMusic*. Available online: https://www.allmusic.com/album/define-the-great-line-mw0000442244 (accessed December 1, 2018).

Moore, Allan F. (2002). "Authenticity as Authentication," *Popular Music*, 21 (2): 209–23.

Moore, R. Laurence (1986). *Religious Outsiders and the Making of America*, New York: Oxford University Press.

Moore, R. Laurence (2003). *Touchdown Jesus: The Mixing of Sacred and Secular in American History*, Louisville: Westminster John Knox Press.

Moore, Ryan. (2004). "Postmodernism and Punk Subculture: Cultures of Authenticity and Deconstruction," *The Communication Review*, 7 (3): 305–27.

Moore, Ryan (2007). "Friends Don't Let Friends Listen to Corporate Rock: Punk as a Field of Cultural Production," *Journal of Contemporary Ethnography*, 36 (4): 438–74.

Moore, Ryan and Michael Roberts (2009). "Do-It-Yourself Mobilization: Punk and Social Movements," *Mobilization: An International Journal*, 14 (3): 273–91.

Morone, James (2003). *Hellfire Nation: The Politics of Sin in American History*, New Haven: Yale University Press.

Mullaney, Jamie L. (2007). "Unity Admirable but Not Necessarily Heeded: Going Rates and Gender Boundaries in the Straight Edge Hardcore Music Scene," *Gender & Society*, 21 (3): 384–408.

Murashko. Alex (2012). "Seattle-Based Megachurch Launches Mars Hill Music," *The Christian Post*, June 7. Available online: https://www.christianpost.com/news/seattle-based-megachurch-launches-mars-hill-music-label-76203/ (accessed December 1, 2018).

Myrick, Nathan (2017). "The Last Goodbyes," *HM Magazine*, February 9. Available online: https://hmmagazine.com/feature/mattie-montgomery-for-today-farewell/ (accessed December 1, 2018).

Myrick, Nathan (2018). "Double Authenticity: Celebrity, Consumption, and the Christian Worship Music Industry," *The Hymn*, 69 (2): 21–7.

Neptune, Alexis Levy (1993). "Christian Punk?" *Thieves and Prostitutes*, 8: 8–9.

Newbigin, Lesslie (1985). *Unfinished Agenda: An Autobiography*, Grand Rapids: Eerdmans.

Niebuhr, H. Richard (1975). *Christ and Culture*, New York: Harper & Row.

Nikolajsen, Jeppe Bach (2013). "Missional Church: A Historical and Theological Analysis of an Ecclesiological Tradition," *International Review of Mission*, 102 (2): 249–61.

O'Brien, Lucy (1999). "The Woman Punk Made Me," in Roger Sabin (ed.), *Punk Rock: So What? The Cultural Legacy of Punk*, 186–98, London: Routledge.

O'Connor, Alan (2008). *Punk Record Labels and the Struggle for Autonomy: The Emergence of DIY*, Lanham, MD: Lexington Books.

Oliveros, Roberto (1993). "History of the Theology of Liberation," in Ignacio Ellacuría and Jon Sobrino (eds.), *Mysterium Liberationis: Fundamental Concepts of Liberation Theology*, 3–32, Maryknoll, NY: Orbis Books.

Ollie Mob (n.d.). "Ollie Mob Registration," Available online: https://form.jotform.com/82406361684156 (accessed December 1, 2018).

Paradox, The (2005). "About Us," *The Paradox*, February 6. Available online: https://web.archive.org/web/20050206224106/http://www.theparadox.org/site/node/view/3 (accessed December 1, 2018).

Parkinson, Tom (2017). "Being Punk in Higher Education: Subcultural Strategies for Academic Practice," *Teaching in Higher Education*, 22 (2): 143–57.

Parmett, Helen Morgan (2015). "'Shredding' the Love: A Feminist Political Economy Critique of Gendered Lifestyle Branding," *Journal of Sport and Social Issues*, 39 (3): 202–24.

Partridge, Christopher and Marcus Moberg (eds.) (2017). *The Bloomsbury Handbook of Religion and Popular Music*, London: Bloomsbury Academic.

Paul VI (1965). *Ad Gentes*. Available online: http://www.vatican.va/archive/hist_councils/ii_vatican_council/documents/vat-ii_decree_19651207_ad-gentes_en.html (accessed December 1, 2018).

Peck, Abe (1985). *Uncovering the Sixties: The Life and Times of the Underground Press*, New York: Pantheon Press.

Peterson, Brian (2009). *Burning Fight: The Nineties Hardcore Revolution in Ethics, Politics, Spirit and Sound*, Huntington Beach: Revelation Records Books.

Plate, S. Brent (2006). *Blasphemy: Art That Offends*, London: Black Dog Press.

Powell, Mark Allan (2002). *The Encyclopedia of Contemporary Christian Music*, Peabody, MA: Hendrickson Publishers.

Pussy Riot (2013). "Virgin Mary, Put Putin Away (A Punk Prayer)," in Pussy Riot (ed.), *Pussy Riot!: A Punk Prayer for Freedom*, 13–14, New York: The Feminist Press.

Putney, Clifford (2001). *Muscular Christianity: Manhood and Sports in Protestant America, 1880–1920*, Cambridge, MA: Harvard University Press.

Rabey, Steve (1998). "Age to Age," *CCM*, July: 19.

Rabinow, Paul (1986). "Representations Are Social Facts: Modernity and Post-Modernity in Anthropology," in James Clifford and George E. Marcus (eds.), *Writing and Culture: The Poetics and Politics of Ethnography*, 234–61, Berkeley: University of California Press.

Rademacher, Heidi E. (2015). "'Men of Iron Will': Idealized Gender in Christian Heavy Metal," *Social Compass*, 62 (4): 632–48.

Radosh, Daniel (2008). *Rapture Ready!: Adventures in the Parallel Universe of Christian Pop Culture*, New York: Scribner.

Rollins, Henry (1997). *Get in the Van: On the Road with Black Flag*, Los Angeles: 12-13-61Press.

Romanowski, William D. (2000). "Evangelicals and Popular Music: The Contemporary Christian Music Industry," in Bruce Forbes and Jeffrey Mahan (eds.), *Religion and Popular Culture in America*, 105–24, Berkeley: University of California Press.

Romanowski, William D. (2001). *Eyes Wide Open: Looking for God in Popular Culture*, Grand Rapids: Brazos Press.

Roof, Wade Clark (1999). *Spiritual Marketplace: Baby Boomers and the Remaking of American Religion*, Princeton: Princeton University Press.

Rossinow, Doug (1998). *The Politics of Authenticity: Liberalism, Christianity, and the New Left in America*, New York: Columbia University Press.

Sabin, Roger (1999). "Introduction," in Roger Sabin (ed.), *Punk Rock: So What? The Cultural Legacy of Punk*, 1–13, London: Routledge.

Salomon, Mark (2005). *Simplicity*, Orlando: Relevant Books.

Sample, Tex (1996). *White Soul: Country Music, the Church and Working Americans*, Nashville: Abingdon Press.

Sanneh, Kelefa (2004). "The Rap against Rockism," *The New York Times*, October 31. Available online: https://www.nytimes.com/2004/10/31/arts/music/the-rap-against-rockism.html (accessed December 1, 2018).

Saunders, Martin (2018). "'Christianity Ruined My Life': Rock Star Slams His Former Faith, But Who's Really to Blame?" *Christian Today*, March 22. Available online: https://www.christiantoday.com/article/christianity-ruined-my-life-rock-star-slams-his-former-faith-but-whos-really-to-blame/127722.htm (accessed December 1, 2018).

Savage, Jon (2002). *England's Dreaming*, 2nd edn, London: Faber.

Savage, Jon (2008). *Teenage: The Prehistory of Youth Culture: 1875–1945*, London: Penguin Books.

Schmidt, Rich (1971). "Can You Dig It?" *Hollywood Free Paper*, 1 (2): 30–3.

Schwalbe, Michael (1996). *Unlocking the Iron Cage: The Men's Movement, Gender Politics, and American Culture*, New York: Oxford University Press.

Sciarretto, Amy (2010). "Interview with Facedown Records Founder Jason Dunn," *Noisecreep*, April 13. Available online: http://noisecreep.com/interview-with-facedown-records-founder-jason-dunn/ (accessed December 1, 2018).

Seay, Davin with Mary Neely (1986). *Stairway to Heaven: The Spiritual Roots of Rock'n'Roll: From the King and Little Richard to Prince and Amy Grant*, New York: Ballantine Books.

Seling, Megan (2002). "Underage: At the Paradox," *The Stranger*, December 12. Available online: http://www.thestranger.com/seattle/underage/Content?oid=12810 (accessed December 1, 2018).

Sheldrake, Philip (2007). *A Brief History of Spirituality*, Oxford: Blackwell.

Sheldrake, Philip (2016). "Constructing Spirituality: The 'Politics' of Definitions and Historical Interpretations," *Religion & Theology*, 23 (1): 15–34.

Shires, Preston (2006). *Hippies of the Religious Right*, Waco: Baylor University Press.

Shuker, Roger (2001). *Understanding Popular Music*, 2nd edn, London: Routledge.

Silverman, Gary (2017). "How the Bible Belt Lost God and Found Trump," *Financial Times*, April 13. Available online: https://www.ft.com/content/b41d0ee6-1e96-11e7-b7d3-163f5a7f229c (accessed December 1, 2018).

Simpson, John H. (1990). "The Stark-Bainbridge Theory of Religion," *Journal for the Scientific Study of Religion*, 29 (3): 367–71.

Sinker, Mark (1999). "Concrete, So as to Self-Destruct: The Etiquette of Punk, Its Habits, Rules, Values and Dilemmas," in Roger Sabin (ed.), *Punk Rock: So What? The Cultural Legacy of Punk*, 120–39, London: Routledge.

Slaughter House (1990). "Title Page," *Slaughter House*, 4: 2.

Small, Christopher (1998). *Musicking: The Meanings of Performing and Listening*, Middleton, CT: Wesleyan University Press.

Smith, Christian (1998). *American Evangelicalism: Embattled and Thriving*, Chicago: University of Chicago Press.

Smith, Christian (2000). *Christian America? What Evangelicals Really Want*, Berkeley: University of California Press.

Smith, Christian (2010). "On 'Moral Therapeutic Deism' as American Teenagers' Actual, Tacit, and De Facto Religious Faith," in Sylvia Collins-Mayo and Pink Dandelion (eds.), *Religion and Youth*, 41–6, Farnham, UK: Ashgate.

Smith, Christian and Melinda Lundquist Denton (2005). *Soul Searching: The Religious and Spiritual Lives of American Teenagers*, New York: Oxford University Press.

Sobrino, Jon (2001). *Christ the Liberator: A View from the Victims*, Maryknoll, NY: Orbis Books.

Sommer, Tim (2017). "You're an Idiot if You're Mad at John Lydon for Praising Trump and Brexit," *Observer*, April 13. Available online: https://observer.com/2017/04/john-lydon-donald-trump-brexit-comments/ (accessed December 1, 2018).

Squip, Tomas (1990). "Tomas Squip," in Martin Sprouse (ed.), *Threat by Example: A Documentation of Inspiration*, 49–52, San Francisco: Pressure Drop Press.

Stark, Rodney and Roger Finke (2000). *Acts of Faith: Explaining the Human Side of Religion*, Berkeley: University of California Press.

Stewart, Francis (2015). "The Anarchist, the Punk Rocker and the Buddhist Walk into a Bar(n): Dharma Punx and Rebel Dharma," *Punk & Post-Punk*, 4 (1): 71–89.

Stewart, Francis (2017). *Punk Rock Is My Religion: Straight Edge Punk and "Religious" Identity*, London: Routledge.

Stowe, David W. (2004). *How Sweet the Sound: Music in the Spiritual Lives of Americans*, Cambridge, MA: Harvard University Press.

Stowe, David W. (2011). *No Sympathy for the Devil: Christian Pop Music and the Transformation of American Evangelicalism*, Chapel Hill: University of North Carolina Press.

Strongman, Phil (2007). *Pretty Vacant: A History of Punk*, London: Orion.

Styll, John W. (1991). "It's Time for a New Revolution," *CCM*, January: 24.

Svenonius, Ian. F. (2007). "Fugazi and Rock 'n' Roll," in *Keep Your Eyes Open: The Fugazi Photographs of Glen E. Friedman*, New York: Burning Flags Press.

Taiz, Lillian (2001). *Hallelujah Lads and Lasses: Remaking the Salvation Army in America, 1880–1930*, Chapel Hill: University of North Carolina Press.

Take a Stand (1987). "Correspondence Directory," *Take a Stand*, December: 5.

Tamás, Gáspár Miklós (2006). "Telling the Truth about Class," *Socialist Register*, 42: 228–68.

Tamás, Gáspár Miklós (2013). "Words from Budapest," *New Left Review (2nd Series)*, 80: 5–23.

Tarazi, Paul N. (1991). *The Old Testament: Prophetic Traditions*, New York: St Vladimir's Seminary Press.

Taylor, Charles (1989). *Sources of the Self: The Making of Modern Identity*, Cambridge, MA: Harvard University Press.

Taylor, Charles (1992). *The Ethics of Authenticity*, Cambridge, MA: Harvard University Press.

Taylor, Charles (2007). *A Secular Age*, Cambridge, MA: Harvard University Press.

Taylor, Jodie (2012). *Playing It Queer: Popular Music, Identity and Queer World-Making*. Bern: Peter Lang.

Taylor, Josh (2006). "Underoath – Define the Great Line," *Jesus Freak Hideout*, June 20. Available online: http://www.jesusfreakhideout.com/cdreviews/DefineTheGreatLine. asp (accessed December 1, 2018).

Taylor, Mark McClain (1996). "Tracking Spirit: Theology as Cultural Critique in America," in Dwight N. Hopkins and Sheila Greeve Davaney (eds.), *Changing Conversations: Religious Reflection and Cultural Analysis*, 123–44, New York: Routledge.

Taylor, Mark Lewis (2003a). "Bringing Noise, Conjuring Spirit: Rap as Spiritual Practice," in Anthony Pinn (ed.), *Noise and Spirit: The Religious and Spiritual Sensibilities of Rap Music*, 107–30, New York: New York University Press.

Taylor, Mark Lewis (2003b). "Subalternity and Advocacy as *Kairos* for Theology," in Joerg Rieger (ed.), *Opting for the Margins: Postmodernity and Liberation in Christian Theology*, 23–44, Oxford: Oxford University Press.

Taylor, Mark Lewis (2004). "Spirit and Liberation: Achieving Postcolonial Theology in the United States," in Catherine Keller, Michael Nausner, and Mayra Rivera (eds.), *Postcolonial Theologies: Divinity and Empire*, 39–55, St. Louis: Chalice Press.

Taylor, Ojo (2012). "Huffington Post Interview – Extended and Unedited," *Ojo Taylor*, October 3. Available online: https://ojotaylor.wordpress.com/2012/10/03/huffington-post-interview-extended-and-unedited/ (accessed December 1, 2018).

Thompson, John J. (2000). *Raised by Wolves: The Story of Christian Rock*, Toronto: ECW Press.

Thompson, Stacy (2004). *Punk Productions: Unfinished Business*, Albany: SUNY Press.

Thornton, Sarah (1995). *Club Cultures: Music, Media, and Subcultural Capital*, Cambridge: Polity.

Throckmorton, Warren (2014). "Twenty-One Former Mars Hill Church Pastors Bring Charges against Mark Driscoll," *Patheos*, August 21. Available online: https://web.archive.org/web/20150215041027/http://www.patheos.com/blogs/warrenthrockmorton/2014/08/21/former-mars-hill-church-pastors-bring-formal-charges-against-mark-driscoll (accessed December 1, 2018).

Till, Rupert (2010). *Pop Cult: Religion and Popular Music*, London: Continuum.

Torrey, R. A. and A. C. Dixon (eds.) (1984 [1917]). *The Fundamentals: A Testimony to the Truth*, 4 vols., Grand Rapids: Baker.

Traber, Daniel (2001). "LA's 'White Minority': Punk and the Contradictions of Self-Marginalization," *Cultural Critique*, 48 (1): 30–64.

Traber, Daniel (2008). "Locating the Punk Preppy (A Speculative Theory)," *Journal of Popular Culture*, 41 (3): 488–508.

Trapp, Philip (2018). "Watch Underoath Share Their Last Words on Christianity," *Alternative Press*, July 24. Available online: https://www.altpress.com/news/underoath-christianity-three-thoughts/ (accessed December 1, 2018).

Tschmuck, Peter (2006). *Creativity and Innovation in the Music Industry*, Dordrecht: Springer.

Turner, John G (2008). *Bill Bright and Campus Crusade for Christ: The Renewal of Evangelicalism in Postwar America*, Chapel Hill: University of North Carolina Press.

Van Steenwyk, Mark (2017). "Take the Politics of Disruption to Church," *Sojourners Online*, February 21. Available online: https://sojo.net/articles/take-politics-disruption-church (accessed December 1, 2018).

Wacker, Grant (2001). *Heaven Below: Early Pentecostals and American Culture*, Cambridge, MA: Harvard University Press.

Waksman, Steve (2009). *This Ain't the Summer of Love: Conflict and Crossover in Heavy Metal and Punk*, Berkeley: University of California Press.

Walser, Robert (1993). *Running with the Devil: Power, Gender, and Madness in Heavy Metal Music*, Middletown, CT: Wesleyan University Press.

Walsh, Steve and Mark Perry (2017 [1976]). "The Very Angry Clash," in Sean Egan (eds.), *The Clash on the Clash: Interviews and Encounters*, 44–54, Chicago: Chicago Review Press.

Warner, R. Stephen (1993). "Work in Progress toward a New Paradigm for the Sociological Study of Religion in the United States," *American Journal of Sociology*, 98 (5): 1044–93.

Warner, R. Stephen (2008). "2007 Presidential Address: Singing and Solidarity," *Journal for the Scientific Study of Religion*, 47 (2): 175–90.

Warner, Rob (2010). *Secularization and Its Discontents*, London: Continuum.

Watts, Galen (2018). "On the Politics of Self-Spirituality: A Canadian Case Study," *Studies in Religion/Sciences Religieuses*, 47 (3): 345–72.

Weber, Max (1992 [1930]). *The Protestant Ethic and the Spirit of Capitalism*, London: Routledge.

Weinstein, Deena (2000). *Heavy Metal: The Music and Its Culture*, 2nd edn, Boston: Da Capo Press.

Weninger, Csilla and J. Patrick Williams (2017). "The Interactional Construction of Social Authenticity: 'Real' Identities and Intergroup Relations in a Transylvania Internet Forum," *Symbolic Interaction*, 40 (2): 169–89.

Wigger, John H. (1994). "Taking Heaven by Storm: Enthusiasm and Early American Methodism, 1770–1820," *Journal of the American Republic*, 14 (2): 167–94.

Wilcox, Melissa M. (2002). "When Sheila's a Lesbian: Religious Individualism among Lesbian, Gay, Bisexual, and Transgender Christians," *Sociology of Religion*, 63 (4): 497–513.

Wilkerson, Rich (1989). "Abortion Is Not the #1 Problem," *Radically Saved*, 1 (4): 3–4.

Williams, Rowan (2001). "Making Moral Decisions," in Robin Gill (ed.), *The Cambridge Companion to Christian Ethics*, 3–15, Cambridge: Cambridge University Press.

Williams, Rowan (2012). *Faith in the Public Square*, London: Bloomsbury Continuum.

Williams, Rowan (2018). *Being Human: Bodies, Minds, Persons*, London: SPCK.

Willis, Susan (1993). "Hardcore: Subculture American Style," *Critical Inquiry*, 19 (2): 365–83.

Wilson, Bryan R. (1966). *Religion in Secular Society*, London: Watts & Co.

Wilson, Bryan R. (1985). "Secularization: The Inherited Model," in Phillip E. Hammond (ed.), *The Sacred in a Secular Age*, 9–21, Berkeley: University of California Press.

Wood, Robert T. (2000). "Threat Transcendence, Ideological Articulation and Frame of Reference Restructuring: Preliminary Concepts for a Theory of Subcultural Schism," *Deviant Behavior*, 21 (1): 23–45.

Wood, Robert T. (2006). *Straightedge: Complexity and Contradictions of a Subculture*, Syracuse, NY: Syracuse University Press.

Woodhead, Linda (2010). "Real Religion and Fuzzy Spirituality? Taking Sides in the Sociology of Religion," in Stef Aupers and Dick Houtman (eds.), *Religions of Modernity: Relocating the Sacred to the Self and the Digital*, 31–48, Leiden: Brill.

Worthen, Molly (2009). "Who Would Jesus Smack Down?" *The New York Times*, January 11. Available online: http://www.nytimes.com/2009/01/11/magazine/11punk-t.html (accessed December 1, 2018).

Wright, David F. (2002). "The Charismatic Movement: The Laicizing of Christianity?," in Deryck W. Lovegrove (ed.), *The Rise of the Laity in Evangelical Protestantism*, 253–63, London: Routledge.

Wuthnow, Robert (1998). *After Heaven: Spirituality in America since the 1950s*, Berkeley: University of California Press.

Yambar, Chris (1989). "Grass Roots (The Basics), Part One," *Different Drummer*, 4: 12–15.

Yetman, Mark (2014). "Paradox," *We Love Mars Hill*, June 28. Available online: https://web.archive.org/web/20140628051829/http://welovemarshill.com/post/89384014008/mark-yetman (accessed December 1, 2018).

Yinger, J. Milton (1982). *Countercultures: The Promise and Peril of a World Turned Upside Down*, New York: Free Press.

Young, Shawn David (2012a). "Evangelical Youth Culture: Christian Music and the Political," *Religion Compass*, 6 (6): 323–38.

Young, Shawn David (2012b). "Into the Grey: The Left, Progressivism, and Christian Rock in Uptown Chicago," *Religions*, 3 (2): 498–522.

Young, Shawn David (2015). *Gray Sabbath: Jesus People USA, the Evangelical Left, and the Evolution of Christian Rock*, New York: Columbia University Press.

Young, Shawn David (2017). "Contemporary Christian Music," in Christopher Partridge and Marcus Moberg (eds.), *The Bloomsbury Handbook of Religion and Popular Music*, 101–10, London: Bloomsbury Academic.

Žižek, Slavoj (2007). *How to Read Lacan*, New York: W. W. Norton.

Žižek, Slavoj (2009). *First as Tragedy, Then as Farce*, London: Verso.

Discography

Altar Boys, *When You're a Rebel*. Broken Records, 1985.

Altar Boys, *Gut Level Music*. Frontline Records, 1986.

Altar Boys, *Against the Grain*. Frontline Records, 1987.

Anti-Flag/The Bad Genes, *Rock'n with Father Mike*. Self-released, 1993.

August Burns Red, *Rescue and Restore*. Solid State/Tooth & Nail, 2013.

August Burns Red, *Found in Far Away Places*. Fearless, 2015.

Ballydowse, *The Land, the Bread, and the People*. Grrr Records, 1998.

Ballydowse, *Out of the Fertile Crescent*. Grrr Records, 2000.

Bad Religion, *Recipe for Hate*. Epitaph, 1993.

Baez, Joan, *Blessed Are ....* Vanguard, 1971.

Carter Family, the, *No Depression in Heaven/There's No One Like Mother to Me*. Decca, 1936.

Chariot, The, *The Fiancée*. Solid State/Tooth & Nail, 2007.

Clash, the, *Complete Control/City of the Dead*. CBS, 1977.

Crashdog, *Mud Angels*. Grrr Records, 1994.

Crashdog, *Cashists, Fascists, and Other Fungus*. Grrr Records, 1995.

Crashdog, *Outer Crust*. Grrr Records, 1998.

Crashdog, *8 Years to Nowhere*. Grrr Records, 1998.

Crass, *Feeding of the 5000*. Small Wonder Records/Crass Records, 1978/1980.

Crass, *Reality Asylum/Shaved Women*. Crass Records, 1979.

Crass, *Stations of the Crass*. Crass Records, 1979.

Crass, *Christ – The Album*. Crass Records, 1982.

Crass, *Yes Sir, I Will*. Crass Records, 1983.

Crucified, the, *Take Up Your Cross*. Self-released, 1986.

Dead Kennedys, *In God We Trust, Inc.*, Alternative Tentacles, 1981.

xDeathstarx, *The Triumph*. Facedown Records, 2008.

Devil Wears Prada, The, *Dead Throne*. Ferret Music, 2011.

Dogwood, *Good Ol' Daze*. Rescue Records, 1996.

Dogwood, *Through Thick and Thin*. Rescue Records, 1997.

Dylan, Bob, *Highway 61 Revisited*. Colombia, 1965.

Eucharist, *Eucharist*. Mountain Records, 1996.

Flatfoot 56, *Knuckles Up*. Self-released, 2004.

Flatfoot 56, *Jungle of the Midwest Sea*. Flicker Records, 2007.

Flatfoot 56, *Black Thorn*. Old Shoe Records, 2010.

Flatfoot 56, *Toil*. Paper + Plastick, 2012.

Flatfoot 56, *Odd Boat*. Sailor's Grave Records, 2017.

For Today, *Portraits*. Facedown Records, 2009.

For Today, *Immortal*. Razor & Tie, 2012.

Fugazi, *13 Songs*. Dischord Records, 1989.

Grant, Amy, *Heart in Motion*. Myrrh/A&M Records, 1991.

Harrison, George, *All Things Must Pass*. Apple, 1970.

Impending Doom, *There Will Be Violence!*. Facedown Records, 2010.

Inside Out, *Inside Out*. Revelation Records, 1990.

Lead, the, *Burn This Record*. R.E.X. Music, 1989.

xLooking Forwardx, *The Path We Tread*. Facedown Records, 2005.

Lungfish, *Love Is Love*. Dischord Records, 2003.

Lust Control, *This Is a Condom Nation*. Self-released, 1988.

Lust Control, *Dancing Naked*. Self-released, 1989.

Lust Control, *We Are Not Ashamed*. Enclave Entertainment, 1992.

Lust Control, *Feminazi*. Self-released, 1994.

Lust Control, *Tiny Little Dots*. Rottweiler Records, 2013.

mewithoutYou, *Catch for Us the Foxes*. Tooth & Nail, 2004.

Minor Threat, *Minor Threat*. Dischord, 1984.

Minutemen, *Double Nickels on the Dime*. SST Records, 1984.

MxPx, *Slowly Going the Way of the Buffalo*. Tooth & Nail/A&M, 1998.

Norman, Larry, *Only Visiting This Planet*. Verve, 1972

Officer Negative, *Zombie Nation*. Screaming Giant Records, 1999.

One Bad Pig, *A Christian Banned*. Porkys Demise, 1986.

One Bad Pig, *Smash*. Pure Metal, 1989.

One Bad Pig, *I Scream Sunday*. Myrrh, 1991.

Peacock, Charlie, *Love Life*. Sparrow, 1991.

People!, *I Love You*. Capitol, 1968.

Repp, Roy, *Mass for Young Americans*. FEL Records, 1966.

Sex Pistols, *Never Mind the Bollocks, Here's the Sex Pistols*. Virgin Records, 1977.

Siouxsie and the Banshees, *Join Hands*. Polydor, 1979.

Team Strike Force, *Tension*. Mars Hill Records, 2001.

Torn Flesh, *Crux of the Mosh*. Pure Metal, 1989.

Uncle Tupelo, *No Depression*. Rockville Records, 1990.

Undercover, *Undercover*. Ministry Resource Centre, 1982.

Undercover, *Boys and Girls Renounce the World*. A&S Records, 1984.

Underoath, *They're Only Chasing Safety*, special edn. Solid State/Tooth & Nail, 2005.

Underoath, *Define the Great Line,* special edn. Solid State/Tooth & Nail, 2006.

Underoath, *Ø (Disambiguation)*. Tooth & Nail, 2010.

Underoath, *Erase Me*. Fearless Records, 2018.

Various Artists, *Jesus Christ Superstar*. Decca, 1970.

Various Artists, *Godspell*. Bell Records, 1971.

Various Artists, *Helpless amongst Friends*. Tooth & Nail, 1994.

Various Artists, *O Brother, Where Art Thou?* Lost Highway/Universal, 2000.

Various Artists, *Bear Tracks*, vols. 1–4. Woobie Bear Music, 2004–2006.

War of Ages, *Return to Life*. Facedown Records, 2012.

Filmography

Friday Night Lights (2007). "Nevermind," NBC, January 3.

Is Demon Hunter a Christian Band? (n.d.). No director indicated. Available online: https://www.youtube.com/watch?v=8Pf-tw2Pibo (accessed December 1, 2018).

Making of Define the Great Line (2006). Directed by Underoath. USA: Tooth & Nail.

O Brother, Where Art Thou? (2000). Directed by Joel Cohen. USA: Touchstone/Universal.

Positive Force: More Than a Witness (2014). Directed by Robin Bell. USA: PM Press.

Punk: Attitude (2005). Directed by Don Letts. UK/USA: 3DD Productions/FremantleMedia.

Salad Days: A Decade of Punk in Washington, DC (1980–1990) (2014). Directed by Scott Crawford. USA: New Rose Films.

SLC Punk! (1998). Directed by James Merendino. USA: Beyond Films.

Underoath: They're Only Chasing Safety (2005). Directed by Shannon Hartman. USA: Tooth & Nail.

Interviews

All names are pseudonyms, except where indicated with an asterisk.

Andy (church musician and pastor), interview with Maren Haynes Marchesini, Tacoma, USA, July 2015.

Bob (Christian music industry executive), interview with Nathan Myrick, Waco, USA, March 2016.

Brad (former Christian record label employee), interview with Andrew Mall, Nashville, USA, September 2010.

Brandon (Christian metalcore vocalist), interview with Amy D. McDowell, Riverside, USA, November 2010.

Chris (church musician), interview with Maren Haynes Marchesini, phone interview, USA, October 2015.

Cliff (punk promoter and Bible study leader), interview with Amy D. McDowell, Indiana, USA, June 2012.

Connor (hardcore musician and collector), interview with Ibrahim Abraham, Cincinnati, USA, June 2010.

David (goth minister), interview with Amy D. McDowell, Maryland, USA, October 2012.

Drees, Steve (the Fringe radio station owner), interview with Nathan Myrick, Waco, USA, April 2016.*

Ethan (punk musician and youth pastor), interview with Ibrahim Abraham, Cape Winelands, South Africa, June 2010.

Gerrard (former Christian record label employee), interview with Andrew Mall, Seattle, USA, March 2010.

Gail (hardcore musician and music venue owner), interview with Francis Stewart, Leeds, UK, January 2010.

Hans (hardcore musician and tattoo artist), interview with Francis Stewart, Berkeley, USA, September 2009.

Ian (ska-punk musician), interview with Ibrahim Abraham, Seattle, USA, December 2010.

Jeff (former grunge musician and current pastor), interview with Ibrahim Abraham, Nashville, USA, December 2010.

Jeremy (former Christian festival organizer), interview with Andrew Mall, Chicago, USA, March and April 2010.

John (punk and church musician), interview with Maren Haynes Marchesini, Seattle, USA, October 2014.

Jono (hardcore musician, promoter, and zine editor), interview with Ibrahim Abraham, Coventry, UK, March 2010.

Josh (post-punk and church musician), interview with Maren Haynes Marchesini, Seattle, USA, August 2015.

Laura (tour promoter and trainee nurse), interview with Francis Stewart, San Francisco, USA, November 2009.

Lucy (former hardcore musician, meditation and yoga teacher), interview with Francis Stewart, San Francisco, USA, November 2009.

Mark (hardcore musician), interview with Ibrahim Abraham, Ventura, USA, September 2010.

Matt (church musician), interview with Maren Haynes Marchesini, Seattle, USA, June 2015.

Melinda (punk Bible study leader and tattoo enthusiast), interview with Amy D. McDowell, Pennsylvania, USA, July 2012.

Michael (punk musician and activist), interview with Francis Stewart, Berkeley, USA, October 2009.

Mitch (ska and punk musician), interview with Ibrahim Abraham, Melbourne, Australia, June 2010.

Nick (Christian hardcore vocalist), interview with Amy D. McDowell, Ohio, USA, July 2010.

Paul (straight edge Christian hardcore vocalist), interview with Amy D. McDowell, Florida, USA, July 2011.

Quiggle, Shannon (Head of Public Relations, Facedown Records), interviews with Nathan Myrick, Waco, USA, April 2016; October 2018.*

Rory (punk musician), interview with Ibrahim Abraham, Glasgow, UK, April 2010.

Sean (punk fan), interview with Amy D. McDowell, Pennsylvania, USA, August 2012.

Stagg, David (owner and editor-in-chief, *HM Magazine*), interviews with Nathan Myrick, Waco, USA, March, April 2016; October 2018.*

Steven (hardcore musician and drug counselor), interview with Francis Stewart, San Francisco, USA, October 2009.

Suvi (metalcore musician), interview with Ibrahim Abraham, Brisbane, Australia, December 2010.

Tim (hardcore musician), interview with Ibrahim Abraham, Nuneaton, UK, April 2010.

Tomas (former hardcore musician and current pastor), interview with Ibrahim Abraham, Atlanta, USA, July 2010.

Ty (punk musician and pastor), interview with Ibrahim Abraham, Glasgow, UK, August 2010.

Welchel, Luke (AudioFeed Festival organizer), interview with Andrew Mall, Urbana, USA, July 2017.*

Will (metalcore and worship musician), interview with Ibrahim Abraham, Sydney, Australia, September 2010.

Index

Lightning Source UK Ltd.
Milton Keynes UK
UKHW021245010821
388027UK00004B/197